New Courses
for the Colorado River

New Courses
for the Colorado River

Major Issues
for the Next Century

Edited by
Gary D. Weatherford and F. Lee Brown

University of New Mexico Press
Albuquerque

Dedication

To Bud and Bert, who helped bring Colorado River water across the deserts, mesas, and coastal plains of Southern California.

To Franklin and Agnes, who spent many days with their son on, in, and near rivers and infused him with a love of their natural energy and beauty.

Library of Congress Cataloging-in-Publication Data
Main entry under title:

New courses for the Colorado River.

Based on proceedings of the Colorado River Working Symposium held at Bishop's Lodge, Santa Fe, New Mexico, May 23–26, 1983.
Includes bibliographies and index.
1. Water consumption—Colorado River Watershed (Colo.-Mexico)—Congresses. 2. Colorado River (Colo.-Mexico)—Water-rights—Congresses. 3. Water quality management—Colorado River Watershed (Colo.-Mexico)—Congresses. 4. Water-supply—Navajo Indian Reservation —Congresses. I. Weatherford, Gary D. II. Brown, F. Lee (Franklin Lee) III. Colorado River Working Symposium (1983: Santa Fe, N.M.)

Library of Congress Cataloging-in-Publication Data

HD1695.C7N49   1986   333.91′009791′3   85-24577
ISBN 0-8263-0854-6
ISBN 0-8263-0855-4 (pbk.)

Contents

Illustrations

Foreword:
The Future of the Colorado River

Governor Bruce Babbitt

It is fitting that in 1983 discussion of the future of the Colorado River occurred in the very city—Santa Fe, New Mexico—and in the same lodge where the constitution of the river, the Colorado River Compact, was fought out and drafted some sixty years ago.

In 1985, the river continues to dominate our economy, our politics, and our lives. One student of the river has written: "Anyone interested, for whatever reason, in the study of water in the West will in the end concentrate on the Colorado, wildest of rivers, foaming, raging, rushing southward—erratic, headlong, incongruous in the desert." The greatest student of the river, John Wesley Powell, warned the Montana constitutional convention back in 1889, "The great values of this region [will] ultimately be measured by you in acre-feet." John Gunther once wrote simply, "Touch water in the West and you touch everything."

The river is a scarce resource in a dry land. The entire Colorado River is scarcely 5 percent of the flow of the Columbia River. It is less than 1 percent of the annual flow of the Mississippi. Today, there is no unused water; the Colorado no longer flows unvexed to the sea. In most months the mouth of the river at the Sea of Cortez is dry, river water replaced by rancid salt flats.

It is thus especially timely that we examine in this volume—and its antecedent symposium—the future of the river than unites us geographically and all too often divides us politically.

We meet in the closing decades of a long and productive century of federally sponsored reclamation of the West. The era of the big reclamation project is nearly finished. The great storage dams— Hoover, Glen Canyon, and Flaming Gorge—are now in place. The great aqueducts, the Colorado River Aqueduct in California, the Central Utah Project, the Central Arizona Project, and the San Juan– Chama diversion, are in place or under construction. With development of remaining projects in the Upper Basin, principally in Colorado, the century of the great reclamation projects will soon come to an end.

Undeniably, river development has been an acrimonious process marked by decades of interstate controversy, prolonged lawsuits, and generations of complex congressional politics. In retrospect, the adversary nature of basin development was probably inevitable, given the federalist nature of the Colorado River Compact, which divided the waters among states rather than by considerations of geography or hydrology.

The waters might have been divided differently. One choice would have been an integrated basin model like the Tennessee Valley Authority. Another choice would have been a strict prior appropriation model without any governmental intervention or state boundaries, as the U.S. Supreme Court originally envisioned in the case of *Wyoming v. Colorado*. But these choices would have diminished state sovereignty to an extent unacceptable to westerners.

And for the most part, westerners have reason for satisfaction about the events that began some sixty years ago. The compact has served us well. Admittedly, the adversary process engendered by state sovereignty has produced some inefficiencies, occasional duplication, and some projects which may not operate at full capacity because of competing demands. Nonetheless, some turbulence and inefficiency is the inevitable price of a federal system that preserved a share of the river for late-developing states.

Moreover, environmental concerns have fared well under the federal-state process of river development, although not without protracted controversy. Environmentalists won big victories at Echo Park, Bridge Canyon, and Marble Canyon, to name a few. And history will be kind to their efforts. The environmental cause lost at Glen Canyon,

an unhappy but perhaps inevitable concession to the storage requirements of the compact.

The second century of the Colorado River, now before us, will
raise issues that no one even thought of back in 1922. Of many such
issues, two stand out as the most urgent and the most difficult to
resolve. The first is justice for the Indian tribes who were bypassed
and ignored during most of the first century of river development. The
second is how we control the increased salinity resulting from intensive
use, which now threatens to destroy many of the economic benefits
generated by reclamation development. Both are issues that will have
to be resolved through new institutions, new laws, and new procedures
adequate for a second century of life in the Colorado River Basin.

Indian Claims

The claims of Indian tribes to a fair share of western water development were passed off as inconsequential by the drafters of the
compact. Only at the insistence of Herbert Hoover, the federal chairman, did the delegates insert Article VII, stating, "Nothing in this
compact shall be construed as affecting the obligations of the United
States of America to Indian tribes." And there the matter lay for forty
years—until 1963.

In 1963 the basin world was turned upside down by the Supreme
Court decision in *Arizona v. California*, a decision which awarded about
900,000 acre-feet of water to five small tribes, constituting scarcely
10,000 individuals, in Arizona and California. Since then, litigation
has proliferated throughout the basin. The test of "practicably irrigable
acreage," adopted by the Court, is still not thoroughly understood or
developed. But one thing is certain: the standard at least in theory
could be applied to defeat every current use from Los Angeles to
Denver, from Tucson to Wyoming, and thereby deed the entire flow
of the river over to tribal development.

The proper framework for discussion of Indian claims and Indian
equity is to recognize that the collision of two incompatible theories
of water law, prior appropriation and reserved rights, is an evolutionary
historical development, compounded by inattention and ignorance,
for which it is difficult to assess too much blame in any quarter. Efforts

to resolve Indian claims will require careful thought and effort to avoid damage to innocent parties on all sides.

The principal difficulty is that piecemeal adjudication of Indian claims, in many different state and federal courts, is not working well. Individual court adjudications, while perhaps plausible on the limited facts of a given case, are beginning to accumulate on a grand scale that cannot be reconciled with the complex realities of basinwide uses developed under the compact. Is it realistic to shut down Los Angeles to develop more alfalfa irrigation on Indian lands? Or to cut off Salt Lake City in favor of a new energy development, whether on Indian or non-Indian land? Of course, these questions are never reached in the context of a single lawsuit. But we are rapidly reaching the point at which an award to any one claimant will necessarily take something from another somewhere in the basin. There is no longer much room for error.

The economic and social stakes for Indian and non-Indian alike seem too high to leave the difficult adjustment of too many claims and too little water to the random accumulation of inconsistent and conflicting judicial decisions. We must begin to move away from the gunfighter ethic of litigation that has dominated western law and seek to harmonize and reconcile claims and uses.

The first step is to explore all possible avenues of negotiation and compromise. There are suggestive precedents in the Ak-Chin Settlement, the Papago legislation, and in the settlement that preceded construction of Navajo Dam. Both Congress and the Interior Department must take a more aggressive approach in search of negotiated solutions, recognizing that in most cases the key to such settlements will be the appropriation of money to transfer paper rights into real, usable water for Indian development.

Beyond negotiation, there is an emerging sentiment among many western groups that Congress should preempt case-by-case adjudication with a comprehensive administrative process for equitable settlement and development in the broader context of basin hydrology and uses. Some groups, such as the Western Regional Council, have drafted specific proposals. It is a subject that deserves more thoughtful consideration and debate than has been generated so far.

Other aspects of the Winters Doctrine deserve careful study outside the judicial process. For example, there is a big difference between outright unqualified ownership of water and various combinations of use rights that can be more easily reconciled with the needs of other users. Such concepts ought to be explored on both the Indian and the non-Indian sides of the ledger. For example, should Winters rights be freely transferable for sale and use off reservations? The social, economic, and equitable arguments on both sides are complex, and in fact the desirable result may differ from state to state and from tribe to tribe.

But one thing is certain: a question of such far-reaching importance to the social and economic future of the West ought to be thoroughly aired and argued somewhere other than in the confines of courtroom adjudications. Such a major question of regional policy ought to involve the political process and the United States Congress.

The West would be well served by congressional hearings into these questions. The Senate Select Committee on Indian Affairs would be a logical place to begin. Concerned westerners on all sides should urge the Select Committee to commence hearings throughout the West and to begin the difficult, controversial process of formulating a rational plan to bring western Indian tribes into the mainstream of water development in the least disruptive and most harmonious way possible.

Salinity Control

The framers of the Colorado River Compact did not even mention the words *salinity* or *water quality*. No one even dreamed in that early time that the river would, a scant thirty years later, be so intensively used that saline water would be killing crops in Mexicali Valley and provoking an international incident.

The Mexican crisis was averted by a treaty guaranteeing Mexican farmers parity with Imperial Valley users, and today a one-quarter-billion-dollar desalting plant is under construction to help make good on that commitment.

But saline contamination, aggravated by each new consumptive withdrawal and by polluted return flows, will continue to advance, relentlessly and inexorably, across the entire basin. Without further control, and assuming further development, salinity at Imperial Dam will again advance to a crop-killing level of 1,000 mg/liter by the end of the century.

For a time in the 1970s, it seemed that salt-control responsibilities would be divided up among the basin states just as waters were divided by the compact. In a little-noticed lawsuit, *Environmental Defense Fund v. Costle,* among the most important cases ever filed in the basin, the Environmental Defense Fund sought to mandate individual water quality standards for each state in the Colorado River Basin.

Had EDF prevailed, basin development, particularly agriculture, would have been severely curtailed. Any variation in state numerical standards, even if subsequently diluted by downstream waters, would have foreclosed. The likely effect would have been to prevent much Upper Basin development in favor of expanded Lower Basin uses in areas such as Imperial Valley where return flows do not reenter the basin drainage.

Instead, the Court approved a model advocated by the states that sets ambient standards for the lower main stem, measured downstream at Hoover, Parker, and Imperial dams. However, this more flexible, basinwide salt control model poses important issues of institutional control. For example, if no one basin state ever bears the onus for violating basin standards, who determines which state and which basin bears the burden of mitigation and cleanup?

The institutional response to this problem is the Colorado River Salinity Control Forum, a cooperative group, appointed by governors of the basin states to plan salt control measures.

Early efforts of the Forum tended to overlook the fact that nearly half the salt load of the river is caused by irrigated agriculture. Instead, the Forum tended to devise expensive and complex structural schemes to control natural pollution from such sources as the Paradox Salt Dome, Las Vegas Wash, and the Little Colorado River. The environmental effects of structural works such as dams, desalting works, and evaporation ponds were neither well publicized nor thoroughly evaluated.

Recently the Forum has shifted efforts to control of irrigation recharge through such techniques as ditch lining. The control of irrigation recharge is an area that requires more effort through the use of such methods as laser leveling, drip irrigation, pumpbacks, and other devices that reduce application and thereby effect water conservation as well as salinity control.

Likewise, the various technologies of direct use of highly saline source water, including the use of that water in energy production, also merit further research.

The future of salt control depends in some measure upon two issues that have not been thoroughly examined: (1) the financing of control measures, and (2) enforcement mechanisms.

Financing

At the present time, 75 percent of salt control measures are financed by the federal government, with 20 percent carried by the Lower Basin Development Fund and 5 percent from the Upper Basin Fund. So long as federal financing remains dominant, interbasin or interstate conflicts are unlikely. If, however, the cost of salinity control were in the future to devolve on the states, the question of interstate cost-sharing could become an urgent topic for discussion.

For a hypothetical example, why should Utah encourage or require modern irrigation practices in the Virgin River Valley if recharge salinity affects only downstrean users in California? Should California in any circumstance be able to compel action to Utah?

In the short run, cost-sharing is more likely to become an issue in the context of modernizing agricultural projects which also produce other benefits that arguably should share in the cost of the modernization.

Enforcement

The ultimate issue before the Salinity Control Forum will be enforcement. Suppose that three oil companies were to announce three oil-shale projects in three basin states, the combined effect of which would be that the third project to reach completion would exceed EPA standards at Imperial Dam. Would or should EPA announce its intention to deny a NPDES discharge permit to one or two of the projects? In which states? Should the projects go ahead on the assumption that the Forum can devise offsetting control projects and then bill 85 percent of the costs to the federal government?

Would one or two of the affected states sue to enjoin development in another state under some claim of equity or priority in time?

Such issues will inevitably arise in one context or another. The important questions today are the institutional issues: Will such conflicts be resolved in the Congress and the federal courts or do the basin states have the capacity to foresee and resolve these problems prior to the onset of crisis?

In summary, the Colorado River Compact has served us reasonably well, but it provides little guidance on the major issues of the next century, namely, the equitable resolution of Indian claims and water quality. The adversary process of case-by-case litigation is not adequate to cope with these issues.

This edited volume and the symposium from which it originated are intended as models for devising cooperative institutional proposals for problem resolution, which we and others will pursue with vigor into the next century.

Acknowledgments

We are pleased to acknowledge the assistance of numerous individuals and organizations without whom neither the Colorado River Working Symposium nor this book would have been possible. First of all, our thanks to all of the symposium participants identified in Appendix A. Most of them either bore the travel and lodging expense themselves or found ingenious ways to be reimbursed. Particular thanks must go to Sally Fairfax, Dick Trudell, Harvey Banks, and Skip Spensley, who additionally served as workshop leaders; to Toby Clark, John Thorson, Tim De Young, and Barbara Andrews, who served as workshop reporters; and to Al Utton, John Sayre, Jeff Fornaciari, and Larry Wolfe, who served as archivists to individual workshops. They all did a superb job. Al Utton also served masterfully as our emcee.

The symposium simply would not have occurred without the financial and moral support provided by the William H. Donner Foundation, Inc., through Don Rickerd, Phil Jessup, and Janet Maughan. A special debt is owed to Phil, vice-president of Donner, who saw the potential for the symposium from among a variety of possible water projects that we discussed with him. Phil also led us to Bob Crawford of Mt. Holly, Vermont, whose experience with organizing conferences and sage advice largely made up for our own inexperience in this regard. When we needed supplemental financial assistance for the symposium, the General Service Foundation came to our aid.

All of the authors-speakers devoted substantial time to the preparation of both their written material and oral presentations. The material they presented provided focus and substance for the workshop sessions. Their roles are briefly summarized in the introductory chapter to this book. Much of the substantive success of the symposium was due to the preparation that each of them brought to the meeting. Additionally, Allen Kneese, Helen Ingram, and Luna Leopold provided important ideas at critical junctures in the planning.

Many of the participants were profuse in their praise for the organizational fluidity with which the symposium was conducted. The credit in this regard goes to Ann Brown and Robin Morgan, whose coordinating skills and attention to detail sustained the proceedings. Randi Beck's contributions from Berkeley were also important in this regard. To Max Linn, Julie Hillis, and Taylor Miller of the John Muir Institute, we express our appreciation for the administrative support and institutional base provided to us.

Then there is this book itself. Despite the excellent written material already prepared for the symposium, a book does not just happen. We are especially appreciative to the Lincoln Institute for Land Policy and to Ann Rockefeller Roberts for the financial assistance that made this book possible. To David Holtby and others at the University of New Mexico Press we express our thanks for the confidence they have shown in this work. Finally, typing and revising were done by Alice Maxwell, Debbie Miller, and Toby Stewart, whose skills and patience we greatly appreciate.

Gary D. Weatherford
Berkeley, California

F. Lee Brown
Albuquerque, New Mexico

New Courses
for the Colorado River

THE COLORADO – RIVER OF CONTROVERSY

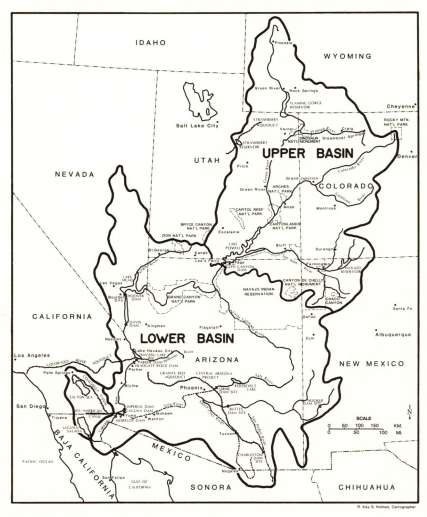

R. Kay S. Holmes, Cartographer

The Colorado—River of Controversy

1 Introduction: A Timely Look at a Timeless River

**Gary D. Weatherford
and F. Lee Brown**

The Colorado River came into being thirty-five million years ago when the headwater erosion of one river system (the Hualapai that flowed into what we now know as the Gulf of California) cut into and diverted another river system (the ancestral Upper Colorado River that had fed the massive inland Lake Bidahochi). The Kaibab Plateau, which had previously divided these river systems, became engraved by this union of water sources, as well as by wind and geologic uplifting, to give us the Grand Canyon.[1]

By comparison, the human imprint on this mighty river system is young but profound. The Colorado was not even mapped until John Wesley Powell's epic exploratory journey in 1869. Yet in the century following Powell's trek we have erected dams on its tributaries and main stem that store more than sixty million acre-feet of water and produce over two million kilowatts of power.[2] Flood surges and millions of tons of sediments are checked by the dams we have placed in its canyons. Hundreds of thousands of farm acres are irrigated by its regulated waters. We yearly export more than five million acre-feet of its flow for use outside its 244,000 square-mile drainage area. Beyond its drainage, the southern California coastal plain and the eastern fans of the Rockies in Colorado receive its waters, as does the middle Rio Grande in New Mexico. Central Arizona will soon become more reliant on the system, and central Utah west of the Wasatch range is scheduled to tap it. And the irrigated fields of the Mexicali Valley in

Mexico continue to depend on its residual flow southward. Beyond question, the roots of regional settlement and economic growth draw extensively on this river.

Changing Water Management Context

Colorado River management occurs within the context of national, regional, state, local, and tribal water policies—all policies which are changing.

The federal government owns 56 percent of the basin's land area, the Indian tribes 16.5 percent, the states 8.5 percent, and private interests only 19 percent.[3] The federal government has a firm control on the operation of the major dams, reservoirs, and hydroelectric power facilities. It is a trustee of Indians, a protector of states' interests, and a promissor under treaty to Mexico. Yet the federal budget is deeply in deficit, and politically it is increasingly difficult to finance water development and management.[4] New project authorizations have slowed; funding for projects under construction has been rescheduled; and water planning and research institutions have been dismantled. A major issue of the day is what degree of cost-sharing by local and state beneficiaries will be required for future federal participation in water resource development and management.[5]

Paralleling the constriction in available capital is the awareness in the arid West that much of the surface water supply is fully appropriated, if not oversubscribed; that irrigated agriculture in many areas faces formidable salt management problems; that the region may be susceptible to longer and more severe droughts than once assumed; and that ground water supplies selectively are being mined and contaminated.

The United States Supreme Court, for its part, is saying that water is fundamentally an article of commerce and that barriers to its interstate movement cannot be legislated by a state except where public health and safety strongly demand it.[6] The private marketing of water across state lines may become a practical result of the Court's decision. While neither Congress nor the courts has decided whether Indian-reserved water rights generally can be leased or sold for off-reservation use, there is now precedent in at least one congressionally approved water rights settlement for the off-reservation leasing of water.[7]

What do all these trends mean? Probably what the National Water Commission alluded to in its 1973 report:[8] a significant shift is occurring away from the *development* of new water supplies to the *management* of existing supplies. Given the limits of available capital and water, two important policy strategies have emerged: conservation and reallocation.[9] To discourage waste, more stringent notions of "beneficial" and "reasonable" use are being urged for state water law systems. Traditional restrictions on the transferability of water rights are being loosened to allow private markets in water to grow. Conservation and reallocation, then, are hallmarks of the emerging western water resource picture, against which the management of the Colorado is likely to be measured.

Challenges for the Colorado

When most of the major decisions were made to divide, dam, desilt, divert, and energize the Colorado, conditions were significantly different from what they are today—and perhaps dramatically different from what they will be tomorrow. Past decisions assumed more reliable flow than subsequent records and research have shown to be true. Past decisions have reflected the particular perspectives, priorities, and political alignments of the day. Time has since elevated the interests of Indians, Mexicans, cities, whitewater recreation, ecology, and environmental quality that were variously unappreciated, forgotten, or neglected in those decisions. Each year more values and interests vie for the limited waters of the Colorado, posing several questions. How should the management institutions of the river respond? What institutional approaches and arrangements might be best suited to the future? Are those institutions capable of accommodating the growing diversity of claims, values, and interests represented in the region served by the river? A water expert suggested, "A pig will fly before the Colorado Compact is amended." Is the management system that intractable?

Such questions prompted the convening of the Colorado River Working Symposium at Bishop's Lodge in Santa Fe, New Mexico, May 23–26, 1983, the proceedings of which are collected for the reader in this volume. Sixty attendees, specially selected to represent the broad array of groups and interests affcted by the river, met, pondered,

and amicably argued on the same ground where the negotiators hammered out the 1922 Colorado Compact under the leadership of Herbert
Hoover. At the first evening session of the symposium, New Mexico's
governor, Toney Anaya, underlined the need for new initiatives in
water policy and introduced the keynote speaker, Bruce Babbitt, governor of Arizona, who gave the group the inspiring charge that appears
as the Preface to this volume. Governor Babbitt has provided dis-
tinctive political leadership on water matters in his state and in the
West. As serviceable as the Colorado River Compact has been, Babbitt
declared that "it provides little guidance on the major issues of the
next century, namely, the equitable resolution of Indian claims and
water quality."

The papers presented at the symposium were designed variously
to provide:

An institutional history of the river

A survey of the key policy issues relating to the river

A preview of hypothetical events that could shock and test the
existing management institutions

A description of probable legal-institutional responses to one of
those shocks (protracted drought)

An assessment of the strengths and weaknesses of the existing
institutions

Speculation about the workability of new institutional forms or
arrangements

Separate arguments for the primacy of economic efficiency, equity,
and environmental quality in management of the river

A summation weaving together the major points and themes of
the meeting

In "The West Against Itself" (chapter 2), Norris Hundley, jr.,
U.C.L.A. professor of history and preeminent historian of the Colorado River (*Water and the West*, 1975; *Dividing the Waters*, 1966),
recounts the conflicts and decisions behind the allocation and management of the river. The prolonged wrangling over water leads him
to conclude:

> Behind the scramble for water in years past was not only its
> obvious necessity for survival in a water-dry country but also
> an obsession with growth—an obsession that equated progress

with obtaining enough water to develop the biggest farms and cities and industries.

Borrowing Hundley's phrase, "River of Controversy," noted water law authorities David Getches and Charles Meyers identify and analyze the Colorado's persistent issues in chapter 3, focusing on the interplay among agricultural, municipal, and industrial users; between the upper and lower basins; among instream, inbasin, and transbasin uses; between surface and groundwater uses; between electric power production and other uses; between Indians and non-Indians; between the states and the federal government; and between the United States and Mexico. Approaches to future problems are assessed, including revision of the "Law of the River," water importation, market pricing, and changes in state water laws. Chapter 4, "Hypothetical Shocks to Water Allocation Institutions," has been fashioned by two insightful and seasoned resource economists, Allen Kneese and Gilbert Bonem. The shocks portrayed include a cutoff in Middle East oil, resulting in massive domestic energy production with attendant water use, the assertion and quantification of substantial Indian water claims, the development of a large-scale interstate market in water rights, and a deep and sustained drought in the Upper Colorado River Basin. One of the most skilled water lawyers in the West, Edward Clyde, follows with an examination of how the river would be operated under such a drought in a piece entitled "Institutional Response to Prolonged Drought" (chapter 5), in which the pecking order of the present scheme is detailed, along with some of the unresolved ambiguities that persist in the "Law of the River."

The fearless water and energy counselor from Washington, D.C., Paul Bloom, next argues that the "Law of the River" (chapter 6) is an "extraordinary legal system," deserving of both respect and reform, the latter through a new federal-interstate compact and acts of Congress mandating the quantification of federal- and Indian-reserved water rights claims.

Numerous legitimate human concerns seek center stage in the management of the Colorado. Broadly, they can be clustered into three sets of values: economic efficiency, equity, and environmental quality. The economic efficiency of private water markets deserves top billing, according to widely published University of California (Davis) professor Delworth Gardner (in chapter 7, "The Untried Market Approach to Water Allocation"), because the current allocative scheme dictated by outmoded law is simply too costly. "Governments might even be useful as brokers to facilitate exchanges until private institutions arise to do so," he suggests. Water is a social good in which the public interest and notions of fairness must remain paramount, counter the authors of the next paper, "Replacing Confusion with Equity" (chapter 8). Helen Ingram and Lawrence Scaff, University of Arizona political scientists, and Leslie Silko, Native American poet and novelist, offer a thoughtful and provocative exposition of the principles inhering in people's notions of equity. The trio suggests that the principles of reciprocity, pluralism, participation, fulfillment of promises, and respect for future generations must continue to be part of the "common sense" of water management in the Colorado River Basin. Counterpoint can be found in the thinking of one of the nation's leading advocates of preservation, University of California (Santa Barbara) professor Roderick Nash, author of *Wilderness and the American Mind* (1967). In "Wilderness Values and the Colorado River" (chapter 9), Nash heralds the importance of the natural scenery and ecology of the basin, noting how the rise in recreational river running through the Grand Canyon reflects a growing popular awareness of the grandeur previously captured in paintings, photographs, poetry, and writings of the western genre.

A lyrical overview and summation of the symposium meeting is provided by the dean of American geographers, Gilbert White, in "A New Confluence in the Life of the River" (chapter 10). An epilog by the editors, "High Water, Carbon Dioxide, and Pig Feathers," surveys postsymposium flooding, climate forecasts, and water policy initiatives.

Notes

1. Merrill D. Beal, *Grand Canyon, The Story Behind the Scenery* (Las Vegas, 1967), pp. 12–13.

2. See, generally, U.S. Department of the Interior, Water and Power Resources Service (Bureau of Reclamation), *Project Data* (Denver, 1981), pp. 79, 119, 251, 293, 297.

3. See U.S. Water Resources Council, Lower Colorado Region Comprehensive Framework Study (June 1971), Appendix 6, p. 49; and Upper

Colorado Region Comprehensive Framework Study (June 1971), Appendix 6, p. 14.

4. See, for example, General Accounting Office, *Water Issues Facing the Nation, An Overview* (CED–82–83, 6 May 1982).

5. See, for example, Congressional Budget Office, *Current Cost-Sharing and Financing Policies for Federal and State Water Resources Development* (July 1983).

6. *Sporhase v. Nebraska,* 102 S. Ct. 3456 (1982).

7. Pub. L. No. 97–293, sec. 306(c), 96 Stat. 1261, 1280.

8. National Water Commission, *Water Policies for the Future* (1973).

9. See Gary Weatherford, ed., *Water and Agriculture in the Western U.S.: Conservation, Reallocation and Markets* (Boulder, 1982).

2 The West Against Itself: The Colorado River— An Institutional History

Norris Hundley, jr.

"River of Controversy" might have been the name if the Spanish explorers could have foreseen the many bitter conflicts over the Colorado. But their attention focused naturally on what first caught their eye, and they christened the river with a name reflecting the ruddy color produced by the enormous quantities of silt—more such sediment than carried by all but a handful of the world's streams. Like the Indians who knew the Colorado by other names and had relied on its waters since time immemorial, the Spaniards, a people from a water-shy country, recognized at once the river's critical importance to the area, although they could only guess at the size of the drainage basin— practically the entire lower left-hand corner of the present United States.

From its headwaters high in the Wind River Mountains of Wyoming, the Colorado meanders 1,400 miles and is the sole dependable water supply for 244,000 square miles, an area embracing parts of seven western states (Wyoming, Colorado, Utah, New Mexico, Nevada, Arizona, California) and Mexico. Though the watershed is vast, the Colorado is not a heavy flowing stream, ranking about sixth among the nation's rivers and having an average annual volume of less than fifteen million acre-feet. This is only a thirty-third that of the Mississippi and a twelfth that of the Columbia, but this modest flow became in the twentieth century the most disputed body of water in the country and probably in the world. The controversies extended far beyond the basin and involved great population centers that have built or are seeking to build aqueducts hundreds of miles long to develop the farms, cities, and industries of Denver and eastern Colorado, Salt Lake City and western Utah, Albuquerque and central New Mexico, and especially the vast megalopolis of Southern California stretching from north of Los Angeles to the Mexican border. Over the years the drive for water significantly altered the appearance and quality of the Colorado's flow, forced domestic and international agreements that sometimes harmonized and just as often exacerbated relations among water users, and created a legacy of laws, court decisions, and water-use patterns that continue to influence the lives of millions of people in the United States and Mexico.

Genesis of an Idea: Arthur Powell Davis

For hundreds of thousands of years, the Colorado and its network of tributaries flowed without interruption to the sea. For a much shorter span, but one still measured in thousands of years, societies made their homes along the watercourses without appreciably changing either river or basin. The coming of the Spaniards in the sixteenth century, Mexico's short hegemony nearly three hundred years later, and the American conquest in the mid-nineteenth century scarcely altered the waterscape. The twentieth century, however, brought dramatic change as hundreds of thousands of newcomers poured into the Southwest and turned their energies toward developing the region's scarce water supplies.

Among the earliest advocates of large-scale development of the Colorado River was Arthur Powell Davis, nephew of the famous explorer and geologist John Wesley Powell. Davis was not the first to advance a sweeping plan, but as a prominent engineer in the U.S. Geological Survey and later in the Reclamation Service, he possessed the skills and connections to draw public attention to the proposal that he first unveiled in 1902. What he sought, he told his fellow engineers, was "the gradual comprehensive development of the Colorado River by a series of large storage reservoirs." The keystone was to be a dam on the lower river built "as high as appears practicable from the local conditions."[1]

Davis was driven by more than an engineer's natural desire to be associated with one of the world's great technological feats. He shared with Henry George and other reformers of the day a concern about the demoralizing effects of land monopoly, the end of the frontier, and urban crime, poverty, and unemployment. While many Americans pointed with pride to growing cities and industries, Davis worried about the seemingly precipitous decline in public morality and advocated a return to the values associated with the independent yeoman farmer so idealized by Thomas Jefferson.[2] To Davis, revitalization of the nation's moral fiber lay in getting more people to work the soil, and a major means to that end would be the reclamation of western lands mistakenly considered useless by many because of lack of water. The task, he recognized, would be enormous, so great and so expensive that only the federal government could overcome the obstacles and provide the necessary overall planning. And the place to begin, he believed, was the Colorado River. "I . . . considered problems in all of the Western States," he later recalled, "but there [was] . . . none which . . . excited my interest and imagination and ambition so much as the development of the Colorado River Basin."[3]

Davis found a vehicle for his ideas in the newly created Reclamation Service, but lack of funds and mercurial public support prevented headway for nearly two decades. Then Californians, first in the Imperial Valley and later in Los Angeles and eventually throughout Southern California, endorsed his plans and set in motion a series of events that profoundly affected the Colorado River Basin.

Imperial Valley and the All-American Canal

Settlers in California's Imperial Valley, an arid but enormously fertile area of 600,000 acres just north of the Mexican border, only slowly became interested in Davis's ambitious scheme. Rather than dams, they wanted a canal—an "All-American Canal," as they called it—that would free them from their dependence on Mexico and assure them enough water to develop their lands. Because of a ridge of sandhills separating the valley from the Colorado, water had been brought in by diverting it south of the border through an old overflow channel of the river. The price exacted by Mexico for this privilege was stiff—the right to take up to half of the diverted water.[4]

At first the price seemed tolerable. Mexican development proceeded slowly while that in the Imperial Valley boomed following the introduction of water in 1901. By 1916 more than 300,000 acres were under cultivation, and valley leaders had plans to expand production even further.[5] But by this time the entire river would occasionally be diverted, especially during the critical low-flow months of summer, and even taking the whole stream often produced insufficient water. While Mexico's water needs remained considerably less than those of U.S. farmers, the reduced flow crossing the line still meant rationing of water in the valley. Alarmed by the threat to their crops and convinced that the situation would deteriorate as Mexico expanded its own agriculture, valley farmers began demanding a delivery system wholly in the U.S. Their clamor grew louder in response to unsettled conditions below the border created by the Mexican Revolution of 1910, refusal of Mexican landowners to share the cost of levees to protect the delivery system, and the duties imposed on equipment used in protective work below the line. Especially galling to valley farmers was the disclosure that the largest single landholder on the Mexican side was a syndicate controlled by Los Angeles businessmen, the most prominent of whom was Harry Chandler, publisher of the *Los Angeles Times.* "These Mexican . . . lands," complained valley residents, "menace us like a great sponge, which threatens to absorb more and more water, until such time as they will take all of the natural flow of the river."[6]

Unable to finance a new canal by themselves, valley farmers in 1917 turned to Washington for help. Operating through the Imperial Irrigation District, a powerful and well-organized public agency in charge of the valley's water system, they persuaded the Secretary of the Interior to investigate the feasibility of an All-American Canal and two years later got Congressman William Kettner to introduce a bill authorizing construction of the aqueduct.[7]

The Kettner Bill immediately attracted the attention of Arthur Powell Davis, who saw it as an opportunity to lobby for his own river development plans. The canal, he told the bill's advocates, would be impractical by itself. It would be at the mercy of the floods that annually menaced settlements along the river and from 1905 to 1907 had actually broken into the Imperial Valley, destroying fields and homes and creating the Salton Sea. But "if we had complete storage," he observed, "the flood menace would be removed." To Davis the issue was clear-cut: "The Imperial Valley problem . . . is inseparably linked with the problem of water storage in the Colorado Basin as a whole."[8]

Strong endorsements of Davis's position came from the engineering team sent by the Secretary of the Interior to investigate the canal's feasibility, from groups supporting the back-to-land movement, and from the League of the Southwest, a highly vocal booster organization representing scores of businesses and local governments. Imperial Valley leaders at first resisted tying the canal to a more grandiose and complicated project, but finally they surrendered to the force of logic and to the pressure from Davis and others. In 1920 they joined with Davis to promote passage of the Kincaid Act, which authorized the government to secure needed field data about the canal and storage sites.[9] These events did not go unnoticed elsewhere.

Enter Los Angeles

Among those following closely the maneuvering in Washington were Los Angeles officials, especially blunt-spoken William Mulholland, chief of the Bureau of Water Works and Supply, and E. F. Scattergood, head of the Bureau of Power and Light. They had spent their lives working to ensure that the city had all the water and electricity that it needed. For a community that had grown by nearly 600 percent during the two decades after 1900, this had been no small accomplishment. The city had fought successfully to gain control of the Los Angeles River, the major local supply, and in 1913 had completed a 233-mile-long aqueduct to the Owens River.[10] By 1920 as the Los Angeles population approached 600,000, Mulholland and Scattergood were turning their attention to the Colorado.

Of concern to city leaders at first was electricity rather than water. The aqueduct to the Owens Valley seemed to guarantee a plentiful water supply, but experts predicted a power shortage within three to five years. Mulholland and Scattergood warned that local plant construction would only temporarily postpone, not prevent, a shortage. They advocated as a solution Arthur Powell Davis's proposal for a dam on the Colorado River. Told that a hydroelectric plant at the dam could provide the city with enough power for "all future needs," the

city council required little persuasion. In August 1920, it endorsed
Davis's plan and boldly proclaimed the city's intention to obtain power
"direct from the Colorado River."[11]

The Los Angeles action delighted Davis and his new allies from
the Imperial Valley, but another city decision a few years later pleased
them even more. In 1923 a dry cycle prompted Los Angeles to look
to the Colorado for water as well as electricity. Such a venture would
require special diversion dams, an aqueduct even longer than the one
to Owens Valley, and pumping stations to raise water over the mountains separating the city from the river. The undertaking was too costly
for the city alone. In 1924 Los Angeles leaders negotiated with nearby
communities for the creation of the Metropolitan Water District of
Southern California (MWD). Three years later the state legislature
approved the new agency and authorized it "to provide a supplemental
water supply to the coastal plain of Southern California."[12] These steps
placed Los Angeles and the twenty-six other agencies that eventually
joined MWD squarely alongside Davis and the Imperial Valley in their
quest to develop the Colorado River.

Upper Basin Alarm and the
Colorado River Compact

Long before Los Angeles entered into an alliance with MWD,
leaders in the Colorado River Basin outside of California had become
troubled. All recognized that the future development of their areas
depended heavily on the Colorado, and they watched uneasily the
advances being made by a state that contributed the least amount of
runoff to the river.

Particularly disturbed were residents in the upper portion of the
basin where the growing season was shorter and the lands less easily
watered than in California or Arizona. The upper states wanted reclamation projects of their own, including some that would benefit
areas outside the basin, especially in western Utah and eastern Colorado. Denver, for example, like Los Angeles, lay outside the basin
and had grown rapidly if not as spectacularly as the southern California
city. From a population of 134,000 in 1900, it had nearly doubled in
size by 1920 and was threatening to precipitate a water war with its
neighbors. "The most serious problem that confronts us at this time,"

warned a Denver official, "is the future water supply. Unless a construction program is formulated . . . that will bring to Denver and the agricultural communities surrounding it more water . . . , any great future growth in Denver's population must be made at the expense of the agricultural communities surrounding it."[13]

Heightening such concern throughout the Upper Basin were a series of events in early 1922. The first occurred in February when the Interior Department issued the long-awaited study called for by the Kincaid Act. Known as the Fall-Davis Report—named for Secretary of the Interior Albert Fall and Arthur Powell Davis, who was now head of the Reclamation Bureau—it recommended construction of an All-American Canal, a storage reservoir "at or near Boulder Canyon," and the development of hydroelectric power to repay the cost of the dam.[14] The next development that disconcerted the upper states took place in April, when Congressman Phil Swing from the Imperial Valley and Senator Hiram Johnson of California introduced a bill to implement the report's recommendations. This Boulder Canyon, or Swing-Johnson, bill met with immediate hostility from Upper Basin representative, who mounted a vigorous campaign against it.[15]

Still another cause for alarm in the upper states occurred two months later. This involved western water law, specifically the doctrine of prior appropriation which gave legal entitlement to the first person using water—"first in time, first in right." This principle was recognized within each basin state, but uncertainty existed over whether it applied to users in two or more states on a common stream. In June 1922 the U.S. Supreme Court, in *Wyoming* v. *Colorado*, eliminated all doubt by announcing that the rule of priority applied regardless of state lines.[16] Now even the law seemed to favor faster-growing states like California. Upper Basin leaders responded to the decision by reaffirming adamant opposition to all reclamation on the lower Colorado until their own interests were safeguarded.

The leader in defining those interests and in devising a protective strategy was Delph Carpenter of Colorado. A brilliant and prominent attorney with years of experience in water litigation, he had long advocated compacts or treaties to resolve interstate disputes. Although no states had demonstrated the practicality of his idea by apportioning water among themselves, Carpenter believed that the usual recourse to litigation was a mistake—it was too costly, too time-consuming, and invariably it created more issues than it resolved. His participation in Colorado's lengthy Supreme Court battle with Wyoming had reinforced these views as had the claims of federal attorneys that the U.S. owned all the unappropriated waters in the West's streams. If the states did not put their houses in order, he feared that the federal government might do it for them, thus "weakening . . . state autonomy on all rivers."[17]

In 1920, at a meeting of the League of the Southwest, Carpenter called for a compact covering the Colorado River. It was an idea whose time had come. The League enthusiastically endorsed his proposal as did the legislatures of all the basin states. In August 1921 Congress consented to the negotiation of a compact.[18] Because the river was an international stream and considered navigable, the federal government sent to the negotiations its own representative, the highly respected Secretary of Commerce, Herbert Hoover. The delegates, now dubbed the Colorado River Commission, invited Hoover to chair the sessions which began in January 1922.

The commissioners spent most of 1922 in fruitless bargaining. They wrangled incessantly, each trying to ensure his state all the water it might need while refusing a similar concession to the others. Finally convinced that they would be unable to settle on a specific volume of water for each state, they decided to concentrate instead on apportioning the river between the upper and lower sections of the basin.[19] But even that decision was more easily reached than implemented. It rested on the assumption that the needs of groups of states could be pegged more easily than those of individual states, and it ignored the possibility of serious conflicts among the states within each basin. Nonetheless, it set the stage for the final round of talks scheduled for November 1922 in New Mexico.

Great pressure for a settlement permeated the negotiations which began on November 9 at Bishop's Lodge, a posh resort near Santa Fe. Californians were driven by their desire for the Swing-Johnson Bill, which had been bottled up in Congress by Upper Basin representatives in control of key reclamation committees. Upper Basin leaders feared that if they did not negotiate a water supply for themselves, a disastrous flood on the lower river might stampede Congress into giving Californians the legislation that they wanted. "We simply *must* use every endeavor to bring about a compact . . . ," pleaded Delph Carpenter, "otherwise . . . we may never again have a like opportunity."[20]

Carpenter had taken the lead in seeking a settlement by circulating, prior to the Santa Fe meeting, a draft proposal allocating the Colorado's waters equally to the Upper and Lower basins. He established the demarcation point between the basins at Lee's Ferry, an old river-crossing station located in northern Arizona's canyon lands not far from the Utah border. While the boundary thus placed parts of several states in both basins, the Upper Basin consisted mainly of Wyoming, Colorado, Utah, and New Mexico and the Lower Basin of Arizona, California, and Nevada.

Discussion of Carpenter's proposal began on an ominous note. Most delegates considered it appealing, but W. S. Norviel of Arizona strongly objected and very nearly brought the proceedings to an end. He sharply criticized the plan for charging the Lower Basin for the water in its tributaries. Though estimates varied, most experts believed those tributaries produced a significant runoff—some two to three million acre-feet—with virtually all of it coming from Arizona streams. Norviel demanded for the Lower Basin all the water in the tributaries, in addition to half the river's flow as measured at Lee's Ferry. He would have preferred that Arizona's tributaries be given specifically to the state, but recognized that the decision to apportion water to basins instead of individual states precluded such an allocation. Besides, he felt Arizona had nothing to fear from the other Lower Basin states— Nevada and California. Nevada's water requests had always been minimal, while California's "ultimate development," he believed, was "definitely well-known" and posed no threat to Arizona.[21]

For days Norviel tenaciously defended his counterproposal, as first one delegate and then another advanced alternatives and sought to bring the conflicting parties together. His intransigence gradually gave way as he found himself standing alone against the pressure for a compromise settlement. The agreement to which he and the others finally gave their approval foresaw the delivery of 7.5 million acre-feet per yer to each basin. Since the bulk of the water originated in the Upper Basin, however, the compact required the upper states to deliver seventy-five million acre-feet at Lee's Ferry every ten years. The ten-year provision allowed the Upper Basin to take advantage of the sometimes severe fluctuations in river flow. In addition to the basic allocation to each basin, the lower states could increase their apportionment by a million acre-feet. This provision reflected Norviel's insistence that the Lower Basin receive compensation for the water in its tributaries. The amount was considerably less than he had sought but high enough to win his grudging approval of the agreement.[22]

The negotiators grounded their water-allocation formula on the Reclamation Bureau's assumption that the average annual flow of the Colorado River at Lee's Ferry was 16.4 million acre-feet. There was no gauging station at Lee's Ferry and this estimate derived from measurements made hundreds of miles downstream at Yuma. It also ignored years of unusually low flow prior to 1905. Nonetheless, the strong desire for a settlement caused no one to challenge the accuracy of the Bureau's estimate—an estimate that indicated 1.4 million acre-feet remained in the main stream as surplus for later allocation.[23]

The few remaining issues were dealt with quickly. The delegates easily agreed to give highest priority to water use for "agricultural and domestic purposes." Hydroelectric power came in for a lesser priority and navigation was made "subservient" to all other uses.[24] As for a possible future treaty with Mexico, the delegates concluded that any such obligation should be met with surplus water, and if that proved insufficient, then the two basins should share equally the burden. This provision reflected a desire to cover an important contingency rather than sympathy for people in Mexico. "We do not believe they ever had any rights," observed Herbert Hoover.[25] The Indians in the Colorado River Basin hardly fared better. Their rights were considered "negligible" and were dealt with perfunctorily in what Hoover called the "wild Indian article": "Nothing in this compact shall be construed as affecting the obligations of the United States of America to Indian tribes."[26]

On Friday, November 24, 1922, after fifteen days of bargaining, the delegates reached agreement on the compact. They adjourned to Santa Fe where formal signing took place in the Palace of the Governors amid much fanfare·and self-congratulation.[27]

A Six-State Pact

The euphoria at Santa Fe was short lived. Within five months every state had ratified the compact except Arizona, but Arizona's

refusal threatened to scuttle the enterprise since only unanimous approval would make the pact effective. Norviel had returned home to
find a new governor in office whose views and those of his closest
advisers were hostile to the agreement. "Arizona cannot afford . . .
to plunge blindly into a contract that may be unfair to her," Governor
George W. P. Hunt cautioned the state legislature.[28] When studies
completed a short time later suggested that Arizona might need the
entire Lower Basin allotment to develop lands in the central part of
the state, Hunt's position hardened. To him, opposition to the compact now became a test of state loyalty. He received strong support
from private utility firms, which were alarmed that the pact would
pave the way for the Boulder Canyon legislation and the construction
of competing public power facilities. Powerful mining interests cho-
rused their opposition because a public power plant would operate tax
free. Since mining companies were shouldering nearly half the Arizona
tax load, they would obtain no relief if the power plants to be built
along the lower river and partially in Arizona were tax exempt.

But the major concern was water. Hunt believed the compact's
"first fundamental error" was its failure to make allocations to individual states.[29] By suspending the law of prior appropriation between
the basins, the compact would protect the Upper Basin from California; but it did nothing to safeguard Arizona from California. The
principle of priority would still prevail among the Lower Basin states.
This posed no problem for Nevada whose small needs were readily
conceded by Arizona and California, but Arizonans became extremely
cautious and then alarmed as they discovered potential uses for water
and hydroelectricity not anticipated earlier. That alarm intensified
when Californians, especially those associated with the Metropolitan
Water District, made similar discoveries. Arizonans found additional
reason for concern in the promise of Upper Basin leaders to withdraw
their opposition to the Boulder Canyon Bill once the compact was in
force. Enactment of the Boulder Canyon legislation would immeas-
urably aid California by authorizing the All-American Canal and especially the high dam that would regulate the river and permit the
MWD to build its own aqueduct and transmission lines. Arizonans,
on the other hand, saw virtually nothing for themselves in the measure. A dam in Boulder Canyon would benefit few Arizona lands unless
other expensive works were also constructed—works viewed by most

experts at the time as economically unfeasible and for which there was no enthusiasm in Congress. Arizonans also worried about what they called the "Mexican threat." A regulated river would enable Mexico to expand its agriculture, and a future treaty might recognize the increased water uses. Put simply, Arizonans feared there would be little water remaining for them after the Upper Basin, California, and Mexico got what they wanted. Those fears, together with Arizona's own ambitious plans for the Colorado, translated soon into implacable opposition to both the compact and the Boulder Canyon legislation.[30]

Arizona's refusal to ratify the compact prompted the other basin states to reassess their earlier insistence on approval by all seven basin states. Delph Carpenter took the lead in campaigning vigorously for a six-state agreement. Some Upper Basin leaders worried about endorsing a compact to which Arizona would not be a party, but Carpenter persuaded them that no practical alternative existed. Because California and Arizona were constantly reevaluating their earlier water needs as too small, it would be folly to attempt to renegotiate the pact and allocate water to each state, as Arizonans were insisting. As a nonsigner, Arizona might try to develop projects that would encroach on the Upper Basin allocation, but success in such a venture would require Washington's approval. The federal government had reserved all the possible dam sites along Arizona's canyons and was unlikely to release any of them without approval of the other basin states. "If . . . the compact were agreed to as binding upon the United States and the six states which have already ratified," reasoned Carpenter, "it would in large measure serve the desired purpose. . . ."[31]

Carpenter's logic proved persuasive. By March 1925 all the upper states and Nevada in the Lower Basin had approved the six-state arrangement. That left only California. Californians favored the reduced requirement for ratification, but only if through it they could absolutely assure themselves the Boulder Canyon Project. Earlier at Santa Fe, they had sought to have such an assurance written into the compact itself, but that had been considered inappropriate. Now, grown weary of waiting for congressional action, they sought that assurance through a different approach. Assemblyman A. C. Finney of the Imperial Valley introduced a resolution in the state legislature making California's approval of the six-state pact dependent upon construction of a high dam on the lower river. Passage of the resolution in April 1925 shifted the major battlefield over the Colorado River to Congress.[32]

Arizona Overwhelmed: The Boulder Canyon Act

In late 1925, when Phil Swing and Hiram Johnson reintroduced in Congress their Boulder Canyon legislation, they included the compact among its provisions. In this way, congressional approval of the compact would mean authorization of lower-river development as well. Swing and Johnson subsequently added other inducements calculated to broaden support—royalties on power to be divided equally between Arizona and Nevada (in lieu of the taxes that those states would collect if the project were built by private capital) and funds authorizing the investigation of possible reclamation projects in every basin state except California.[33]

Congress at first balked at the measure, bowing not only to Arizona's protests but also to those of easterners and others unsympathetic to expensive reclamation and public power projects. In addition, many legislators felt that Arizona and California should be given more time to resolve their differences and to negotiate a Lower Basin apportionment of water. Such opposition lessened over the next two years as both states persisted in their refusal to reach agreement and as Californians launched a campaign dramatically highlighting the flood dangers and water and power needs along the lower river.

Upper Basin leaders were pleased that the Boulder Canyon Bill included the compact among its provisions, but their earlier anxieties returned as the prolonged debates on the measure rekindled their fears of both California and Arizona and reawakened their earlier preference for a seven-state compact. They finally agreed to support the bill, but only if California would promise to limit its use of Colorado River water. Without such a limitation, California could be expected to increase its uses until little remained for Arizona. That state, in turn, would obviously do everything possible to develop projects of its own—projects that would take water meant for the Upper Basin. Arizona would have to overcome serious economic and political obstacles to build such projects, but so long as the state possessed even a remote chance of doing so, the Upper Basin felt threatened. If, on the other hand, California would limit itself and leave a significant volume of Lower Basin water for Arizona, then the threat to the Upper Basin would be reduced considerably. "The States of the upper-basin much prefer a "seven-state compact," observed a Colorado congressman, "but they desire a compact of some kind, and with a provision under which one of the lower basin States—California—practically steps into the position of guarantor, so that the upper-basin [states] would be reasonably assured . . . that they could go ahead safely in developing their irrigation enterprises."[34]

California agreed, but only reluctantly and after much haggling over the precise restriction on its uses. Congress finally settled on 4.4 million acre-feet plus no more than half of any surplus water unapportioned by the compact. Congress then went further in trying to harmonize basin rivalries by adding still another provision to the Boulder Canyon Bill giving prior approval to a Lower Basin pact. The suggested agreement would apportion 0.3 million acre-feet to Nevada, 4.4 million acre-feet and half the surplus to California, and 2.8 million acre-feet plus half the surplus to Arizona. In addition, all the waters of the Gila (Arizona's principal Colorado tributary) would go to Arizona and be exempted from any future Mexican treaty. Many objected to the proposal as an infringement on states' rights, but its author disagreed, insisting that it was merely a suggestion and "not the request of the Congress." "If California and Nevada and Arizona do not like this agreement," he explained, "they do not have to approve it."[35] With that assurance, the proposal won adoption and paved the way for a final vote on the bill.

Over Arizona's continued vigorous objections, Congress approved the Boulder Canyon Bill in December 1928. Two months later the California legislature agreed to the limitation imposed by Congress and on June 25, 1929, President Herbert Hoover declared the act effective.[36]

"Arizona v. California: Round One"

Enactment of the Boulder Canyon legislation meant approval of the Colorado River Compact and authorization of the All-American Canal and a high dam on the lower river. Under the terms of the new law, construction of the dam could not begin until the federal government had obtained contracts for the hydroelectric power needed to pay for the project. Since Nevada had no market for Boulder Canyon power and Arizona had neither a market nor a desire for one, Californians in 1930 obligated themselves to purchase all the electricity and thereby underwrite the cost of the dam and power plant. The contracts permitted the federal government to draw back 36 percent of the power for use in Arizona and Nevada any time during the fifty years required to pay for the project, but until the two states asked for power, California agencies had to take all of it.[37]

The Great Depression of the 1930s slowed construction, but in 1935 Hoover Dam was completed (in more suitable Black Canyon, rather than in Boulder Canyon as originally planned) and a year later hydroelectric power reached southern California communities. In June 1941 the Metropolitan Water District of Southern California began delivering water to the coastal plain, and the next Imperial Valley residents received their first supplies through the All-American Canal. Californians delighted in these developments, which during the next three decades allowed Los Angeles to grow to three million inhabitants and the four coastal counties to attract a population in excess of ten million.[38]

Arizonans looked angrily on California's rapid growth. Their state also grew during the same period, but the increases in people and economic development paled in comparison to those of California which they accused of taking water that rightly belonged to them. At first Arizonans returned to the negotiating table and tried to hammer out a Lower Basin compact with California, but the two states repeatedly failed to harmonize their differences and neither state was satisfied with the pact suggested by Congress in the Boulder Canyon Act.

When bargaining collapsed, Arizonans turned to the U.S. Supreme Court for help. In 1930 in the first of a series of *Arizona v. California* cases, they asked the courts to declare unconstitutional the Boulder Canyon Act because it violated Arizona's "quasi-sovereign rights" by authorizing construction of a dam partially in Arizona without the state's permission. Congress's claim that it had acted to improve navigation was a "subterfuge and false pretense." The Court was unimpressed: authorization of the dam came clearly within the government's power to improve navigation and represented a "valid . . . exercise of the Constitutional power."[39] Four years later Arizonans returned to the Court and asked it to certify for later use some oral testimony on the meaning of certain sections of the Colorado River Compact. They planned to use the testimony in a future suit against California. Again the Court disappointed them: "The meaning of the Compact . . . can never be material . . . since Arizona refused to ratify."[40] Still unwilling to admit defeat, Arizonans turned once more to the Court a year later. In 1935 they asked for a judicial apportionment of the lower Colorado in which Arizona would receive an "equitable share of the water." But, as before, the justices threw out the case. The technical reason was Arizona's failure to make the U.S. government a party to the suit. Yet even if the U.S. had been included, the Court left little doubt that the outcome would have been the same. Unless Arizona could show that it was actually being deprived of water to which it held title, there would be no "justiciable controversy."[41] With hundreds of millions of gallons flowing unused in the river, Arizona stood little chance of demonstrating that harm had been done.

Convinced at last that the Court would not provide a satisfactory solution, Arizonans reopened bargaining with California. But here, too, the old patterns of intransigence reemerged. Arizonans had not endeared themselves to their rival when in 1933 they had sent their National Guard to prevent construction of MWD's diversion works on the Colorado. The shutdown proved temporary, but the incident had hardened differences that became further embittered as first one and then another of California's projects were completed.[42] By the early 1940s the accumulated setbacks prompted some leading Arizonans to reassess the state's water policy—a policy grounded on opposition to the Colorado River Compact.

California's advances naturally played a role in Arizona thinking, but so, too, did developments at home. The state's population had more than doubled in the two decades following the drafting of the compact. By 1944 the number of people stood at 700,000 with most of them congregated in the central part of the state near the rapidly growing cities of Phoenix and Tucson. Local water supplies were inadequate for the growth envisaged by state leaders, and in some places wells had gone dry while in others pumping had led to land subsidence.

Electricity was in even shorter supply than water. In 1939 the Bureau of Reclamation responded to Arizona's plea for emergency power by establishing a line to Hoover Dam.[43]

Arizona's decision to accept Hoover Dam electricity marked a major change in the state's policy. Leaders had delayed taking power as long as possible on the grounds that doing so would compromise their opposition to the compact. They had found support for such resistance from private power companies that were not anxious to compete with cheaper public power. But the need for electricity proved eventually too strong to resist. In time so did the desire for water. Many Arizonans began arguing that if the state was to win support in Congress for reclamation projects of its own, Arizona would have to ratify the compact. Taking this message directly to the people of the state was Governor Sidney Osborn. "With the passage by Congress of the Boulder Canyon Project Act in 1928," Osborn declared in 1943, "the era of theorizing about the Colorado's riches has ended. Whatever our previous opinion about the best place and the best plan for utilizing its water . . . , we now can only recognize that the decisions have been made, and the dam has been constructed."[44]

On February 24, 1944, the Arizona legislature unconditionally ratified the compact and reversed twenty-two years of opposition.[45] State leaders then began working closely with the Reclamation Bureau to devise a major reclamation project for Arizona. The struggle now entered a new phase.

The Mexican Water Treaty

Reenforcing Arizona's decision to ratify the compact was a treaty signed three weeks earlier by the United States and Mexico. On February 3, 1944, the two countries had ended nearly a half century of controversy by agreeing to divide the waters of the Colorado River. Some two thousand square miles of Mexican territory lay within the Colorado Basin, a modest amount of land when compared to the U.S. drainage area, but it included the Mexicali Valley, one of the richest agricultural regions in Mexico.

The Mexicali Valley lies just across the border from California's Imperial Valley, and the development of the two areas was closely intertwined from the outset. The need to divert water south of the line and to allow landholders in Mexico up to half the flow fostered farming in the Mexicali Valley while also stimulating demands in the U.S. for the All-American Canal. Some leaders in both countries early advocated a treaty dividing the river's waters, but negotiations seldom got beyond the preliminary stage. Complicating the task were attempts to reach a similar agreement on the lower Rio Grande, the other major river shared by the U.S. and Mexico. In 1906, the two countries had arrived at a settlement on the waters of the upper Rio Grande (the area north of Fort Quitman, a demarcation point just below El Paso and Juárez), but talks on the lower river stalled and became increasingly tangled with those on the Colorado. While virtually all the waters of the Colorado originated in the U.S., the situation was almost the reverse on the lower Rio Grande where more than 70 percent of the runoff came from Mexico. The situation contained the elements for a horse trade, but neither country would compromise enough to reach a settlement. Each nation tended to approach the rivers separately and to seek the superior settlement even when this meant adopting a legal position on one river at odds with the position advanced on the other stream. During extended talks in 1929 and 1930, the U.S. offered Mexico 0.75 million acre-feet of Colorado River water, the maximum amount she had used in any one year up to that time, but Mexico insisted on more than four times as much. When the talks collapsed, Mexico expanded her agriculture below the border while Imperial Valley farmers looked forward to the completion of the All-American Canal with which they hoped to force a settlement on Mexico.[46]

By the early 1940s both countries were anxious for an accord. The completion of the All-American Canal in 1942 and plans for a project on the lower Rio Grande that would neutralize Mexico's superior position there brought Mexican officials to the bargaining table. The U.S. sought to put a limit on Mexico's Colorado River uses, which had doubled during the previous decade and could be expected to increase further as a result of Hoover Dam's regulation of the river. Only when Americans began using virtually the entire flow—and that might not be for decades—could the All-American Canal become an effective weapon. The U.S. government, enmeshed in the crisis of World War II, also believed that a settlement of the water dispute would significantly advance the Good Neighbor Policy of President Franklin D. Roosevelt.

After months of bargaining during which the State Department consulted frequently with leaders in the Colorado Basin states, the two nations signed a treaty in February 1944. Mexico received 1.5 million acre-feet, an amount slightly less than the State Department believed that country was then using.[47]

Californians greeted the news with anger. They claimed Mexico deserved only 0.75 million acre-feet, the maximum amount that it had used prior to the completion of Hoover Dam in 1935 and the amount offered in the unsuccessful negotiations of 1929 and 1930. Behind California's strong opposition was the belief that Mexico was being given water that would mostly come from California. The state had limited itself to 4.4 million acre-feet plus half the surplus, and California was currently using nearly a million acre-feet of surplus water. California's calculations indicated there would be little or no surplus remaining if Mexico received the amount promised in the treaty.[48]

While Californians fought vigorously to prevent U.S. Senate approval of the agreement, the other basin states advocated ratification. They feared that Mexican uses would increase further and perhaps encroach on the basic compact allocations if a settlement were not obtained. Even Arizona, which also had designs on surplus water, endorsed the treaty. Arizonans, unlike Californians, had not built expensive aqueducts with capacities to carry surplus waters to the state. Moreover, Arizonans, who had now ratified the compact, shared the upper states' desire to safeguard the basic allocations in that agreement. Support also came from those worried about the harm that would be done to the Good Neighbor Policy by a rejection of the treaty. Repercussions would be more serious than in earlier years since Mexicans, not American capitalists, were now farming the Mexicali Valley. In 1938 the Mexican government had expropriated most of the land belonging to the Chandler syndicate and the remainder had been disposed of a few years later. Additional advocates of the treaty were Texans on the lower Rio Grande who were pleased with the provisions allocating water on that stream and providing for orderly international development.

The broad support, together with pressure from the White House, overwhelmed the California opposition. On April 18, 1945, the Senate approved the treaty by a vote of seventy-six to ten. Five months later, on September 27, the Mexican Senate voted unanimous approval.[49]

Upper Basin Compact: Harbinger of Development

The Mexican treaty, Arizona's ratification of the compact, and California's rapidly increasing uses of Colorado River water forcefully reminded the upper states of their own reclamation ambitions. Colorado had already taken the lead in 1937 by winning congressional approval of the Colorado–Big Thompson Project, a plan for transporting water out of the basin to the cities and farms on the eastern slope of the Rockies. Other projects awaited a feasibility study authorized by the Boulder Canyon Act but delayed by the onset of World War II. Finally, in March 1946, the Reclamation Bureau issued the long-awaited study. The message proved disconcerting: many possible projects existed on the headwaters but there was not enough water for all of them. Until the upper states determined their individual rights the Bureau refused to approve any projects.[50]

Within four months, the governors of the Upper Basin states had authorized negotiation of a compact to apportion their share of the river's waters. After two years of gathering data and holding public hearings, delegates gathered in Vernal, Utah, in July 1948 to draft an agreement. Three weeks of negotiations produced a pact apportioning the Upper Basin water on a percentage basis: 51.75 percent to Colorado, 23 percent to Utah, 14 percent to Wyoming, and 11.25 percent to New Mexico. The use of percentages reflected uncertainty over how much water would remain after the Upper Basin had fulfilled its obligation to the lower states and, if the surplus proved insufficient, to Mexico. Only Arizona, which had a small section of the state in the Upper Basin, received a specific volume—fifty thousand acre-feet. Unlike the compact of 1922, the Upper Basin agreement provided for the creation of an interstate agency, the Upper Colorado River Commission, charged with determining the water uses of each state and with reducing diversions if that should become necessary to meet the obligations to the Lower Basin.[51]

The delegates circulated the draft agreement among their respective state governments, which gave the go-ahead for the formal signing in Santa Fe on October 11, 1948. By early 1949, the pact had received the approval of all the upper-state legislatures and Congress.[52] Upper Basin leaders now joined with Reclamation Bureau officials to obtain major new reclamation projects for their region.

In early 1952 the first Colorado River Storage Project Bill reached Congress. It called for a billion-dollar dam-building program with major reservoirs at Echo Park on the Green River and at Glen Canyon on the main stream near the Arizona-Utah border. The bill immediately aroused opposition from southern Californians who viewed any significant developments on the upper river as threats to their own water uses. More recent measurements of flow had been calling into question the rosy forecasts on which the 1922 compact had been based. Major opposition also emerged nationwide and focused on the Echo Park reservoir, which would flood the unique and beautiful canyons of Dinosaur National Monument. The alarm escalated into the biggest battle over wilderness preservation since John Muir had tried to keep a dam out of Hetch Hetchy Valley at the turn of the century. The contest was essentially a civil war in which both sides labeled themselves "conservationists." While one side campaigned for conservation for use through dams and hydroelectric power, the other argued for conservation through preservation of unique wilderness areas. The struggle took on added intensity when opponents elevated Echo Park to the status of a test case that they believed would shape national policy for decades.[53]

After several years of struggle, the bill's advocates finally conceded that Echo Park would have to go. Opposition in the House proved unmovable, and preservationists began threatening to campaign against other dam sites mentioned in the bill. The measure that finally cleared Congress in 1956 eliminated Echo Park and seemed to reflect an unequivocal preservationist victory: "It is the intention of Congress that no dam or reservoir constructed under the authorization of the Act shall be within any National Park or Monument."[54] Within a short time, however, it became clear that the victory was far from complete. Preservationists viewed their acquiescence to the other major dam in the bill at Glen Canyon as a serious mistake that cost the loss of a remarkable wilderness area. Their disappointment intensified several years later when they failed to prevent the water rising behind

Glen Canyon Dam from flooding Rainbow Bridge National Monument in southern Utah.[55] The congressional proviso in the 1956 measure appeared to be a dead letter.

Under the resulting Colorado River Storage Project Act of 1956, Glen Canyon became the "cash register" generating most of the revenue through the sale of hydroelectric power to build a dozen so-called participating projects elsewhere in the Upper Basin. The largest was the Central Utah Project outside the basin, which was to receive water for nearly 144,000 acres of new land and a supplementary supply for almost 243,000 acres. By 1963 Glen Canyon Dam had been completed and Lake Powell had been brought into existence behind it. The act also authorized dams for three tributaries—Blue Mesa on the Gunnison, Flaming Gorge on the Green, and Navajo on the San Juan. Additional legislation in 1962 and 1964 further rounded out Upper Basin desires by authorizing the San Juan–Chama, Navajo, Fryingpan-Arkansas, Savery–Pot Hook, Bostwick Park, and Fruitland Mesa projects.[56]

"Arizona v. California: Round Two"

The Upper Basin's success in obtaining reclamation projects aroused envy and concern in Arizona. That state had approved the compact in 1944 and three years later greeted enthusiastically the Reclamation Bureau's plan for a massive undertaking, the Central Arizona Project (CAP). The plan resurrected and now deemed economically feasible the old high-line canal scheme advocated by former Governor Hunt. The project called for a 241-mile-long aqueduct to transport some 1.2 million acre-feet to the rapidly growing Phoenix and Tucson areas. When Arizonans introduced a bill in Congress to authorize the CAP, they encountered stiff opposition from Californians who argued that Arizona was attempting to use water that did not belong to the state. This time dissension centered on conflicting interpretations of the 1922 compact. The differing claims caused Congress to refuse approval of the CAP until the two states had resolved their differences. Congress did not want to invest in a project for which there might be no water.[57]

The news bitterly disappointed Arizonans. While the Upper Basin, California, and Mexico were moving ahead with their projects,

Arizonans had remained stymied. They believed their only recourse was to appeal once more to the U.S. Supreme Court.

When Arizona filed suit in 1952, it asked the Court for a judicial apportionment of the Lower Basin's water. When it had made a similar plea in 1935 the Court had refused to act on the grounds that no actual harm was being done since the volume of water exceeded current uses. Seventeen years later the flow still exceeded uses, but this time Arizona succeeded in persuading the justices that the state would suffer serious harm if the dispute with California were not resolved.

The subsequent trial proved to be among the most complicated and hotly contested in Supreme Court history. It lasted eleven years, required the services of a special master, cost nearly five million dollars, and resulted in major shifts in position as the two states jockeyed for advantage. Some 340 witnesses testified and nearly 50 lawyers participated before the opinion was finally announced on June 3, 1963, followed by the decree on March 9, 1964.

The decision represented a tremendous victory for Arizona, although the nature of the victory took nearly everyone by surprise. The Court grounded its opinion not on the compact, but rather on the Boulder Canyon Act. In that measure, declared the Court in its five-to-three decision, Congress "intended to and did create its own comprehensive scheme for . . . apportionment." According to the justices, Congress in 1928 had not merely suggested a Lower Basin compact; it had actually authorized the Secretary of the Interior to use his contract power to implement a Lower Basin agreement—an agreement "leaving each State its tributaries" and an agreement in which "Congress decided that a fair division of the first 7,500,000 acre-feet of . . . mainstream waters would give 4,400,000 acre-feet to California, 2,800,000 acre-feet to Arizona, and 300,000 to Nevada."[58] By awarding Arizona all the water in its tributaries plus 2.8 million acre-feet, the Court gave the state virtually everything that it had unsuccessfully sought during the negotiations for the 1922 compact.

Californians reacted angrily to the decision, accusing the Court of misreading the intent of Congress and eroding the rights of the states. They correctly noted that the decision represented the first time that the Court had interpreted an act of Congress as apportioning rights to interstate streams. Water rights had earlier been determined only by interstate compact or by the Supreme Court itself. Now a third way had won approval, even though it would have amazed the Congress of thirty-five years earlier to know what it was supposed to have done.[59]

Another surprise was the Court's decision on how future surpluses and shortages would be allocated. Responsibility would rest with the Secretary of the Interior, who would not only apportion surpluses and shortages among the states but also among the users *within* each state. The latter marked an especially sharp break with tradition. Since states had always determined the water laws applicable to their citizens, they had naturally also determined the water rights of those citizens. But now the Court held that Congress had empowered the Secretary of the Interior to determine those rights when water had been secured by contract from federal reclamation projects.

In explaining Congress's authority over apportionment, the Court pointed to the navigation clause of the Constitution, but it also hinted that Congress could invoke the "general welfare" clause to divide the waters of nonnavigable as well as navigable streams.[60] The decision thus increased dramatically Congress's authority over the nation's rivers. More importantly from the point of view of Arizonans, it seemed at long last to pave the way for the Central Arizona Project.

"Arizona v. California" and the American Indian

The decision in *Arizona v. California* proved almost as much a victory for American Indians as for Arizona. The Indians had long been overlooked in Colorado River matters, but following World War II they reemerged in the public consciousness as white Americans grappled uneasily with the social and economic inequities of the nation's ethnic minorities. When Arizona filed suit in 1952, the federal government intervened to protect its interests and also to defend the rights of the Indians living on the twenty-five reservations in the Lower Basin. Government lawyers asked for sufficient water to maintain not only Indian reservations, but, in addition, the national forests, parks, recreational areas, and other governmental holdings. Specifically for the Indians, the government demanded enough water to develop all the irrigable lands on the reservations.

The Court upheld the contentions of the federal attorneys, although in doing so it restricted its decision to the five reservations along or near the main stream—Chemehuevi, Cocopah, Yuma, Colorado River, and Fort Mohave—and left to the future the ultimate fate of the other reservations. Implicitly, however the opinion had far-reaching implications for Indians elsewhere. Invoking a principle laid down in the 1908 case of *Winters v. United States,* the justices held that the five lower-river reservations "were not limited to land but included waters as well. . . . It is impossible to believe that when Congress created the great Colorado River Indian Reservation and when the Executive Department of this Nation created the other reservations they were unaware that most of the lands were of the desert kind—hot, scorching sands—and that water from the river would be essential to the life of the Indian people and to the animals they hunted and the crops they raised." In determining the volume of water set aside, the Court adopted the government's position. "How many Indians there will be and what their future needs will be can only be guessed. We have concluded . . . that the only feasible and fair way by which reserved water for the reservations can be measured is irrigable acreage."[61] Although the measurement of the right was irrigable acreage, the Court held in a later supplemental decree that the Indians were not restricted in the uses to which they could put their water.[62] Reason, rather than agriculture, seemed to emerge as the ultimate test.

The 1963 decision also stipulated that Indian uses were to be charged against the state in which a reservation was located. This especially disturbed Arizona where most of the Indian land was located, but it pleased none of the basin states. In addition, the Court held that the Indian rights dated from the establishment of a reservation and was superior to later non-Indian rights, including those rights based on uses initiated before the Indians had begun diverting water. Thus the Court held (and in so doing reaffirmed the earlier *Winters* decision) that the Indian rights existed whether or not the Indians were actually using water and continued unimpaired even if the Indians should cease their uses. Since some of the Indian lands along the lower river had been set aside as early as 1865 and none later than 1917, the decision left the Indians in an almost impregnable legal position.

But the Indians soon learned that a legal right did not guarantee them water. A decade after the decision, the Indians were farming only about half their irrigable acreage. By the later 1970s the amount was closer to 60 percent, but the Indians themselves had developed less than 8 percent. The remainder was in the hands of non-Indian leaseholders. The major reasons for this situation were Indian poverty and non-Indian pressure on the federal government. The Indians were unable to finance expensive irrigation projects themselves, and Congress was reluctant to help because of pressure from non-Indians opposed to Indian projects that would divert water from their cities and farms. The Colorado River Indian Irrigation Project, for example, was initiated in 1865 but remains uncompleted primarily because of lack of funds. Not surprisingly, when Indian lands on the lower river have been developed, it has usually been because tribes have entered into long-term leasing arrangements with non-Indians.[63]

Another disappointment to Indians on the lower Colorado was the 1983 Supreme Court decision on the extent of the irrigable acreage on the reservations. For two decades Indians and non-Indians debated sharply, with the Indians offering one set of figures and the non-Indians insisting on another and lower set. In 1979 the Supreme Court turned the dispute over to a special master who three years later recommended that the Court uphold Indian claims that would permit them to receive some 1.2 million acre-feet or about a third more water than had been awarded nearly twenty years earlier in *Arizona* v. *California.* In a five-to-three decision, the Court in 1983 rejected the recommendation, explaining that it violated the spirit of *res judicata:* "Recalculating the amount of practicably irrigable acreage runs directly counter to the strong interest in finality in this case." Besides, the Court observed, more water for the Indians "cannot help but exacerbate potential water shortage problems" for non-Indians.[64]

Elsewhere in the Colorado River Basin, Indians have sometimes bargained away potential rights in order to obtain congressional support for projects. The Navajos, the nation's largest tribe, did so in 1957 when the tribal council, in exchange for congressional approval of the Navajo Indian Irrigation Project, agreed to waive its priority on the San Juan River and to share water shortages proportionately with non-Indians. A decade later the Navajos entered into still another agreement which compromised their claims and became the subject of sharp controversy. In exchange for the construction of a power plant on the reservation and the jobs and revenue it would provide, the

Navajos agreed to limit their demands to the water of the upper Colorado to fifty thousand acre-feet. The limitation was for the life of the power plant (now in operation) or for fifty years, whichever ended first. Many Navajos subsequently attacked the agreement, claiming that the federal government failed to fully inform the tribal council about valuable potential rights that it was surrendering.[65] In recent years, the Navajos have employed engineers and attorneys to prepare a water rights case against the basin states and the federal government. Some observers believe that the suit, if filed, will be for at least five million acre-feet.[66] The outcome of such litigation, as well as of suits now being contemplated by other tribes, is impossible to determine. What is clear is that Indians can no longer be ignored in future planning for the Colorado River.

The CAP: Catalyst for Basinwide Development

Arizona v. *California* proved a boon—at least legally—for Indians, but Arizonans were the major beneficiaries. As victors in their decade-old struggle with California, they optimistically returned to Congress for authorization of the Central Arizona Project. Approval did not come easily, however. Californians had lost the Supreme Court battle in 1963, but their large delegation in the House of Representatives doggedly held up the Arizona project for five years. Behind the California resistance was the conviction of state leaders that earlier estimates of stream flow had been grossly overestimated. Instead of 16.4 million acre-feet at Lee's Ferry, the runoff, according to more recent estimates, was closer to fourteen million acre-feet. This meant that under conditions of full development, the Lower Basin would receive at Lee's Ferry only the seventy-five million acre-feet over a ten-year period as guaranteed in the 1922 compact. Adjustments for evaporation losses, Indian claims, and the Mexican treaty obligation could be expected to reduce the available supply even further.[67]

But Californians were willing to bargain. As the price for dropping their opposition to CAP, they demanded a first priority for California's apportionment of 4.4 million acre-feet. In effect, Arizonans would have to promise to regulate CAP diversions so that Californians never received less than that amount. No one missed the point: California boldly sought to regain some of the ground lost in the 1963 Court decision.

Arizonans reluctantly acquiesced. Like Californians, they were uneasy about the adequacy of the water supply, but their desire for the CAP outweighed their uneasiness. The water diverted to the CAP, they promised Californians in a provision added to the bill, "shall be so limited as to assure the availability" of the 4.4 million acre-feet allocated to California.

Arizona had to mollify more than California. The concern about the water supply had spread to the Upper Basin. If the river flow at Lee's Ferry was only about fourteen million acre-feet, as many now suspected, then the upper states, after fulfilling their obligation to the Lower Basin, would receive 6.5 million acre-feet, a million acre-feet less than anticipated in the 1922 compact. Their share could drop even further after allowing for evaporation losses, the Mexican treaty, and Indian claims. Worried that such water-supply estimates might later prevent them from obtaining projects on their own, they tied their fortunes to the Arizona bill. They agreed to support it but only in exchange for a provision authorizing five projects for the Upper Basin—Animas-LaPlata, Dolores, Dallas, West Divide, and San Miguel. This would bring to twenty-one the number of "participating projects" authorized by Congress for the Upper Basin since 1956.[68]

The maneuvering for concessions produced a bill authorizing projects for which the water supply was likely to be inadequate. This possibility prompted the basin states to close ranks behind another provision directing the Bureau of Reclamation to study ways of bringing water into the Colorado River Basin from other river systems. Strong opposition came from environmentalists and especially from leaders in the Pacific Northwest who knew that Bureau officials viewed the Columbia River as the probable source of a supplementary supply. Although the opponents failed to delete the provision, they succeeded in obtaining a ten-year ban on interbasin studies.

Satisfying the various water interests in the basin proved to be only one of the obstacles facing the CAP advocates. In the public's mind, the most controversial aspect of the legislation involved two proposed dams, one at Marble Canyon just east of the main gorge of the Grand Canyon, and the other at Bridge Canyon, a short distance west of Grand Canyon. The principal purpose of the dams would be to generate hydroelectricity to provide revenue for building the CAP and power to pump the water into Central Arizona. Both dams would flood scenic areas, and the reservoir behind Bridge Canyon would inundate portions of Grand Canyon National Park and Grand Canyon National Monument. Environmentalists waged a vigorous, national campaign against the dams that was reminiscent of the struggle over Echo Park. The furor finally forced the deletion of the dams. In their place was substituted a coal-fired power plant to be built at Page in northern Arizona.[69]

As finally amended, the CAP legislation emerged as the Colorado River Basin Project Bill. In September 1968, the billion-dollar-plus package of compromises received congressional approval.[70]

Uncertainty over the adequacy of the water supply for the CAP as well as concern about the project's impact on the environment resulted in only small annual appropriations for actual construction. By the early 1980s the slowdown in the nation's economy had added to the delay, but by then the coal-fired plant had been built (emitting air pollutants over Grand Canyon, Zion, Cedar Breaks, and Bryce that caused environmentalists to regret having given their earlier approval) and completion of the CAP to the Phoenix area was scheduled for late 1985 and to the Tucson area for the early 1990s. In the Upper Basin, nine of the twenty-one participating projects had been completed by 1971 and work was continuing on most of the others in the early 1980s. Construction crews on the ambitious Central Utah Project had by early 1985 finished a tunnel through the Continental Divide and were under contract to complete the final segments of the 37-mile-long Strawberry Aqueduct.[71]

Salinity Controversy with Mexico

Even before construction had begun on the CAP or on most Upper Basin projects, the United States had become embroiled once more in a controversy with Mexico, this time over the quality of the runoff reaching that country. The 1944 treaty had guaranteed Mexico 1.5 million acre-feet, but the agreement said nothing specific about water quality. The seriousness of the omission had become apparent even before ratification and while hearings were being held on the treaty in the U.S. and Mexico. American negotiators claimed that the Mexican obligation could be met with water of any quality, while Mexico's diplomats told their senators that the treaty guaranteed water of "good quality." The issue had arisen because studies indicated that water reaching Mexico during certain future periods would consist almost entirely of heavily saline drainage from irrigated fields in the U.S. Such concern failed to dampen the enthusiasm of treaty advocates who feared that attempts to clarify the agreement through reservations or renegotiation would result in no treaty at all.[72] Sixteen years later water quality emerged as a bitter issue between Mexico and the U.S.

In 1961 the Wellton-Mohawk Irrigation District, located along the lower Gila River in Arizona, completed a channel discharging drainage water into the Colorado just above Mexico's diversion canal. This water was exceptionally heavy in salt content since its source was an underground basin possessing no outlet and containing water that had been used and reused over the years until it had declined sharply in quality. The introduction into the Wellton-Mohawk Valley of a new supply from the Colorado River in the 1950s had raised the water table and damaged fields, causing farmers to take the Reclamation Bureau's advice and install wells to pump the polluted groundwater to the surface and channel it into the main stream. When this drainage water reached the Colorado in February 1961 it caused the average annual salinity of the flow crossing the border to nearly double. Resulting crop losses in Mexico produced a loud outcry. Mexican officials accused the U.S. of violating the 1944 treaty, demanded compensation for damages, insisted on water as good as that going to the Imperial Valley, and threatened to take the issue to the International Court of Justice if the protests went unheeded. The U.S. denied that the treaty imposed any obligation "with respect to the quality of the water," but nonetheless took steps to alleviate the problem. Fresher water was released from American dams and a channel was constructed in 1965 to divert the Wellton-Mohawk drainage around the Mexican intake.[73]

The situation improved, but both countries recognized the improvement as temporary. It would be only a matter of time before evaporation from American reservoirs and completion of projects already authorized would seriously impair the quality of water crossing the border. The two nations sought a negotiated settlement, and on

August 30, 1973, they signed an agreement known as Minute 242 of the International Boundary and Water Commission.[74]

Both governments hailed the agreement as "the permanent and definitive solution of the salinity problem," an expression more of hope than of reality. Minute 242 promised Mexico that most of its water (1.36 million acre-feet) would have an average annual salinity of no more than 115 parts per million (plus or minus 33 ppm) over the salinity of the water going to the Imperial Valley. The balance of Mexico's water (0.14 million acre-feet), which had traditionally been delivered at San Luis on the Arizona-Sonora land boundary, would continue "with a salinity substantially the same as that of the waters customarily delivered there." The agreement obligated the U.S. to assume all the costs necessary to maintain the agreed-upon salinity levels. In addition, the U.S. pledged to finance the installation of tile drains in the Mexicali Valley and to fund any other "rehabilitation" measures necessary to eliminate the "salinity problem" there.

As far as Mexico was concerned, Minute 242 would represent a "permanent and definitive solution" only so long as water quality remained substantially as it was at that time (approximately 1,000 ppm). The American negotiator of the agreement candidly acknowledged that unless the U.S. immediately took steps to control salinity within its borders another dispute with Mexico was inevitable.[75]

Congress took the hint. In June 1974 the Colorado River Basin Salinity Control Act received the overwhelming approval of both House and Senate. The measure authorized upstream salt-control projects in Nevada, Utah, and Colorado, as well as one of the world's largest desalination plants near Yuma. The plant is now under construction and scheduled for completion in 1989 or 1990. Only time will reveal the success or failure of the efforts.[76]

Retrospect

"A river no more" is one current assessment of the Colorado.[77] It is difficult to argue with such an observation. The dams and aqueducts already in place have permanently altered the river's appearance and, for more than two decades, have prevented virtually any water from flowing to the Gulf of California.[78] Completion of projects already authorized can only further control a river that long ago ceased to be wild. The wonder is that the Colorado has been so transformed in light of the monumental battles over its waters during the last three-quarters of a century. But those controversies reflect not only the preciousness of water in an arid land, but more importantly, the almost frenzied determination of the combatants to use water as quickly as possible and thereby strengthen their claim to it.

The determination to use rivers has shaped the major western institutions dealing with water in general and the Colorado in particular. The law of prior appropriation is an obvious reverberation, but so too are the Colorado River Compact, the Boulder Canyon Act, the Mexican treaty, the Upper Basin compact, the 1963 *Arizona v. California* decision, and the other actions, which, taken together, have made the Colorado what it is today. Each represents for its time what was perceived by its advocates as the best way of dealing with the river. The best way, of course, did not always mean the most efficient, the most environmentally sound, or the fairest way to proceed.

Some would now like to undo past decisions or at least to chart a future less constrained by those actions. In the Upper Basin are those who advocate rewriting the 1922 compact so as to reflect more recent estimates of stream flow and to assure themselves enough water to develop their oil-shale and other mineral reserves. Indians want a larger share of the river. Environmentalists wish to prevent additional development and to sidetrack some authorized but uncompleted projects. More significantly, they would like to change popular attitudes which view every drop of water reaching the ocean as a drop wasted and which tend to overlook aesthetic and recreational values associated with uncontrolled streams.

There are, in addition, those convinced that the only way to proceed is to augment the Colorado River with water from elsewhere. In 1978 the ten-year moratorium on studies to bring in water from other basins was renewed for another ten years. When it was first imposed, most eyes were on the Columbia River, but the emergence of the environmental movement and the costly pumping requirements projected in studies of the Columbia have dampened enthusiasm for such a transfer—at least for the time being.

Ten years ago many experts predicted that desalination of ocean water would become a major source for meeting municipal and industrial needs. Since then, declining public support for nuclear plants and skyrocketing costs of oil for conventional facilities have seriously undermined this possibility for the foreseeable future. The energy cost in oil for desalting an acre-foot of ocean water in southern California is more than six times that for an equivalent volume of Colorado River water brought in by aqueduct.[79]

A by-product of the soaring cost of energy has been intensified competition for the relatively cheap power produced at Hoover Dam. The original power contracts were scheduled to come up for renewal in 1987. California by the mid-1980s was receiving nearly 65 percent of the electricity, while Arizona and Nevada were getting 17.6 percent apiece. At first, California insisted that the new contracts reaffirm the old arrangement, but Arizona and Nevada demanded an equal allocation among the three states, arguing that they needed the additional electricity, that the Boulder Canyon Act entitled them to it, and that the dam's location in the two states warranted a larger share. Californians disagreed, contending that their decision to take the power provided the revenue to build the dam and that "it's not right that Nevada and Arizona can come back 50 years later wanting to take two thirds of the power."[80] Others, especially in the East, objected to maintaining the current rate structure, arguing that the cost of Hoover electricity was significantly below that of power elsewhere in the nation and hence represented an unwarranted governmental subsidy. Anxious to forestall the growing demands for a rate increase and to avoid a protracted court battle among themselves, the three lower states in 1984 hammered out a compromise based upon increasing the capacity of Hoover Dam's generators, the surrendering by California of a small amount of energy, the obtaining of additional power from other sources, and the retention of the current basis for computing the cost of power. (Despite agreement on the last point, the actual cost of power to the public could be expected to rise significantly as a result of the changes to Hoover's generators and the obtaining of the additional power from elsewhere.) With the western states voting almost as a block, Congress approved the agreement and in late summer the President signed into law the Hoover Power Plant Act under which the new contracts would not again come up for renewal until the year 2017.[81]

Although the dispute over power has captured recent headlines, concern over the water supply remains a fundamental issues. Representatives of basin states with incomplete water projects become nervous during public discussions about possible water shortages. Receiving much attention is weather modification through cloud-seeding as a way to augment river supplies. The results of the Bureau of Reclamation's pilot program in the San Juan mountains of Colorado suggest that cloud-seeding throughout the Upper Basin mountains would increase runoff by 1.3 million acre-feet a year. Although some find these claims encouraging, the overall feasibility of weather modification as a significant source of water must await the completion of current studies.[82] Also receiving emphasis are programs to control more effectively weeds along water courses and to encourage more widespread use of laser land-leveling technology, drip irrigation, and sprinkling rather than flooding.

Behind the scramble for water in years past was not only its obvious necessity for survival in a water-shy country but also an obsession with growth—an obsession that equated progress with obtaining enough water to develop the biggest farms and cities and industries. Many now question that fascination with growth, but even they tend to forget that water is a finite commodity. Ten years or a hundred years or a hundred thousand years from now, the world's supply will remain the same. Such an assertion cannot be made about the world's population or about mankind's capacity for devising technologies to use—and abuse—the limited water supply. Put another way, the fate of all natural bodies of water is inseparably tied to human values about the quality of life and the number of people any part of the world can properly support. Seen from this perspective, the Colorado River is a microcosm of the world's water supply. Lessons learned from its past and policies adopted for its future are of fundamental importance not only for those dependent on the river, but also for peoples everywhere.

Notes

1. Arthur Powell Davis to J. B. Lippincott, 10 October 1902, Colorado River Project, 1902–1919, Bureau of Reclamation Papers, Record Group 115, File 187, National Archives.

2. Arthur Powell Davis, *The Single Tax from the Farmer's Standpoint* (Minneapolis, 1897); Davis to Gifford Pinchot, 14 May 1912, Arthur Powell Davis Papers, Western History Research Center, University of Wyoming, Laramie; Gene Gressley, "Arthur Powell Davis, Reclamation, and the West," *Agricultural History* 42 (1968), pp. 241–57.

3. League of the Southwest, "Minutes" (Denver, 25–27 August 1920), p. 34, copy in Box 477, Imperial Irrigation District Papers, Imperial, Calif.

4. This agreement was reached in 1904, three years after water was brought through Mexico to the Imperial Valley. For the complex developments leading to it, see Norris Hundley, jr., "The Politics of Reclamation: California, the Federal Government, and the Origins of the Boulder Canyon Act—A Second Look," *California Historical Quarterly* 52 (1973), pp. 300–304.

5. "Report of the American Section of the International Water Commission, United States and Mexico," *H. Doc. 359*, 71st Cong., 2d sess. (1930), p. 103; Otis Tout, *The First Thirty Years, 1901–1931* (San Diego, 1931), passim; House Committee on Irrigation of Arid Lands, *Hearings on All-American Canal in Imperial County, Calif.*, H.R. 6044, 66th Cong., 1st sess. (1919), pp. 121, 139, 143, passim.

6. House Committee on Irrigation of Arid Lands, *Hearings on All-American Canal in Imperial County, Calif.*, H.R. 6044, p. 116.

7. Imperial Irrigation District Board of Directors, "Minutes"(13 November 1917), vol. 3, p. 92; *El Centro Progress*, 11 November 1917; U.S. Department of the Interior, *Seventeenth Annual Report of the Reclamation Service, 1917–1918* (Washington, D.C., 1918), p. 382; *Cong. Rec.*, 66th Cong., 1st sess. (1919), p. 1258.

8. "Report on H.R. 6044 for Relief of Imperial Valley, California," 21 August 1919, p. 13, File 711.1216M/494, Records of the Department of State, National Archives; House Committee on Irrigation of Arid Lands, *Hearings on All-American Canal in Imperial and Coachella Valleys, Calif.*, H.R. 6044 and H.R. 11553, 66th Cong. (1920), pp. 94, 142, 261, 290, passim.

9. *Cong. Rec.*, 66th Cong., 2d sess. (1920), p. 7360.

10. William L. Kahrl, *Water and Power: The Conflict over Los Angeles' Water Supply in the Owens Valley* (Berkeley and Los Angeles, 1982); Abraham Hoffman, *Vision or Villainy: Origins of the Owens Valley–Los Angeles Water Controversy* (College Station, Tex., 1981).

11. "Problems of Imperial Valley and Vicinity," *S. Doc. 142*, 67th Cong., 2d sess. (1922), pp. 282–83.

12. Metropolitan Water District of Southern California, *Metropolitan Water District Act* (Los Angeles, 1947).

13. Colorado River Commission, "Hearings" (Denver, 31 March 1922), p. 70, copy in Colorado River Project, Bureau of Reclamation Papers, Record Group 115, File 032, National Archives.

14. "Problems of Imperial Valley and Vicinity," *S. Doc. 142*, 67th Cong., 2d sess. (1922), p. 21.

15. *Cong. Rec.*, 67th Cong., 2d sess. (1922), pp. 5929, 5985.

16. *Wyoming v. Colorado*, 259 U.S. 419 (1922).

17. Delph Carpenter, "The Colorado River Compact," p. 21, file 1–M/366, Herbert Hoover Papers, Hoover Presidential Library, West Branch, Iowa; "Proceedings of the League of the Southwest, Denver, Colorado, August 25, 26, 27, 1920" (typescript [1920]), pp. 287–90, copy in Papers of the Utah State Engineer, Utah State Archives, Salt Lake City.

18. *U.S. Statutes at Large* 42 (1921), p. 171.

19. See Colorado River Commission, "Minutes," in Colorado River Project, Bureau of Reclamation Papers, Record Group 115, file 032, National Archives.

20. Delph Carpenter to Frank C. Emerson, 7 September 1922, Papers of the Wyoming State Engineer, Wyoming State Archives, Cheyenne.

21. See, especially, Colorado River Commission, "Minutes of the Seventeenth Meeting" (15 November 1922), pp. 8–12; "Minutes of the Nineteenth Meeting" (19 November 1922), pt. 1, pp. 4, 8; W. S. Norviel, "Report of W. S. Norviel, Colorado River Commissioner, State of Arizona" [1923], p. 6, file 1–M/315, Hoover Papers; Richard E. Sloan, "Pact Criticism Is Largely on What It Does Not Say," *Arizona Mining Journal* 6 (15 January 1923), p. 58. For a detailed discussion of the negotiations, see Norris Hundley, jr., *Water and the West: The Colorado River Compact and the Politics of Water in the American Way* (Berkeley and Los Angeles, 1975), pp. 187–214.

22. Colorado River Commission, "Minutes of the Twenty-first Meeting" (20 November 1922); "Minutes of the Twenty-second Meeting" (22 November 1922).

23. See, especially, the minutes of the Colorado River Commission for the eleventh through the twenty-second meetings; Delph Carpenter to Frank C. Emerson, 19 August 1922, Papers of the Wyoming State Engineer; "Problems of the Imperial Valley and Vicinity," *S. Doc. 142*, pp. 2, 5; "Report of the Colorado River Board on the Boulder Dam Project," *H. Doc. 446*, 70th Cong., 2d sess. (1928), pp. 9, 12.

24. "Colorado River Compact," *H. Doc. 605*, 67th Cong., 4th sess. (1923), Article IV. For a later legal analysis of the compact and much more, see Charles J. Meyers, "The Colorado River," *Stanford Law Review* 19 (1966–67), pp. 1–75.

25. Colorado River Commission, "Minutes of the Nineteenth Meeting" (19 November 1922), pt. 2, p. 2; "Minutes of the Twentieth Meeting" (19 November 1922), p. 2.

26. Colorado River Commission, "Minutes of the Twentieth Meeting"

(19 November 1922), pp. 39–40; Delph Carpenter, *Report . . . in re Colorado River Compact* (n.p. [15 December 1922]), p. 7, copy in file 032, Colorado River Compact, Bureau of Reclamation Papers; "Colorado River Compact," Article VII.

27. Colorado River Commission, "Minutes of the Twenty-seventh Meeting" (24 November 1922), p. 8; *Santa Fe New Mexican,* 25 and 28 November 1922.

28. *Journal of the Arizona Senate: Sixth Legislature, 1923,* p. 22.

29. George W. P. Hunt, *Arizona's Viewpoint on the Colorado River* (Phoenix, 17 August 1925), p. 1.

30. Hundley, *Water and the West,* chap. 8.

31. Delph Carpenter to R. T. McKisick, 23 December 1924, A. T. Hannett Papers, New Mexico State Archives, Santa Fe.

32. *Journal of the California Assembly, 1925,* p. 1031; *Journal of the California Senate, 1925,* pp. 1135–36.

33. House Committee on Irrigation and Reclamation, *Hearings on Colorado River Basin, H.R. 6251 and H.R. 9826,* 69th Cong., 1st sess. (1926); Senate Committee on Irrigation and Reclamation, *Hearings on Colorado River Basin, S. 728 and S. 1274,* 70th Cong., 1st sess. (1928); Hiram Johnson to C. K. McClatchy, 17 March 1928, Hiram Johnson Papers, Bancroft Library, University of California, Berkeley.

34. *Cong. Rec.,* 70th Cong., 2d sess. (1928), pp. 382, 389.

35. Ibid., pp. 470, 471. For a close analysis of the congressional discussion of this suggested agreement, see Norris Hundley, jr., "Clio Nods: *Arizona v. California* and the Boulder Canyon Act: A Reassessment," *Western Historical Quarterly* 3 (1972), pp. 17–51.

36. *U.S. Statutes at Large* 45 (1928), pp. 1057–66; 46 (1929), p. 3000; *Calif. Stats.* (4 March 1929), chaps. 15–16, pp. 37–39.

37. "Hoover Dam Documents," *H. Doc. 717,* 80th Cong., 2d sess. (1948), pp. 65–69.

38. William L. Kahrl, ed., *The California Water Atlas* (Sacramento, 1979), pp. 41–42.

39. *Arizona v. California,* 283 U.S. 423 (1931).

40. *Arizona v. California,* 292 U.S. 341 (1934).

41. *Arizona v. California,* 298 U.S. 558 (1936).

42. Hundley, *Water and the West,* pp. 294–95, passim.

43. Ibid., pp. 297–98. For a perceptive analysis of Arizona water politics into the early 1960s, see Dean E. Mann, *The Politics of Water in Arizona* (Tucson, 1963).

44. *Journal of the Arizona Senate, 1943,* pp. 89–90.

45. *Journal of the Arizona Senate, 1944,* pp. 38–39; *Journal of the Arizona House, 1944,* p. 60.

46. Norris Hundley, jr., *Dividing the Waters: A Century of Controversy Between the United States and Mexico* (Berkeley and Los Angeles, 1966), chaps. 2–4.

47. Ibid., p. 147.

48. For a detailed account of the debate over the treaty in the United States and Mexico, see ibid., chap. 6. A careful legal analysis of the treaty may be found in Charles J. Meyers and Richard L. Noble, "The Colorado River: The Treaty with Mexico," *Stanford Law Review* 19 (1966–67), pp. 367–419.

49. *Cong. Rec.,* 79th Cong., 1st sess. (1945), pp. 3491–92; *Excelsior* (México, D.F.), 28 September 1945.

50. U.S. Bureau of Reclamation, *The Colorado River: A Comprehensive Departmental Report on the Development of the Water Resources of the Colorado River Basin for Review Prior to Submission to the Congress* (Washington, D.C., 1946), p. 21. For discussion of the Colorado–Big Thompson Project, see Donald B. Cole, "Transmountain Water Diversion in Colorado," *Colorado Magazine* 25 (1948), pp. 49–65, 118–33; William Kelly, "Colorado–Big Thompson Initiation, 1933–1938," ibid., 34 (1957), pp. 66–74; and Oliver Knight, "Correcting Nature's Error: The Colorado–Big Thompson Project," *Agricultural History* 30 (1956), pp. 157–69.

51. Jean S. Breitenstein, "The Upper Colorado River Basin Compact," *State Government* 22 (1949), pp. 214–16, 225.

52. *U.S. Statutes at Large* 63 (1949), p. 31.

53. Senate Committee on Interior and Insular Affairs, *Hearings on Colorado River Storage Project, S. 1555,* 83d Cong., 2d sess. (1954); Roderick Nash, *Wilderness and the American Mind,* 3d ed. (New Haven, 1982), pp. 209–19; Dean Mann, Gary D. Weatherford, and Phillip Nichols, "Legal Political History of Water Resource Development in the Upper Colorado River Basin," *Lake Powell Research Project Bulletin No. 4* (Los Angeles, September 1974).

54. For discussion of the controversy, see the items cited in the preceding note as well as "Echo Park Controversy Resolved," *Living Wilderness* 20 (1955–56), pp. 23–43; David Perlman, "Our Winning Fight for Dinosaur," *Sierra Club Bulletin* 41 (1956), pp. 5–8; Owen Stratton and Phillip Sirotkin, "The Echo Park Controversy," *Inter-University Case Program No. 46* (University, Ala., 1959); Richard E. Baird, "The Politics of Echo Park and Other Development Projects in the Upper Colorado River Basin" (Ph.D. diss., Uni-

versity of Illinois, 1960); Elmo Richardson, *Dams, Parks and Politics* (Lexington, Ky., 1973).

55. Eliot Porter, *The Place No One Knew: Glen Canyon on the Colorado* (San Francisco, 1963); Francois Leydet, *Time and River Flowing: Grand Canyon* (San Francisco, 1964); Nash, *Wilderness and the American Mind*, p. 229; Dean E. Mann, "Conflict and Coalition: Political Variables Underlying Water Resource Development in the Upper Colorado River Basin," *Natural Resources Journal* 15 (1975), pp. 166–67.

56. *U.S. Statutes at Large* 76 (1962), p. 96; 78 (1964), p. 852.

57. House Committee on Interior and Insular Affairs, *Hearings on the Central Arizona Project, H.R. 1500 and H.R. 1501*, 82d Cong., 1st sess. (1951), pp. 739–56, passim.

58. *Arizona v. California et al.*, 373 U.S. 564, 565 (1963).

59. See Hundley, "Clio Nods: *Arizona v. California* and the Boulder Canyon Act," pp. 17–51.

60. *Arizona v. California et al.*, 373 U.S. 587 (1963).

61. Ibid., 373 U.S. 596, 598–601 (1963). See also *Winters v. United States*, 207 U.S. 564 (1908); and Norris Hundley, jr., "The 'Winters' Decision and Indian Water Rights: A Mystery Reexamined," *Western Historical Quarterly* 13 (1982), pp. 17–42.

62. *Arizona v. California et al.*, 439 U.S. 422 (1979).

63. Norris Hundley, jr., "The Dark and Bloody Ground of Indian Water Rights: Confusion Elevated to Principle," *Western Historical Quarterly* 9 (1978), pp. 478–79; Acting Assistant Director, Phoenix Area Office, U.S. Bureau of Indian Affairs, to author, 18 January 1983.

64. *Arizona v. California*, 51 LW 4329 (1983); *Los Angeles Times*, 19 March 1982 and 31 March 1983; Acting Assistant Director, Phoenix Area Office, U.S. Bureau of Indian Affairs, to author, 18 January 1983.

65. Monroe E. Price and Gary D. Weatherford, "Indian Water Rights in Theory and Practice: Navajo Experience in the Colorado River Basin," *Law and Contemporary Problems* 40 (1976), pp. 108–31; James P. Merchant and David M. Dornbusch, *The Importance of Water Supply to Indian Economic Development* (prepared for the Office of Water Research and Technology, U.S. Dept. of the Interior, 1977), pp. 64–65; interviews with members of the Navajo Tribal Council, 2 May 1977.

66. Metropolitan Water District of Southern California, *INFO* (Los Angeles, October 1977), p. 27.

67. House Committee on Interior and Insular Affairs, *Hearings on Lower Colorado River Basin Project, H.R. 4671 and Similar Bills*, 89th Cong. (1965–1966); *Hearings on Colorado River Basin Project*, 90th Cong., 1st sess. (1967);

Hearings on Colorado River Basin Project, Part II, 90th Cong., 2d sess. (1968).
For an advocate's inside view of the struggle for the CAP, see Rich Johnson,
The Central Arizona Project, 1918–1968 (Tucson, 1977).

68. Ibid. For a perceptive analysis of the bargaining for projects, see
Helen M. Ingram, *Patterns of Politics in Water Resource Development: A Case
Study of New Mexico's Role in the Colorado River Basin Bill* (Albuquerque,
1969).

69. Nash, *Wilderness and the American Mind*, pp. 227–35; *Congressional
Quarterly Fact Sheet* (1 November 1969), pp. 3019–31.

70. *U.S. Statutes at Large* 82 (1968), p. 885.

71. Upper Colorado River Commission, *Thirty-second Annual Report*
(Salt Lake City, 30 September 1980), pp. 47–56; Central Utah Water Conservancy District, *Annual Report, 1981* (Salt Lake City, 1982); interview with
Vernon Valantine of the Colorado River Board of California, 15 May 1984,
and 21 February 1983; *Los Angeles Times*, 19 February 1985. For concern
about the air pollution caused by the coal-fired plant, see *Los Angeles Times*,
9 February 1975; Alfred Runte, *National Parks: The American Experience* (Lincoln, 1979), p. 185.

72. Senate Committee on Foreign Relations, *Hearings on Water Treaty
with Mexico*, 79th Cong., 1st sess. (1945), pp. 323–38, 1109, 1704, passim;
Hundley, *Dividing the Waters*, pp. 153–59, passim; Hundley, "The Colorado
Waters Dispute," *Foreign Affairs* 42 (1963–64), pp. 495–500. For a Mexican
perspective that, although polemical in outlook, reproduces many Mexican
documents, see Ernesto Enriquez Coyro, *El Tratado entre México y los Estados
Unidos de América sobre Ríos Internationales: Una Lucha Nacion a 1 de Noventa
Años*, 2 vols. (México, D.F., 1975).

73. Joseph F. Friedkin, Commissioner of the U.S. Section, International Boundary and Water Commission, to the author, 6 June 1983; Hundley,
Dividing the Waters, pp. 172–80.

74. For a copy of the English and Spanish versions of Minute 242, see
the January 1975 issue of *National Resources Journal*, pp. 2–9. This issue also
contains a valuable collection of articles which analyze the salinity problem
and Minute 242.

75. *El Universal* (México, D.F.), 30 August 1973; House Committee
on Interior and Insular Affairs, *Hearings on Colorado River Basin Salinity Control, H.R. 12165*, 93d Cong., 2d sess. (1974), p. 107; Myron Holburt, "International Problems of the Colorado River," *Natural Resources Journal* 15
(1975), pp. 21–22.

76. *U.S. Statutes at Large* 88 (1974), p. 266; U.S. Section, International
Boundary and Water Commission, *Joint Projects of the United States and Mexico*

through the International Boundary and Water Commission, 1983 (n.p., [1982]), p. 30; Hundley, *Water and the West*, pp. 316–17; interview with Vernon Valantine of the Colorado River Board of California, 15 May 1984. See, also, "Symposium on Anticipating Transboundary Resource Needs and Issues in the U.S.–Mexico Border Region to the Year 2000," *Natural Resources Journal* 22 (October 1982), passim.

77. Philip L. Fradkin, *A River No More: The Colorado River and the West* (New York, 1981).

78. Metropolitan Water District, *INFO*, p. 30.

79. Ibid., p. 21.

80. *Los Angeles Times*, 9 November 1982.

81. *Federal Register*, 9 May 1983, pp. 20872–89; memo from MWD Director of Contracts Administration to Assistant General Manager David N. Kennedy, 19 May 1983, copy in possession of author; interview with Vernon Valantine of the Colorado River Board of California, 1 July 1983, 15 May 1984, and 21 February 1985; Colorado River Association, *CRA Newsletter*, 19, no. 3 (1984), p. 3; *Los Angeles Times*, 9 August 1984.

82. Colorado River Board of California, *Annual Report, 1979* (Los Angeles, 1980), p. 12; Metropolitan Water District, *INFO*, pp. 23–24.

3 The River of Controversy: Persistent Issues

David H. Getches
and Charles J. Meyers

The Colorado River is a national symbol of the highest order. The lifeline of much of the arid West, it is a sobering reminder of our fragile dependence on water supplies that are as ephemeral as the weather. It embodies the West's history of struggles with nature and among rivals vying for scarce resources. It demonstrates the paradoxical western attitude that allows a distrust and distaste for intrusions of the federal government to coexist with constant demands for federal assistance. As the most intensively managed river of its size in the world, the Colorado stands for the ability to maximize use of a natural resource. It reveals the interplay for technology, politics, and social goals. The purpose of this chapter is to call on the river's past to anticipate the river's future problems and how to deal with them.

In little over half a century, the might of the river has been harnessed and its appearance and chemistry radically changed. Ingenuity and determination have enabled humanity to triumph over natural elements. Millions dwell comfortably in former deserts, their thirst quenched by waters piped from the river and their industries animated by energy generated by the river's force. This is the new West. Yet, in rural areas a now characteristic, deeply romantic ideal of the old West has been perpetuated. A solid ranching and farming society is founded on a common dedication to hard work and self-reliance, inspired by communion with the land. The rural life-style of long ago would have become a bit of nostalgia but for regular water supplies.

Instead, that life-style has spread throughout the West, expanding even to places where crops could not have survived and where natural forage was long ago depleted. Marginal areas have been nourished by irrigation, sustained through dry seasons by water stored behind dams and moved hundreds of miles through canals, over mountains, and across state lines.

The Colorado River epitomizes the way in which the new West has met the old West. The meeting has been far from congenial, but the most visible disputes have not simply pitted old West agricultural interests against new West industrial and municipal interests. The battles more often have been among states with various and changing mixes of both interests. Yet the same states have made tentative alliances with their adversaries to pursue common advantages from water projects that only the federal government could afford to build.

The voices of Indian tribes have been raised in the fight over the river, insisting that their needs not be overlooked. As descendants of the aboriginal sovereigns of the entire territory, the tribes claim formidable legal rights for the vestiges of their domain. The exercise of Indian rights could severely limit the growth of non-Indian uses. That possibility may tempt Congress to exercise its superior political authority to curb Indian rights, a prospect complicated by concerns for justice and national honor.

In recent years, as the river's native elegance has become scarcer, the zeal for its total exploitation has been tempered. Citizen's groups have become increasingly vocal, insisting that some of the West's natural amenities be saved from subjugation to human enterprise. The enchantment of the early explorers has been rekindled in those who insist that some of the river belongs to wildlife and that stretches must be preserved so that unborn generations can have glimpses of what enthralled John Wesley Powell in his epic 1869 scientific exploration.[1]

Of the speculations that may be made about the Colorado River's future, perhaps the most reliable is that there will be continuing conflict. Inevitable tensions are created by fundamental demands for equity, for environmental quality, and for efficiency in the face of natural limitations. These tensions test the fiber of our existing political and economic institutions. They try not only the stability of institutional arrangements created for managing the river, but also some of the basic concepts of our polity, such as federalism. Conflicts over the river, indeed, go beyond the matter of who gets to use a particular quantity of water, to encompass values that run to the core of our social organization. The effects of decisions on water allocation, on pricing of power, on how to value instream uses, and on the degree of enforcement of water-quality laws reach far beyond their immediate targets. The results can be dramatic: New industry may supplant a pastoral society; the quality of life in a vast land area may rise or fall; major demographic shifts may occur; nature's plan for an entire region may be forever obscured; ancient Indian cultures may live or die.

Here we explore a number of issues that have plagued the river and surely will continue to do so for the foreseeable future. They are grouped under three categories: competition among uses; Indian and federal reserved rights; and federal-state relations. We then examine some of the possible approaches to the issues.

Competition Among Uses

Can Agricultural Uses Compete Politically and Economically with Municipal and Industrial Uses?

Congress was strongly motivated by a desire to assist agriculture in authorizing expenditures of hundreds of millions of dollars to subsidize a system of dams and intricate delivery systems on the Colorado. The "Law of the River" bristles with favoritism for agricultural interests.

Although river development historically has been tailored to accommodate agriculture, the area's demographics and economy have radically changed. Agriculture has ceased to expand significantly and urban growth abounds. Population centers outside the Colorado River Basin[2]—like Los Angeles and San Diego, Denver, Phoenix and Tucson, and Salt Lake City—place heavy demands on the river. More than half of the Colorado River water used in the United States is exported from the basin.[3] Users elsewhere can pay enough to make it advantageous for farmers and ranchers in the basin to sell their rights plus enough to transport the water hundreds of miles.

Even in rural areas of the Upper Basin, increased water demands are projected for industrial development. Energy-related projects, such as oil-shale development and coal-slurry pipelines, can justify prices for water which amount to hundreds of times the prices irrigators now pay.[4] Many projects are temporarily stayed by economic conditions, but once revived, they could tap huge supplies now used for agriculture.

Although there are strong economic forces that may influence the shift away from irrigated agriculture, legal and political forces may prevent transactions. Many state laws limit transfers of water rights.[5] In addition, federal projects operate under reclamation laws that erect barriers to market transfers of water.[6] Legal obstacles to changing water use from agriculture to municipal and industrial uses are inspired, at least in part, by a desire to protect farming and ranching interests. The same policy may create resistance to allocating large amounts of unappropriated waters to a major project that would prevent future agricultural development. A good example is the proliferation of legislative attempts to control or prevent water use for slurry pipelines.

A strong proagriculture spirit lives in the breast of western society. The tradition of western agriculture is so powerful that it even moves urban dwellers to oppose water developments that would be in their interests. And it moves western politicians to champion farm preservation when economically more beneficial industrial or municipal uses compete for water, although the electorate is concentrated in the cities.

Agriculture enjoys substantial economic advantages as well as receiving an effective subsidy from favorable political and legal inertia. Benefits accrue to irrigators using water from facilities that are financed by the government. Project costs are repaid interest free or at below market rates and amortized over an extended period.[7] Feasibility studies done in connection with major reclamation projects do not use a cost-benefit analysis that considers all the values that would be attributed in a free market. Furthermore, hydroelectric power revenues are used to defray much of the cost of irrigation water. Also, the value of flood control, navigation, and other public benefits may be overstated, reducing the repayment obligation of irrigators.[8] Environmental costs are often ignored and alternative uses—industrial municipal uses, or the adjustment of stream flow for wildlife maintenance, recreation, and aesthetics—are rarely fully considered.[9]

How far should a calculus of external costs of water use be carried? At a minimum, an informed decision-making process should consider known market costs and alternative uses. Significant external costs

and external benefits also should be identified. Nonmarket values that
surround agriculture and other uses should be considered too in water
policy-making.

Is the Law of the River Inequitable to the Upper Basin?

Water from the Colorado is shared among the seven basin states
in a way that bears almost no relation to the amounts of water each
contributes to the river's flow. The 1922 compact,[10] the first interstate
water compact, was intended to strike an accommodation between
the expanding demands of the Lower Basin and the need to preserve
adequate water for future use in the less-developed Upper Basin, the
source of almost all the river's water. The compact would enable
construction of storage facilities to protect the Lower Basin from floods
and to make use of water needed for a growing population. The Upper
Basin states—Colorado, New Mexico, Wyoming, and Utah—saw the
compact as a way of preventing river water from being monopolized
by California and Arizona through the establishment of legal priorities
based on their earlier usage.

The compact assured the Lower Basin states—Arizona, California, and Nevada—a guaranteed flow of seventy-five million acre-feet
over a progressive series of ten-year periods. The contemplation of the
drafters was that an average of 7.5 million acre-feet a year would give
each basin, upper and lower, an approximately equal share of the flow;
in years when the flow permitted, the faster developing Lower Basin
would be able to use any water that the Upper Basin could not use,
but the compact effectively set a ceiling on the quantity of rights that
could be perfected.[11] Further, the two basins were to share equally any
burden there might be to deliver water to Mexico, an obligation later
set at 1.5 million acre-feet.[12]

Physical realities provoke a number of questions, the answer to
which could have serious consequences for the Upper Basin. The most
stunning reality is that the allocation of the river was made on the
incorrect assumption that there would be annual flow of at least 16.5
million acre-feet.[13] In fact, data spanning three centuries reveal an
average flow of about 13.5 million acre-feet.[14] Furthermore, annual
flows are erratic, ranging from 4.4 million acre-feet to over 22 million
acre-feet.[15] The compact's decennial guarantee of 75 million acre-feet

of water to the Lower Basin arguably places a servitude on all Upper Basin storage facilities for delivery requirements to the Lower Basin, thus reducing their utility to the Upper Basin. As Edward Clyde explains, the consequences of several successive drought years could be disastrous to the Upper Basin if it is obligated to use stored water to simulate "normal" flows for the Lower Basin.[16]

If the various uncertainties about the obligations of the Upper Basin under the compact[17] are resolved against the Upper Basin, there may be dire consequences in terms of limiting growth, of managing facilities efficiently, and of generation of electric power. Even favorable resolutions do not answer the ultimate question: How to build a future on the right to leftovers? The problem has not yet been presented sharply because Upper Basin uses have not approached the point where the limits on water supplies from the river have impacted the realization of the Upper Basin's growth potential.[18]

The Lower Basin, already heavily developed, can make claims to a larger share of water. The understanding implicit in the agreement was that each basin should be able to develop at its own pace with a predictable supply guaranteed when development occurs.[19] But the Upper Basin states fear that the Lower Basin's "temporary" reliance on this water could ripen into necessity and ultimately into recognized rights. Since the water is surplus in the Upper Basin now, the possibility of harm is largely hypothetical. The Upper Basin must determine how to protect itself from the threat of Lower Basin encroachment on supplies, an encroachment that could come from adverse interpretations of the law of the river combined with a growing Lower Basin dependence on the lion's share of the river's water.

A traditional answer to the Upper Basin's problem has been the development of more storage projects and more water-intensive uses. Impressing the Upper Basin entitlement with new demands for consumptive use and by physically retaining it has a crude but appealing logic. Informed leaders recognize that this solution ignores the need to optimize the use of water and the pressures to move existing rights to more productive, more efficient uses.[20]

Damming Upper Basin streams to the maximum extent possibile could provide insurance against the consequences of major drought. Yet further investment (doubtless of public money) before Upper Basin water demands are real is perhaps best justified by storage benefits to the overdeveloped Lower Basin. The ostensible purpose of such projects would be to give Upper Basin states the means to expand their future uses while satisfying their compact obligation to the Lower Basin. Until the new uses develop, however, the Lower Basin has a right under the compact to demand all the water it needs for current uses. Moreover, construction of new storage facilities is limited by the paucity of feasible sites. Some sites have been ruled out because of the destructive effects that dam building would have on natural assets.[21] Even the most attractive remaining projects have been stalled because they are difficult to justify economically.

Unless there are significant unexplored sites for storage facilities— an unlikely possibility—only a handful of new projects will be built in the Upper Basin. Without promise of substantial economic benefits, private enterprise will not undertake a project. In an era of freer access to what many consider a federal "pork barrel," a state's grandiose plans for a pet water storage project may have had a chance for acceptance without much scrutiny of the economics involved. That era is surely in decline, if not dead. Federal funding is almost certain to depend to some degree on economic justification. Of course, an Upper Basin state may itself decide to finance a project that has little immediate utility in order to protect future access to supplies. But the staggering costs are likely to thwart most projects, for state finances in the Upper Basin have suffered considerably in recent years. State fiscal recovery probably will depend on a rebound in energy and mineral development or on a resurgence in industrial and population growth. These phenomena could bring with them not only increased tax revenues, but also increased private investment in water projects.

Short of building new water projects, what can the Upper Basin do to protect its interests? One possibility would be to seek revision of the law of the river. Clarification of several issues could resolve the most vexing uncertainties. The Upper Basin states could initiate negotiations with the Lower Basin states. Or they might seek congressional intervention. The chief obstacle to either approach is a lack of bargaining power. California was able to get Congress to revise the law of the river as a part of the Central Arizona Project authorization. It won first priority to 4.4 million acre-feet per year of the Lower Basin share as the price of giving political support to Arizona's needed project. The Upper Basin states exacted a price too: authorization of five additional Upper Basin projects. Perhaps clarification of some of the compact ambiguities also should have been sought.[22]

A legal argument that has not yet been tried would reform or void the Upper Basin's compact obligation because it was based on a mutual mistake of fact. The intent of the compact was to divide the river's waters equally, assuming an average annual runoff based on the few, extraordinarily wet years just before 1922 when the compact was negotiated. It is now known that the assumptions underlying the compact were wrong. Applying established principles of contract law could lead to reformation of the compact to reflect accurate flow statistics; if the compact negotiator's approach of dividing water equally were followed, the Upper Basin obligation to the Lower Basin would be reduced by more than a million acre-feet per year.

The compact is a crucial foundation of the law of the river, and that law has been an integral part of decisions to fund projects costing billions of dollars. The allocations in the compact also formed part of the backdrop for the United States Supreme Court's 1963 *Arizona v. California* decision. Only the Supreme Court would have the temerity to manipulate this intricate legal web. And that Court may fear the upsets and dislocations it would bring. Still, the argument is credible enough that it might prod the Lower Basin states to consider con-senting to a revision of the compact or an elucidation of its meaning.

If the precise obligations of the Upper Basin states were known, planning for growth and for future water projects could be done more intelligently. Certainty would also facilitate economic adjustments between the two basins. An Upper Basin state could plan development of its share of water, but if a Lower Basin state believes it has more valuable uses, a lease or other agreement might be negotiated to allow use of the Upper Basin water in the Lower Basin state. The Lower Basin state would effectively pay the Upper Basin state to forego the development and thereby secure a larger, more reliable supply. But unless the parties know their obligations and entitlements such trans-fers are unlikely.

How Can Inbasin and Instream Uses Be Balanced against Water Needs Outside the Basin?

Colorado River water has been allocated among the Lower Basin states by Congress[23] and among the Upper Basin states by compact.[24]

Each state can allocate its share of water as it wishes. It should not be surprising, then, that most Colorado River water is used outside the watershed that produces the resource. Extrabasin use of Colorado River water creates an interdependence with many other watersheds in the West. River-dependent areas must look beyond the basin to augment supplies as their entitlements or obligations under the law of the river limit the amount of Colorado water available to them.

To the extent that river water is inadequate for Southern California, water must be drawn from the California State Water Project, which is supplied by river systems hundreds of miles to the North. At one point Exxon eyed imports from the Missouri River Basin in its planning for oil-shale development in western Colorado. From time to time the Southwest has focused on the far North as a potential source of imported water. Projects to move water from distant basins such as the Snake, the Columbia, the Mackenzie, and the Yukon have been discussed.

If water is not put to its most productive use in the Colorado River Basin, water availability and use in other areas may be affected. Ultimately, this means finding the highest economic uses. Serious conflicts may arise over two types of uses. First, agriculture, the principal inbasin use, has difficulty in competing economically with municipal and industrial uses that attract water out of the basin.[25] Second, instream uses tend to get short shrift.[26] Maintaining stream flow is essential in preserving a habitat for fish and wildlife, in supporting many types of water-based recreation, and in satisfying aesthetic preferences. But instream values may be overlooked or treated as unimportant when compared to many extrabasin uses. The importance of instream uses also reaches beyond the basin. Those who benefit from instream values may live far away but visit the basin occasionally. And wildlife that depends on habitat in the basin may use it in connection with a migration of several thousand miles.

The interdependence between inbasin and out-of-basin uses suggests some mutuality of interests among water users throughout the West. Most of the West could be considered as a single water "market," subject only to the economic reach of water transfer facilities and compact limitations. Political barriers may also exist. (The issue of state prohibitions against interstate transfers is raised later in this chapter.)

Can Management of Colorado River Water Be Considered Apart from Groundwater Use?

There is little question that pumping of groundwater hydrologically connected with the river is included in its management regime. While it went unmentioned in the 1922 compact, related groundwater was interpreted by the Supreme Court to be within the scope of management authority in the Boulder Canyon Project Act.[27] A now common understanding of the fundamentals of hydrology demands that groundwater be regulated along with the river flow that it affects.[28] Indeed, most basin states manage "tributary" groundwater as a part of the surface system to which it is connected.[29]

Use of groundwater by basin states is important for river management even if the groundwater source is not connected with the river. Just as there is an interrelationship between basin and nonbasin sources, groundwater use is related to the use of river water. Use of one can supplant the need for the other. In 1968 Colorado River Basin Project Act requires conservation in groundwater development.[30] If sources are to be complementary, it is essential that they be developed and used with great care. Heavy uses of groundwater in Arizona place increased demands on the river as the aquifer is threatened with depletion. Thus, extractions and overdrafts of groundwater in the Lower Basin may actually be "paid for" by Upper Basin states. Congress was aware of this prospect. Before funds were appropriated for the long-awaited Central Arizona Project, Arizona had to show that it was making significant efforts to conserve all its water resources.[31] The state responded by enacting in 1980 one of the nation's strictest groundwater conservation laws.[32]

As demands on the river become more intense, Congress may perceive a national interest in ensuring that all the waters of the basin states are wisely used. Federal legislation could invade turf traditionally reserved to the states by regulating groundwater allocation and use. That possibility was foreshadowed by a 1982 Supreme Court decision[33] in which the Court stated that "ground water overdraft is a national problem and Congress has the power to deal with it on that scale."[34]

Can Use of the River for Power Production Be Reconciled with Optimum Management for Water Delivery?

Management of the river and the timing of releases from dams to respond to demands of water users and to satisfy upper basin–lower basin obligations may be inconsistent with efficient power generation. A further problem is the impact of hydroelectric dam operations on recreational activity and on fish and wildlife. Recreational users have objected to proposals to operate dams on the river to meet periodic needs for peak power loads.[35]

The Secretary of the Interior, as manager of the Colorado River dam system, has been allowed to elect to maximize the production of electricity, to maximize the reliability of water supplies, or to optimize the availability of both.[36] The 1922 compact expresses a clear preference for domestic and agricultural uses over power production in Article IV(b). Energy uses simply were not as important then as they are today. Perhaps it could be argued that the authorization of newer projects that are feasible only as hydroelectric facilities reflects a congressional awareness of changing times. The 1968 Colorado River Basin Project Act, however, states preferences for uses other than power production.[37]

For several reasons, electrical generation is an important option today. Upper Basin power generation can justify dams that will provide more storage upriver and return significant revenues. Lower Basin interests may also favor such development as prospective customers of the power.

Questions are rife as to the rights and obligations of the two basins with respect to power generation and the preferences expressed in the law of the river. Can the Lower Basin demand delivery of its share of water when it is not needed for agricultural and domestic uses so that it can be used for hydroelectric power generation? Does it matter whether such deliveries will result in reduction of Upper Basin agricultural and domestic uses or whether they can be accommodated simply by releases of stored water?[38] Can the Lower Basin demand that excess stored waters (over the compact entitlement) be delivered solely for power generation?[39] Can the Upper Basin have credit against its compact obligation for any excess releases made to generate power but not demanded for Lower Basin uses?

Water users who are obliged to repay development costs for the dam system may favor generation because power revenues are applied to reduce the repayment obligation. Yet because some of the largest water customers on the Colorado use vast amounts of power to pump their water to distant locations, there is no clear division of interests. Indeed, influential water users press to keep power prices low. For instance, the Metropolitan Water District (MWD), which uses more of the Lower Basin's share of water than any but the vast combined agricultural interests of the Imperial Valley,[40] is also one of the largest power consumers.[41] It has much more to gain from a contract for extremely low-priced power than from infinitesimal reductions in capital obligations. The Department of Energy has developed criteria for marketing power from Hoover Dam and other dams on the Lower Colorado upon expiration of the existing contracts,[42] but there is no suggestion of departing from the present system of rates based on recovery of costs of constructing and operating projects, a matter that would require congressional legislation.

The federal government could react to national energy needs by attempting to appropriate the flow of the Colorado for power generation. Government management of the timing and amount of river flows solely to meet power needs could jeopardize water-diversion patterns. A decision to manage the river primarily for power might be within the ambit of constitutional power over navigable waters and hence not a taking of property subject to compensation, but under the law of the river it would be difficult to maintain.[43]

Indian and Federal Reserved Rights

How Can Colorado River Basin Water Users Cope with Uncertainties Caused by the Existence of Reserved Rights?

In its 1963 *Arizona* v. *California* decision, the Supreme Court allocated about 900,000 acre-feet of the Colorado River to the five Indian tribes located along the river and 79,000 acre-feet for federal lands in the vicinity. The allocation was based not on prior use but upon the doctrine of reserved rights. The doctrine teaches that when federal or Indian lands are reserved the rights to sufficient water to fulfill the purposes of the reservation are also reserved.[44] The needs to be met are those which existed at the time that the reservation was set aside as well as any that may arise in the future. Later uses can displace uses by others who commenced their uses after the reservations were established.

The Court found that agriculture was one of the principal purposes underlying the creation of the five Colorado River Indian reservations,[45] and it fixed the tribes' entitlement at an amount sufficient to irrigate all "practicably irrigable acreage" on the reservations.[46] This enabled the quantification of reserved rights, thus facilitating planning by the tribes and by other river water users. Yet uncertainties remain.

In order to rectify what they perceived to be errors and changed circumstances since 1963, the tribes, which had been represented only by the United States, recently sought to invervene in and to reopen *Arizona v. California*. With the support of the United States on most points, the tribes requested an expanded allocation of water rights, presenting evidence that lands had been erroneously omitted from the 1964 calculation of practicably irrigable acreage and that other lands have since been determined to lie within their reservations.[47]

The Court allowed the tribes to intervene, but it refused to expand their entitlement based on the government's failure to claim certain lands as "practicably irrigable" in the earlier litigation. The Court said that there is a "strong interest in finality," noting that "certainty of rights is particularly important with respect to water rights in the Western United States."[48] By invoking this policy the Court closed the door on about two-thirds of the claims to additional irrigable acreage.[49] The Court did allow for enlarged entitlements in the future when boundary disputes left open in the 1964 decree are finally decided by a court. This effectively continues uncertainty as to water rights for several thousand irrigable acres.

The Indian rights have not yet been fully utilized.[50] This is partly due to a notorious lack of diversion and distribution facilities.[51] As Indian use continues to expand it could cut into the ability of the states to take the river water they need. The effort by the tribes to develop needed facilities may be limited by their cost and the availability of capital.[52] But tribes, restrained only by the quantity of water allocated to them and not by the agricultural purposes used to calculate that quantity,[53] have begun to develop more productive uses. These uses could displace existing non-Indian water uses in California and Arizona.

Tribes other than the five that were represented in *Arizona* v. *California* may have far greater reserved rights to Colorado River Basin waters. Quantification of reserved rights of the huge Navajo Reservation and others such as the Ute, the Gila River, and the Papago could significantly affect reliability rights of others in the river.[54] Congress has failed to enact legislation to determine Indian reserved rights,[55] but litigation[56] and negotiations[57] are being pursued in a number of places outside the basin. If there is quantification of Indian rights in the basin it will probably be on a case-by-case basis rather than through some sweeping exercise of congressional authority. Circumstances differ radically from reservation to reservation and so do the necessity and appropriateness of quantifying tribal rights. A tribe with little need for water or no practicable means for using it poses little threat to other users. But on reservations where the tribe or an industry stands ready to put huge quantities of water to use, established non-Indian users may be faced with great dislocations.

One way of resolving the haunting uncertainties of Indian-reserved rights is through agreements between tribes and other users. Several examples exist in the basin states. The Utes of the Unitah and Ouray Reservation in Utah signed a deferral agreement to enable the Central Utah Project to be constructed.[58] In 1968 the Navajos were persuaded to agree not to develop any more than 50,000 acre-feet of water for fifty years in the Upper Basin, where more than half of the huge reservation is located. The agreement was made to facilitate construction of a coal-burning power plant on the reservation, which promised a number of jobs for Navajos and increased revenues for the tribe.[59] By another agreement made in 1957 the Navajos waived their early priority date on the San Juan River, the price of congressional approval of the Navajo Indian Irrigation Project.[60]

Tribal agreements to forego use of water rights have been surrounded by political and legal problems. The wisdom of both Navajo agreements has been cast into considerable doubt,[61] and the Ute deferral agreement has been challenged as unlawful. Interests in Indian real property cannot lawfully be transferred without congressional consent.[62] A contract to defer use of water rights, while not strictly a "transfer," effectively leases rights to others and probably comes within the prohibition.[63] Because no statute authorizes federal officials to approve a lease or other transfer of Indian water rights, a particular agreement may be subject to challenge by the Indian parties. Challenges should be expected where the benefits of deferral are questionable or nonexistent. Thus, reliance cannot be placed on negotiated agreements unless Congress consents to them, but when the interests of all concerned are served and a fair agreement is negotiated, congressional assent is likely. If water is more valuable to non-Indians such agreements are possible.

One way of addressing Southern California's expected shortfall in available water supplies would be for Metropolitan Water District or other interests to contract with some of the tribes. They could be assured of a reliable supply, free of the spectre of being displaced by an initiation of Indian uses.[64] Leases and other transfers of Indian water rights could be made for an appropriate sum or for other considerations (such as a trade for irrigable land elsewhere, construction of irrigation facilities to serve part of the reservation, a share of the electric power produced, or an interest in a business).

A basic question to be considered in connection with contracts regarding Indian-reserved water rights is whether those rights should be alienable at all. An outright transfer of a reserved right, such as a sale or a long-term lease, is difficult to justify. The right is an asset that exists only to the extent necessary to fulfill the purpose of the reservation. On the other hand, a temporary arrangement may help to preserve the asset for future Indian use at the expiration of the agreement by having the principal competitors for its use acknowledge that it exists. Indeed, the essential purpose of Indian reservations— "civilizing" the Indians and making the Indians self-sufficient—may best be fulfilled by letting them market their water resources.

At the present time, tribes may be better off receiving payments instead of water, and others may be quite willing to pay for the assurance of a supply not subject to interruption by future exercise of reserved rights. But many believe that Indian rights to water are strictly tied to its use on the reservations, thus throwing the idea of conveyances into serious question. Even if other users of the river formally acknowledge Indian rights, and the Indians have only deferred their claims, would the water ever be available to the tribes for reservation uses should they need it there? And what are the tradeoffs in terms of coherent social structure and community life? A community could be built on a developed agricultural use of water, but probably it could not be founded on a common interest in collection and distribution of periodic payments made by others for the tribe to forego such uses. As in other Indian policy debates, the ultimate question is to what extent should Indians be assimilated into the larger society?

Federal-State Relations

Will Federal Pollution Laws Affect the Quantity of Water Available to Colorado River Users?

Growing assertions of national control over water quality under a plethora of statutes portends a serious federalism conflict on the Colorado River. The basic quality problem on the river is salinity—increased pickup and concentration of dissolved solids.[65] The salinity problem has many natural causes but is exacerbated by human activity. Already highly saline water is made worse by the evaporation of water stored and slowed by dams, which causes exposure of larger surfaces for longer times, and by the addition of agricultural return flows that become increasingly concentrated as waters are reused and as they leach salts from cultivated fields.

The federal government has dealt with water quality problems selectively. The federal role in controlling water pollution is greatest under the Clean Water Act.[66] The act requires the government to set effluent standards in restricting the amounts of various pollutants that can be discharged from "point sources" such as pipes and ditches. Irrigation return flows contain agricultural chemicals (as well as dissolved solids) that can cause serious pollution problems,[67] but for political reasons Congress has chosen not to regulate agricultural return flows, thereby removing them from the definition of "point sources" under the Clean Water Act.[68] It is possible, though not likely, that Congress will close this, the largest gap in the coverage of the act. Doing so could have dramatic effects on irrigation practices. Return flows either would have to be treated or irrigators would be limited in the amount of land that could be irrigated.

The Clean Water Act also includes a provision for the federal exercise of authority to control the overall water quality of streams.[69] The job belongs in the first instance to the states, but if they do not take sufficient action to preserve water quality, the United States may intercede; it has declined to do so on the Colorado.[70] Diversion of too much water from the stream, combined with evaporation and transpiration, can increase the concentration of pollutants in the water and thereby decrease water quality. A provision in the Clean Water Act, which states that it should not impair the states' authority to allocate water,[71] arguably does not prevent the United States Environmental Protection Agency from setting minimum water quality levels in order to establish requirements. This could test the reach of federal authority if it meant limiting the amount of water diverted under state authority. So far, the only federal attempts to limit state water allocation to assure water quality have been under Section 404 of the act, which gives the government authority to issue "dredge and fill" permits for any waters or wetlands.[72]

Statutes other than the Clean Water Act can be vehicles for asserting federal supremacy over the state control of water use. The Endangered Species Act can be enforced independently of the Clean Water Act if the habitat of an endangered or threatened species is harmed or if the species itself is "harassed" or "taken" within the meaning of the statute.[73] The United States Fish and Wildlife Service has declared that several indigenous fish of the Upper Colorado River are in "jeopardy," not from increasing salt loads but from inadequate flows. Consequently the Service proposed to restrict diversions from the Upper Colorado system. Federal agencies with responsibility over new depletions, including issuing permits for water development such as under Section 404, cannot allow water use until the jeopardy opinion is removed. The serious conflict with ability to use water rights established under state law has brought the Upper Basin states and the Fish and Wildlife Service to the negotiating table in an attempt to find ways to accommodate future water use without destroying fish habitat.

The Fish and Wildlife Coordination Act demands that there be special consideration of the effects of federal water projects.[74] This is less likely to produce a head-on confrontation with state-controlled water resources, but it could seriously affect the way a new federal project is developed or how an existing project is operated.

How Will the Water Quality Burdens of Meeting the Mexican Treaty Obligation Be Met?

The 1944 treaty entitling Mexico to 1.5 million acre-feet a year of Colorado River water did not address the issue of water quality.[75] In 1961, water quality had so degenerated that water was not suitable for irrigation by the time it reached Mexico at the foot of the river.[76] Mexico protested. A series of negotiations resulted in agreements that assured Mexico of water deliveries of a certain quality.[77] Costly measures have been instituted to protect water quality, including an expensive desalination plant now being constructed near the border.[78] The federal government need not rely on construction of such works to clean up salinity. Instead it could choose to satisfy its promises to Mexico by regulating the manner in which water is used for irrigation, especially in the Lower Basin.[79]

What Is the Future of Federal Participation in Water Projects on the Colorado River?

The federal government has been generous in its largess for water projects for over seventy years; over half of all the money spent by the Bureau of Reclamation's national construction budget, since the agency started in 1902, has been spent in the basin.[80] There was consensus that water development on the river was a national need to be satisfied by national expenditures. The early water projects on the river transformed much of the West from what explorers thought was an uninhabitable waste to an area of tremendous importance for the nation's economy as well as a recreational haven for millions. However, the efficacy of new projects is limited.

Although problems remain that might be addressed by the construction of water projects to provide physical solutions to shortages and allay dissension among the states and user groups, the federal approach to these problems probably will be different. Strong bipartisan sentiment now exists for rethinking the role of the United States in new endeavors and for curtailing further federal investments. Policy is in flux for several related reasons. First, the non-Indian projects that remain to be built—mainly Upper Basin storage facilities—are difficult to justify economically and would not directly benefit large numbers of people. In an era when nondefense spending is being constricted, few new water projects will be federally financed.[81]

Second, there is a trend toward demanding financial participation by states and by the beneficiaries of projects.[82] States are being pressed to hold the line on tax rates, and at the same time they face downturns in revenues because of an economic recession. Thus, they are not equipped to accept the responsibility for major water development projects. Private efforts may become possible as the economy improves, at least for projects that have the promise of profitability—mostly nonagricultural enterprises.

Third, the United States has a responsibility as the steward of vast public lands and waters throughout the Colorado River Basin. Congress has repeatedly reaffirmed a commitment to preserve wildlife and recreational opportunities. Projects that may jeopardize these goals are unlikely to receive federal support. As the manager of existing projects on the river and as the primary building agency for water projects, the Department of the Interior is bound to consider the effects of its actions on the environment.[83] Values should be attached to uses for fishing, hunting, camping, and the simple enjoyment of open, unspoiled areas. However, valuation of these amenities is difficult to include alongside the more tangible benefits of industrial use, agriculture, and electrical generation.[84]

Requiring financial soundness of federal projects could have implications for existing projects needing repairs or renovation; it could also scuttle proposed new projects. A reform of project operations also could be forced if the Secretary of the Interior imposed new operating criteria as expiring contracts are renegotiated. Legislation to require market pricing of power might be enacted, and reclamation law could be amended to impose user charges for irrigation water at market levels. Price increases for either product would greatly increase costs to both municipal and agricultural users. The relative inelasticity of the municipal demand for water would probably mean that there would be little effect on water use for that purpose but that greater dislocations could occur among agricultural users. Unless increased costs can be reflected in the prices of agricultural commodities (especially beef, which consumes most of the crops grown with Colorado River Basin water)[85] many farmers and ranchers could be put out of business. Alternatively, these agricultural users must find ways to use less water— a suggestion with considerable promise for girding them against increased competition.[86]

Approaches to Future Problems

There are several approaches that might cut across and address the range of issues raised in this paper. Some have been mentioned in the discussions of particular issues. These approaches are suggested, though not necessarily advocated, as ways that ought to be considered in dealing with the river's future.

Revising the Law of the River

Most problems concerning the allocation and management of river resources ideally would be resolved by mutual agreement of the states acted on by Congress (that is, by compact).[87] History has shown that the requisite assent of the parties is tremendously difficult to obtain. Further compacts among the Colorado River Basin states perhaps have the greatest promise where the parties already are in general agreement and have a common ground for implementing their intentions.

Congress could take unilateral action to revise or interpret the "Law of the River." The prospects that it will do so are slight unless considerable injustice to some state or other entity can be shown. Perhaps Congress might listen to the argument that the Colorado River Compact is invalid and unenforceable because it is based on an erroneous estimate of the reliable flow of the river. But Congress will not perceive the problem as serious until the fulfillment of compact obligations by the Upper Basin is shown to limit the ability of the basin to grow and flourish.

Another way to alter or to construe the law of the river lies in the exercise of the Supreme Court's original jurisdiction over interstate disputes.[88] The Court is a forum in which mutual-mistake arguments might have a hearing on the ground that the compact is contrary to the Court's doctrine of equitable apportionment. But the Court has shown a strong bias against resolving interstate issues between states, especially when the resolution requires complex political adjustments and detailed future administration.[89] The Court has regularly declined to exercise its original jurisdiction, often finding that the dispute raises no threat of present or imminent harm to a party.[90]

There is a risk to the Upper Basin in asking the Supreme Court to reform the compact based on equitable apportionment principles. Now, while water remains underutilized in the Upper Basin, the Lower Basin states are able to put river water to valuable and productive uses. Thus, the Court could decide that the Lower Basin states, with their heavy demands, ought to be entitled to even more water. Such a conclusion would be outrageous from the perspective of the Upper Basin states, but it could find some justification in the standards employed by the Court in other interstate water allocation cases. A major overhaul of the law of the river would be more hospitably received if the Upper Basin could demonstrate immediate hardship. A dramatic permanent reduction in supply, actual growth or concrete plans, not hopeful speculation, may well induce the Court or Congress to act. Although there are long-term predictions of growth and reduced supplies, even including declines of river flow by as much as 60 percent of present average flows,[91] significant changes in the law seem remote now. Whether or not Congress or the Court will engage in a major revision of the law of the river, they may be called upon in the near future to deal with interpretive problems. Several issues arising in the Colorado River Basin[92] may be the forerunners of attempts to reform the 1922 compact on the ground of mutual mistake.

The most likely change in the law of the river is a determination of Indian water rights. Congress could call for widespread quantifications of tribal water rights, but it is more probable that there will be a combination of judicial, congressional, and negotiated determinations. This will leave some uncertainties. The prospect of Congress or the Supreme Court extinguishing reserved rights on a massive scale exists, but it is slim given the political reality and recent judicial reaffirmations.

Importation of New Supplies

One means of quelling the battles over Colorado River water would be to augment the river's flow with water from other sources, a possibility discussed sporadically for most of the century. Politics has ruled out consideration of tapping the Columbia River Basin for much of the recent past.[93] The future may see new thinking about that and other possible sources of supply as the "rights" built on Colorado River water outstrip available supply. But a project of the magnitude needed to sustain the levels of use anticipated for the river without changes in how water is allocated and managed may take from thirty to forty years to plan and build. Both economic feasibility and timing would dim the prospects of relying on imports to solve basin shortages.

Market Pricing of Water

If the price of water reflected the cost of developing and distributing it, several results would follow. Surely the cost of water would be far higher. This would be an incentive to greater water conservation.[94] Unproductive irrigation practices would be discontinued and some crops would not be produced as demand declined in response to rising prices.

Market pricing is inhibited by political resistance, especially where it would cause difficulties for farmers and ranchers. Yet the surviving agricultural enterprises might enjoy a strong, profitable business if prices for their products reflected the increased costs. This depends in part on whether they could or would need to compete with similar products from other regions. A boost to market pricing could result from major transfers from agricultural to municipal or industrial users (such as from Imperial Valley users to the Metropolitan Water District), or from payments to Indian tribes by other users. These arrangements put a value on water that has been lacking in the past.

Changes in State Water Law

Western water law is little more than a century old and it has evolved considerably during its short life. It remains dynamic, responding to changing conditions and new needs. There are some identifiable trends in water law today that may affect management of the Colorado River in the future.

Conservation and Waste. The conservation of water can alleviate many present and future water requirements, posing a partial solution to the problems of feared shortages in the Colorado River Basin. Just as the United States "found" a significant supply of oil through conservation during the energy crisis of the 1970s, more water can be found through water-saving measures.

One has never had a right to waste water under the prior appropriation system; the right is only to put water to a "beneficial use." And definitions of "waste" and "beneficial use" are relative.[95] A recent trend in the West is to redefine "beneficial use" in light of today's technology and conditions. Thus, a leaky, unlined irrigation ditch that was the state of the art seventy-five years ago may be deemed wasteful today.[96] Water lost by the ditch might be counted against one's right to use water.[97] Judicial and legislation can penalize waste from antiquated irrigation and storage works, poor water-use practices, phreatophytes, and the like, and can reward salvage in a variety of ways.

Millions of acre-feet of water might be saved in the basin states through conservative agricultural water-use practices.[98] But there are impediments to conservation, some of which are inherent in the law of the river. The guaranteed annual flow formula provides a disincentive to conserve in the Upper Basin states when the first call on surpluses belongs to the Lower Basin. Consequently, Upper Basin states are moved to search for new uses of water to prevent it from being "lost" to downsteram users.

Shifts in Preferred Uses. As demographics change and as the economies of western states become more dependent on water for nonagricultural uses, laws will be changed to express new preferences. Arizona's new groundwater law is a prime example.[99] It gives strong preference to municipal and industrial uses and is a patent attempt to phase out low-valued, highly consumptive agricultural uses.

Anti-Export Legislation. Efforts to protect water originating in a state from being transported out of state are likely to increase. Protective legislation affecting exports to nonbasin states may be a way of providing more reliable supplies for states in the basin. The Supreme Court has held that laws regulating water export must pass constitutional muster under the commerce clause.[100] This may allow restrictions on the use of water out of state only when the state strictly regulates water use within state borders. Thus, a state's evenhanded measures, which are demanded by shortages to protect "the health of its citizens . . . not simply the health of its economy," will be given deference.[101] Further, anti-export legislation, which is needed to fa-

cilitate compliance with the law of the river, may not be subject to
the same limitations as other embargoes. The Constitution allows
Congress to restrain or regulate interstate commerce as it sees fit or
to authorize the states to do so. Because Congress has been intimately
involved in allocating the interstate waters of the Colorado, state
restrictions needed to carry out the congressionally approved allocation
scheme are not subject to the implied restraints of the commerce clause
that normally inhibit state action.[102]

Conclusion

We have attempted only to suggest some future problems of the
river and some possible solutions. We are confident that there *will* be
clashes among those who have "rights" under compact, under state
law, or under acts of Congress. Some will not get water. The consequences of denial will be less painful and the costs will be lower if
problems can be anticipated before a crisis arises. It is necessary that
the river's great resource be allocated and used with a keen awareness
of their limitations and their great value to the West and to the nation.
That awareness can be reflected in deliberate changes in the law of
the river, in changes in state water laws, and in the emergence of a
free market in water rights; or it can be a drought-induced accident.
The task is to focus on how best the future of the river can be confronted and its resources used efficiently, with an appropriate regard
for environmental values and with fairness to those who have reason
to expect to receive water from the river.

Notes

1. John Wesley Powell, *The Explorations of the Colorado River and Its
Canyons* (New York, 1961).
2. Phoenix and Tucson are technically within the drainage of the Colorado River. They are in the Gila River watershed which has for many years
contributed nothing to the river's flow. Thus, we include these cities as
effectively outside the basin.
3. United States General Accounting Office, *Colorado River Basin Water
Problems: How to Reduce Their Impact*, GAO Report No. B–122053, LED–
79–11 (1979), p. 9.

4. Western States Water Council, *Water for Energy Development, Update 1977* (1977), p. 17; Nathaniel Wollman, *The Value of Water in Alternative Uses* (Albuquerque, 1962), p. xvii.

5. See Clayton K. Yuetter, "A Legal-Economic Critique of Nebraska Watercourse Law," *Nebraska Law Review* 44 (1965), pp. 11, 35; George A. Gould, "Conversion of Agricultural Rights to Industrial Use," *Rocky Mountain Mineral Law Institute* 27B (1982), pp. 1791, 1804–5. See Allen V. Kneese and F. Lee Brown, *Southwest Under Stress* (Baltimore, 1981), pp. 89–94; L. M. Hartman and Don Seastone, *Water Transfers: Economic Efficiency and Alternative Institutions* (Baltimore, 1970); Gary D. Weatherford, *Water and Agriculture in the Western U.S.: Conservation, Reallocation, and Markets* (Boulder, 1982), pp. 215–23; Comment, "Water Law—Legal Impediments to Transfers of Water Rights," *Natural Resources Journal* 7 (1967), p. 433.

6. Joseph Sax, "Selling Reclamation Water Rights: A Case Study in Federal Subsidy Policy," *Michigan Law Review* 64 (1965), p. 13; Willis Ellis and Charles Du Mars, "The Two-Tiered Market in Western Water," *Nebraska Law Review* 57 (1978), p. 333; George Pringle and Laurence Edelman, "Reclamation Law Constraints on Energy/Industrial Uses of Western Water," *Natural Resources Lawyer* 8 (1976), p. 297.

7. Comment, "Reclamation Subsidies and Their Present-Day Impact," *Arizona State Law Journal* (1980), pp. 497, 518–20; Comment, "Desert Survival: The Evolving Western Irrigation District," *Arizona State Law Journal* (1982), pp. 377, 387–89.

8. Ibid.; H. S. Burness, R. G. Cummings, W. D. Gorman and R. R. Lansford, "United States Reclamation Policy and Indian Water Rights," *Natural Resources Journal* 20 (1980), p. 807; Paul E. Roberts, "Benefit-Cost Analysis: Its Use (Misuse) in Evaluating Water Resource Projects," *American Business Law Journal* (1976), pp. 73, 81–83.

9. Roberts, "Benefit-Cost Analysis," p. 74; A. B. Jaffe, "Benefit-Cost Analysis and Multi-Objective Evaluation of Federal Water Projects," *Harvard Environmental Law Review* 4 (1980), pp. 58, 60, 61; Richard L. Berkman and W. Kip Viscusi, *Damming the West* (New York, 1973), pp. 55–62.

10. The Colorado River Compact was negotiated in 1922 under authority of the act of 19 August 1921, ch. 72, 42 Stat. 171. It was approved by Congress in Sec. 13(a) of the Boulder Canyon Project Act of 1928, 45 Stat. 1064, 43 U.S.C. Sec. 6171. It was proclaimed by President Hoover on 25 June 1929, 46 Stat. 3000. See Ray Wilbur and Northcutt Ely, *The Hoover Dam Documents*, H.R. Doc. No. 717, 80th Cong., 2d sess. (Washington, D.C., 1948), p. 22.

11. The Lower Basin was permitted by Article III(b) to expand uses by no more than a million acre-feet beyond the 7.5 million acre-feet, but no obligation to deliver the additional water is created.

12. The obligation to Mexico was quantified in the 1944 treaty with Mexico, 59 Stat. 1219, T.S. No. 944, 3 February 1944.

13. Articles III(a) and (b) of the compact contemplated annual use of sixteen million acre-feet. Article III(c) allowed for further allocation of river water for Mexico and Article III(f), which provided for later equitable apportionment of water not otherwise allocated by the compact. Furthermore, Article I makes it clear that the compact signatories thought they were only making "an apportionment of the use of part of the water of the Colorado River System. . . ." The compact negotiators proceeded on the assumption that there was an annual supply in the Colorado River system of some twenty-one million acre-feet. Simon H. Rifkind, *Report of the Special Master, Arizona v. California,* United States Supreme Court, 5 December 1960 (approved in part, *Arizona v. California,* 373 U.S. 546 [1963]), p. 17 n.56.

14. Gary D. Weatherford and Gordon C. Jacoby, "Impact of Energy Development on the Law of the Colorado River," *Natural Resources Journal* 15 (1975), pp. 171, 183–85. The authors explain a study of tree-ring widths and reconstructed virgin-flow data to develop estimates going back to 1570. A Bureau of Reclamation estimate for the period from 1906 to 1973 was reported to be 14.9 million acre-feet a year. The progressive ten-year running average peaked about the time the compact was signed. Since 1933 there has been only one year (1950) in which the ten-year progressive running average flow at Lee Ferry reached 15 million acre-feet. Average annual virgin flow for the period from 1922 to 1982 has been 13.9 million acre-feet. Upper Colorado River Commission, *Thirty-fourth Annual Report* (Salt Lake City, 1982), pp. 21–27.

15. Rifkind, *Report of the Special Master,* p. 18.

16. See Edward W. Clyde, "Institutional Response to Prolonged Drought."

17. Several of the interpretive problems regarding interbasin obligations and rights are discussed elsewhere. Charles J. Meyers, "The Colorado River," *Stanford Law Review* 19 (1966), pp. 1, 12–26; Edward W. Clyde, "Conflicts between the Upper and Lower Basins on the Colorado River," *Resources Development: Frontiers for Research* (Boulder, 1960), p. 113.

18. Total consumptive water use from the Colorado River in the Upper Basin was 3.5 million acre-feet in 1980. United States Department of the Interior, *Quality of Water, Colorado River Basin,* Progress Report no. 11 (January 1983), p. 10.

19. See *Arizona v. California,* 377 U.S. 546, 555–59 (1963).

20. Colorado Governor Richard Lamm has stated: "We are in a transition period moving from the development and storage of water to a period which will see conflicts between the agricultural uses of water and municipal, industrial, recreational, and other environmental uses. We will not be as preoccupied with the development of new water supplies as we have been in the past." Lamm, "Colorado, Water, and Planning for the Future," *Denver Journal of International Law and Policy* 6 (1976), pp. 441, 447.

21. Dean E. Mann, "Conflict and Coalition: Political Variables Underlying Water Resource Development in the Upper Colorado River Basin," *Natural Resources Journal* 15 (1975), pp. 141, 154–56, 158–61.

22. In retrospect, it appears that legal clarification could have been far more valuable than the project authorizations that the Upper Basin got. After fifteen years only two of the five projects are under construction (Dolores and Dallas Creek), two appear to be dead (San Miguel and West Divide), and only one has a reasonable hope of being constructed (Animas-LaPlata).

23. Allocation of the Lower Basin share is governed by the Boulder Canyon Project Act, 43 U.S.C. Secs. 617–617f, as interpreted in *Arizona v. California*, 373 U.S. 546 (1963). This gives Arizona 2.8 million acre-feet, California 4.4 million acre-feet, and Nevada 300,000 acre-feet of the first 7.5 million acre-feet. Deliveries in excess of that amount are apportioned 46 percent to Arizona, 50 percent to California, and 4 percent to Nevada.

24. Upper Colorado River Basin Compact, act of 6 April 1949, ch. 48, 63 Stat. 31. The states got the following shares of the Upper Basin allocation: Colorado, 51.75 percent; Utah, 23 percent; Wyoming, 14 percent; New Mexico, 11.25 percent; Arizona, 50,000 acre-feet.

25. See Gilbert Bonem, M. Gisser, J. Myers, and M. Resta, *Water Demand and Supply in the Albuquerque Urban Area 1975–2030* (Albuquerque, 1977), pp. 24–27.

26. Appropriations for instream flow purposes historically have not been allowed although a number of states have now permitted government agencies to appropriate streamflows for the preservation of fish and wildlife habitat and for recreational needs. See Colorado Revised Statutes Sec. 37–92–103. See, generally, A. Dan Tarlock, "The Recognition of Instream Flow Rights: 'New' Public Western Water Rights," *Rocky Mountain Mineral Law Institute* 25 (1979), p. 24–64.

27. *Arizona v. California*, 376 U.S. 340, 347–50 (1964).

28. National Water Commission, *Water Policies for the Future—Final Report to the President and to the Congress of the United States* (Washington, D.C., 1973), pp. 480–81.

29. See Frank J. Trelease, "Conjunctive Use of Groundwater and Sur-

face Water," *Rocky Mountain Mineral Law Institute* 273 (1981), pp. 1853, 1856–63.

30. 43 U.S.C. Sec. 1524c. See *United States Code Congressional and Administrative News* (St. Paul, Minn., 1968), pp. 3666–87.

31. See Desmond D. Connall, "A History of the Arizona Groundwater Management Act," *Arizona State Law Journal* (1982), pp. 313; James W. Johnson, "The 1980 Arizona Groundwater Management Act and Trends in Western States Groundwater Administration: A Minerals Industry Perspective," *Rocky Mountain Mineral Law Institute* 26 (1980), pp. 1031, 1059–60; Weatherford, *Water and Agriculture in the Western U.S.*, pp. 153, 158.

32. Arizona Revised Statutes Secs. 45–401 *et seq.*

33. *Sporhase v. Nebraska*, 458 U.S. 941, 102 S. Ct. 3456 (1982).

34. 102 S. Ct. at 3463.

35. John Roberts, "Dam Is Killing the Grand Canyon," *National Parks* 55 (July–August 1981), p. 18 (expanded use of Glen Canyon Dam for peaking power could destroy the 12 million dollar river-running industry in the Grand Canyon as well as endangering fish and wildlife and damaging the physical environment).

36. *Yuma Mesa Irrig. & Drainage Dist. v. Udall*, 253 F. Supp. 548 (D.D.C. 1966): *Yuma County Water Users Assn'n v. Udall*, 231 F. Supp. 548 (D.D.C. 1964) (sustaining Secretary's power to curtail impoundment of water in Glen Canyon Dam in order to provide water sufficient to satisfy power generation contract obligations of Hoover Dam downstream). See also *Arizona v. California*, 373 U.S. 546, 590 (1963) (affirming the extensive powers of the Secretary in managing the river). The Secretary was expressly empowered to adopt criteria for operation of the federal dams on the Colorado in the Colorado River Basin Act of 1968, 43 U.S.C. Sec. 1552.

37. 43 U.S.C. Sec. 1501.

38. See Meyers, "The Colorado River," p. 21.

39. See Edward W. Clyde, "Conflicts Between the Upper and Lower Basins on the Colorado River," *Resources Development: Frontiers for Research* (Boulder, 1960), pp. 113, 119–23. The upper and lower basins have agreed on principles to guide the exercise of that discretion, which were essentially adopted by the Secretary as a statement of priorities for releases from Glen Canyon Dam in the Colorado River Basin Project Act, 43 U.S.C. Sec. 1501.

40. Seven-Party Water Agreement, 18 August 1931, Art. I Secs. 1–4, in Wilbur and Ely, *Hoover Dam Documents*, p. A480.

41. MWD is entitled to 35 percent of the basic energy produced from Hoover Dam. In addition, it has the first right to use any secondary energy produced from the dam. "General Regulations for Generation and Sale of

Power in Accordance with the Boulder Canyon Project Adjustment Act," 20 May 1941, Secretary of the Interior, in Wilbur ad Ely, *Hoover Dam Documents*, pp. A279–A286.

42. 48 F.R. 20872, 9 May 1983.

43. Sections 5 and 8(b) of the Boulder Canyon Project Act provide that the Secretary may contract for sale of stored waters from the Colorado. 43 U.S.C. Sec. 617d, 617g(b). Congress delegated "full power to control, manage, and operate the government's Colorado River works and to make contracts for the sale and delivery of water" to the Secretary of the Interior in the Boulder Canyon Project Act, *Arizona v. California*, 373 U.S. 546 (1963). To the extent that the Secretary violates a contract by use of water for power generation, the deprived party should be able to assert a breach of contract claim against the United States under the Tucker Act. 28 U.S.C. Sec. 1346(a)(2). That Congress intended such action by the United States to be compensable in damages is shown by the fact that reclamation law requires that water rights needed for projects must be condemned. See *United States v. Gerlach Live Stock Co.*, 339 U.S. 725 (1950). There may be problems under Article I, Section 10, Clause 1 of the Constitution, which prohibits impairment of the obligation of contracts if the United States abrogated existing contractual arrangements.

44. See, generally, Harold Ranquist, "The Winters Doctrine and How It Grew: Federal Reservation of Rights to the Use of Water," *Brigham Young University Law Review* (1975), p. 639.

45. The tribes whose claims were decided in *Arizona v. California* were the Chemehuevi tribe, Cocopah tribe, Colorado River tribe, Fort Mojave tribe, and Quechan tribe.

46. 373 U.S. at 600–601. The Court approved the report of the Special Master who had found: "The reservations of water were made for the purpose of enabling the Indians to develop a viable agricultural economy. . . ." Rifkind, *Report of the Special Master*, p. 265.

47. A Special Master appointed by the Court held lengthy hearings and issued a 315-page report. Elbert P. Tuttle, *Report of the Special Master, Arizona v. California* (22 February 1982).

48. *Arizona v. California*, U.S. 103 S. Ct. 1382, 1392 (1983).

49. See Tuttle, *op. cit.*, pp. 106–11, for a summary of the claims to additional irrigable acreage.

50. One tribe, Fort Mojave, has diverted an average of about 77 percent of its entitlement. Another, Chemehuevi, has diverted none. *Arizona v. California*, 103 S. Ct. 1382, 1409 n.8 (1983).

51. Tremendous capital expenditures would be required to make full

use of the tribes' entitlements. Federal assistance in developing the means to irrigate Indian land has been lacking while the government has provided copious aid to the tribes' competitors for water from the same sources. This situation was forcefully criticized by the National Water Commission. National Water Commission, *Water Policies for the Future,* pp. 474–75.

52. The 1982 Special Master's report in *Arizona v. California* showed that many of the lands considered to be "practicably irrigable" could barely be profitable when used for agriculture, even under the most favorable assumptions. Tuttle, *Report of the Special Master,* pp. 192 et seq.

53. *Arizona v. California,* 439 U.S. 419, 422 (1979) (Indian water rights that were quantified based on irrigable acreage need not be confined to agricultural uses); Rifkind, *Report of the Special Master,* pp. 265–66.

54. Navajo claims alone could range as high as 50 million acre-feet, far more than the entire river produces annually. A modest estimate of what a court might award the Navajos solely based on the practicably irrigable acreage formula would be 2 million acre-feet. (Arizona's compact share is only 2.8 million acre-feet.) See William D. Back and Jeffery S. Taylor, "Navajo Water Rights: Pulling the Plug on the Colorado River?," *Natural Resources Journal* 20 (1980), pp. 71, 74 n.12. The tribe may claim more water for purposes other than irrigation, consistent with the broad purposes of the reservation.

55. Several bills have been introduced that would lead to quantification of reserved rights. They generally have avoided dealing with Indian reserved rights. All have died before coming to a vote in Congress. See Note, "A Proposal for the Quantification of Reserved Indian Water Rights," *Columbia Law Review* 74 (1974), pp. 1299, 1301. Commentators citing the one available example, the Navajos' rights in the San Juan River, have warned that congressional quantification is doomed to failure unless the interests of all parties are reflected and represented, a difficult objective when politically powerful interests are pitted against Indian tribes. See Charles Du Mars and Helen Ingram, "Congressional Quantification of Indian Reserved Rights: A Definitive Solution or a Mirage?," *Natural Resources Journal* 20 (1980), p. 17.

56. More than thirty lawsuits raising questions of Indian water rights were pending before state and federal courts in 1981. David H. Getches, Daniel M. Rosenfelt, and Charles F. Wilkinson, *1983 Supplement to Federal Indian Law* (St. Paul, Minn., 1983), p. 161.

57. Montana has established a Reserved Water Rights Compact Commission to negotiate with Indian tribes and the federal government for quantification of reserved rights. Montana Session Laws, ch. 697, 11 May 1979. Congress has approved settlements of water disputes, usually with as-

sistance from the federal treasury, or at least from federal water projects. An arrangement was approved under which the Ak-Chin Indian community in Arizona would forego asserting its rights against non-Indians in return for a promise of 85,000 acre-feet of irrigation water to be furnished by the Secretary of the Interior from a federal project. Act of 28 July 1978, Pub. L. No. 95–328, 92 Stat. 409.

After an initial veto by President Reagan, an act was passed approving settlement of claims by Arizona's Papago Indian tribe against groundwater users in the Tucson area. Public Law No. 97–293, 96 Stat. 1261.

58. Ute Indian Deferral Agreement of 20 September 1965 (Bureau of Reclamation Contract No. 14–06–W–194); see Edward W. Clyde, "Special Considerations Involving Indian Water Rights," *Natural Resources Lawyer* 8 (1975), pp. 250–51.

59. Act of 30 September 1968, Pub. L. No. 90–537, Sec. 303, 82 Stat. 889, as amended, 43 U.S.C. Sec. 1523. See Monroe E. Price and Gary D. Weatherford, "Indian Water Rights in Theory and Practice: Navajo Experience in the Colorado River Basin," *Law and Contemporary Problems* 40, pp. 109–14.

60. Ibid., pp. 119–25.

61. Ibid., pp. 114–19, 125–30; Back and Taylor, "Navajo Water Rights," pp. 71, 87–88; Du Mars and Ingram, "Congressional Quantification of Indian Reserved Rights," p. 17.

62. F. Cohen, *Handbook of Federal Indian Law* (Charlottesville, Va., 1982), pp. 510–22.

63. *New Mexico v. Aamodt*, 537 F. 2d 1102, 1110 (10th Cir. 1976), *cert. denied*, 429 U.S. 1121 (1977); *United States v. Ahtanum Irrig. Dist.*, 236 F. 2d 321, 334 (9th Cir. 1956), *cert. denied*, 352 U.S. 988 (1957).

64. Jack D. Palma, "Considerations and Conclusions Concerning the Transferability of Indian Water Rights," *Natural Resources Journal* 20 (1980), pp. 91, 95–96.

65. Allen V. Kneese and F. Lee Brown, *The Southwest Under Stress* (Baltimore, 1981), pp. 46–47. See Environmental Protection Agency, *The Mineral Quality Problem in the Colorado River Basin—Summary Report* (1971).

66. 33 U.S.C. Secs. 1251, et seq.

67. National Water Commission, *Water Policies for the Future*, pp. 66–67.

68. 33 U.S.C. Sec. 1362(14). For legislative history, see 1977 *U.S. Code Congressional and Administrative News*, p. 4326.

69. 33 U.S.C. Secs. 1251(b), 1313(c). A broad, federal supervisory authority over water-quality standards, including discretion in the adminis-

trator to promulgate substitute standards, has been sustained. For example, see *Mississippi Commission on Natural Resources* v. *Costle*, 625 F. 2d 1269 (5th Cir. 1980).

70. Water-quality standards have not been set by each of the seven states on the Colorado River, but the states joined together in 1973 to form the Colorado River Basin Salinity Control Forum. The Forum set salinity standards for three locations on the river in 1975 and developed an implementation plan for controlling salinity levels. The plan, which relies largely on federally funded construction of salinity control projects authorized by the Colorado River Salinity Control Act of 1974, was revised in 1978. Success of the Forum's plan depends on construction of several projects so that water quality standards can be met. See U.S. General Accounting Office, *Colorado River Basin Water Problems: How to Reduce Their Impact*, GAO Report No. B–122053, CED–79–11 (1979), pp. 32–34. The Bureau of Reclamation determined that further measures would be needed if the standards were to be met. Many of these measures, such as land use controls, conversion from irrigation to other uses, and imposition of use charges for reclamation project water, would have to be taken by state and local governments.

The basinwide approach to water quality, without even state line salinity standards or monitoring, was challenged as a violation of the Clean Water Act. *Environmental Defense Fund* v. *Costle*, 657 F. 2d 275 (9th Cir. 1981). The plaintiff sought to compel the Environmental Protection Agency to exercise its authority to set standards when a state fails to do so. Claims also were made under the Colorado River Basin Salinity Control Act and the National Environmental Policy Act. The court rejected all the claims, but expressed concern for the massive salinity problem in the river.

71. 33 U.S.C. Sec. 1251(g). The provision, known as the Wallop Amendment after its Senate sponsor, stated: "Legitimate water quality measures authorized by this act may at times have some effect on the method of water usage. . . . It is not the purpose of this amendment to prohibit those incidental effects. . . . [The amendment] is designed to protect historic rights from mischievous abrogation by those who would use an act, designed solely to protect water quality and wetlands for other purposes. It does not interfere with the legitimate purposes for which the act was designed." U.S. Congress, *Congressional Record* 123 (Washington, D.C., 1977), p. 39212.

72. 33 U.S.C. Sec. 1344. See, for example, *United States* v. *Byrd*, 609 F. 2d 1204 (7th Cir. 1979).

73. 16 U.S.C. Secs. 1531, et seq.

74. 16 U.S.C. Secs. 661–66b.

75. Treaty with Mexico, 3 February 1944, T.S. No. 994, 59 Stat. 1219. See Charles J. Meyers and Richard L. Noble, "The Colorado River: The Treaty with Mexico," *Stanford Law Review* 19 (1967), p. 367.

76. Michael Bulson, "Colorado River Salinity Problem: Has a Solution Been Found?," *International Lawyer* 9 (1975), pp. 283, 285; Herbert Brownell and Samuel Eaton, "The Colorado River Salinity Problem with Mexico," *American Journal of International Law* 69 (1975), pp. 255, 256.

77. Minute 218, *International Legal Materials*, 84, vol. 4 (1965), p. 545; *Department of State Bulletin* 55 (1965), p. 555. This led to the construction of elaborate drainage works. After some remedial measures were taken, concentrations of dissolved solids reaching Mexico in 1968 were measured at 1269 ppm; while about twenty miles upstream at the Imperial Dam in the United States concentrations were 811 ppm. See William E. Martin, "Economic Magnitudes and Economic Alternatives in Lower Basin Use of Colorado River Water," *Natural Resources Journal* 15 (1975), p. 229. In 1972 the agreement was modified by a new one requiring that the United States substitute higher quality water for the drainage water sent south of the border. Minute 241, *Department of State Bulletin* 67 (1972), p. 198. Then, in 1973, the United States agreed with Mexico that it would construct a desalination plant above Morelos Dam. Minute 242, *International Legal Materials* 12 (1973), p. 1105; *Department of State Bulletin* 69 (1973), p. 395.

The history and issues concerning the salinity problem are thoroughly covered in the several articles appearing in the "International Symposium on the Salinity of the Colorado River," *Natural Resources Journal* 15 (1975), pp. 1–239.

78. The package of controls was included in the 1974 Colorado River Basin Salinity Control Act passed by Congress in 1974. 43 U.S.C. Sec. 1591.

79. See Dean E. Mann, "Politics in the United States and the Salinity Problem of the Colorado River," *Natural Resources Journal* 15 (1975), pp. 113, 126–27.

80. Federal expenditures for contruction of water projects in the Colorado River Basin for the period 1903–1980 exceeded 3.66 billion dollars. The full Reclamation Bureau budget for the basin during the same period was 4.92 billion dollars. U.S. Bureau of Reclamation budget, *1980 Annual Report* (Washington, D.C., 1981), app. 2.

81. The Bureau of Reclamation budget dropped from 778 million dollars in 1981 to 773 million dollars in 1982. The largest cuts were in the construction budget. *Budget of the United States Government, Appendix* (Washington, D.C., 1981, 1982). The budget for fiscal year 1984 shows an increase

of 80 percent in defense spending, while the budget for all nondefense purposes has grown by only 35.9 percent. Executive Office of the President,
Office of Management and Budget, *Budget of the United States, Fiscal Year
1984* (Washington, D.C., 1982), pp. 9.3, 9.5.

82. In 1981 Senator Peter Domenici, Republican, of New Mexico, and
Senator Daniel Patrick Moynihan, Democrat, of New York, introduced a bill
to require state contributions of 25 percent to be paid at the beginning of
water projects, and federal contributions to be made in the form of subsequent
block grants. U.S. Senate, Committee on Environment and Public Works,
S.621, 97th Cong., 1st sess. (introduced 5 March 1981).

83. For example, the National Environmental Policy Act requires a
consideration of the significant environmental effects of actions taken by
federal agencies before the actions may be taken; 42 U.S.C. Sec. 4331(c)(2).
It has been held that the act makes environmental protection part of the
mission of every agency. *Calvert Cliffs Coordinating Committee* v. *United States
Atomic Energy Commission*, 449 F. 2d 1109 (D.C. Cir. 1971).

84. See Notes 9, 21, above.

85. B. Delworth Gardner and Clyde E. Stewart, "Agriculture and Salinity Control in the Colorado River Basin," *Natural Resources Journal* 15
(1975), pp. 63, 64. It is reported that 90 percent of all water used in the
Upper Basin states is for crop irrigation and 88 percent of the irrigated land
produces livestock feed. The Lower Basin states use 85 percent of their water
for agriculture. Fradkin, *A River No More* (New York, 1981), pp. 31–32.
Gardner and Stewart state that 58 percent of the irrigated lands in the Lower
Basin are dedicated to growing forage and grain.

86. Tremendous inefficiency in present irrigation water use is well doc-
umented. It has been estimated that irrigation water waste alone, mostly
from evaporation and phreatophytes, amounts to 24 million acre-feet a year.
U.S. Soil Conservation Service, *Crop Consumptive Irrigation Requirements and
Irrigation Efficiency Coefficients for the United States*, appendix to the National
Analysis, Second National Water Assessment (Washington, D.C., 1976).

Analysts of water policy uniformly urge the importance of water con-
servation. See, for example, National Water Commission, *Water Policies for
the Future* (Washington, D.C., 1973), pp. 227–30; U.S. Department of the
Interior, Westwide Study Report on Critical Water Problems Facing the
Eleven Western States (Washington, D.C., 1975); United States Water Resources Council, *The Nation's Water Resources 1975–2000)* (Washington,
D.C., 1978); State of California, *Final Report, Governor's Commission to
Review California Water Rights Law* (Sacramento, 1978), pp. 71–72 (list of
measures recommended to increase efficiency of water use). See Ronald D.

Lacewell and Glenn S. Collins, "Implications and Management Alternatives for Western Irrigated Agriculture," Technical Article 17807 of the Texas Agricultural Experiment Station (College Station, Tex., unpublished, undated).

87. The most influential source on interstate compacts is Felix Frankfurter and James M. Landis, "The Compact Clause of the Constitution—A Study in Interstate Adjustments," *Yale Law Journal* 34 (1925), p. 684. On interstate water compacts see Jerome Muys, *Interstate Water Contracts: The Interstate Compact and Federal-Interstate Compact*, National Water Commission Legal Study no. 14 (Arlington, Va., 1971). Congress must approve a compact for it to be valid. United States Constitution, Article III, Section 3, Clause 2.

88. Congress does not surrender or limit its sovereign power by consenting to an interstate compact. *Pennsylvania v. Wheeling & Belmont Brige*, 59 U.S. (18 How.) 421, 433 (1856).

89. The Court has indicated in a dispute over waters of an interstate stream that "mutual accommodation and agreement should, if possible, be the medium of settlment, instead of invocation of our adjudicatory power." *Colorado v. Kansas*, 320 U.S. 383, 392 (1943).

90. *Arizona v. California*, 283 U.S. 423 (1931); *Kansas v. Colorado*, 206 U.S. 46 (1907).

91. A noted climatologist has suggested that a global warming trend caused by carbon dioxide loading of the atmosphere could result in such a decline in river flow. Walter Orr Roberts, "It Is Time to Prepare for Global Climate Changes," *Conservation Foundation Letter* (April 1983). See also the various scenarios discussed by Dr. Kneese in Chapter 4.

92. For example, some say it is unclear whether the 1922 compact or the Upper Colorado River Basin Compact of 1948, Pub. L. No. 37–48, 63 Stat. 31, apportioned the White River in Colorado. Also, the overlapping coverage of the Upper Basin Compact and the Animas–La Plata Project Compact, approved in the Colorado River Basin Project Act, Pub. L. No. 90–537, Sec. 501, 82 Stat. 896, could require interpretive action to determine whether the latter amended the former compact.

93. Protectionist sentiment in the Columbia River Basin led Senator Henry Jackson to press for and obtain a twenty-year moratorium on further research or planning for transbasin diversions from that area. Colorado River Basin Project Act, 43 U.S.C. Sec. 12511; see also Reclamation Safety of Dams Act, Pub. L. No. 95–578, Sec. 10, 92 Stat. 2471.

94. Charles J. Meyers and Richard Posner, "Toward an Improved Market in Water Resources," Legal Study no. 4 (Washington, D.C., 1971).

95. See Note, "Water Waste-Ascertainment and Abatement," *Utah Law Review* (1973), p. 449.

96. *In re Willow Creek*, 74 Ore. 592, 144 P. 505 (1914). Compare *A & B Cattle Co. v. United States*, 589 P. 2d 57 (Colo. 1978).

97. *Glenn Dale Ranches, Inc. v. Straub*, 94 Idaho 585, 494 P. 2d 1029 (1972).

98. For example, see U.S. Comptroller General, *More and Better Uses Could Be Made of Billions of Gallons of Water by Improving Irrigation Delivery Systems* (GAP CED–77–117) (Washington, D.C., 1977); U.S. General Accounting Office, *Better Water Management Possible—But Constraints Need to Be Overcome* (GAO CED–79–1) (Washington, D.C., 1978).

99. Arizona Revised Statutes Secs. 45–101—45–631.

100. *Sporhase v. Nebraska*, 458 U.S. 941, 102 S. Ct. 3456 (1982).

101. Ibid., 102 S. Ct. at 3464.

102. Ibid., 102 S. Ct. at 3466.

4 Hypothetical Shocks to Water Allocation Institutions in the Colorado Basin

Allen V. Kneese and Gilbert Bonem

Water allocation institutions in the Colorado River Basin were built up during a period of rapid water development and were designed to foster and aid that development. This is also the case for the West more broadly. Prior appropriation law helped to provide a degree of security of supply so that private developers of irrigation had the incentive to commit capital and labor to the construction of diversion and distribution systems. But the relationships between law, institutions, and development did not stop there.

Even after water courses were fully appropriated, agriculture continued to expand by developing supplies through the federal program to reclaim the arid West. The era of reclaiming arid lands began in the late nineteenth century, and the 1902 Reclamation Act established this objective as a national goal. The period following the Reclamation Act was one of heavily subsidized and increasingly centralized, large-scale irrigation projects. Long-term, interest-free financing based on "ability to pay" further institutionalized the notion that unappropriated and undeveloped water was itself free, with its only cost being the capital cost of constructing works and the subsequent operation and maintenance cost. The Bureau of Reclamation provided dams and diversion works on most major waterways in the West. Transbasin diversion projects were also commonplace. Accompanying the reclamation program was the creation of special water districts as entities responsible for repayment, operation, and maintenance functions with

respect to these public works. If projects experienced hardships, contract obligations were deferred. Regions that had political clout in
Congress were usually treated most generously. Frequently, hydroelectric power production was part of these projects and was used as
the "cash register" to subsidize irrigation water development.[1]

But the West is rapidly undergoing a major transformation with
respect to water. Increasing water scarcity already has brought changes
in western development and water-use patterns, and much greater
changes are likely to occur in the future. In particular, the expansion
of irrigated agriculture based on the availability of inexpensive water
is ending.

Just a few decades ago supplies were sufficient to satisfy a rapid
growth of water use throughout virtually all of the West. More recently,
however, high costs and limited opportunities for developing new
supplies have severely constrained the growth of offstream water use
in many areas, especially where users are heavily dependent on diminishing supplies of groundwater. Total water withdrawals for all but
hydroelectric generation rose 4.6 percent per annum from 1950 to
1960, compared to only 1.4 percent per annum from 1970 to 1980.
Excluding the northern plains states of Kansas, Nebraska, and North
and South Dakota, where water withdrawals nearly doubled over the
last decade, water withdrawals rose only 0.9 percent per annum from
1970 to 1980.[2]

Rights to most of the surface waters have been allocated, and
with rising frequency, potential users are forced to compete for the
same water. This competition has been intensified by the rising value
that society is placing on instream water uses. In nearly half of the
West's water resource subregions, the sum of instream use (defined as
the flow at the discharge point of the subregion required to satisfy the
higher of minimum needs to maintain fish and wildlife populations or
navigational needs) and offstream consumption exceeds average yearly
streamflow.[3] And since current levels of water consumption result in
the groundwater mining of about 22.4 million acre-feet per year,[4]
future competition over supplies likely will intensify even in the absence of further growth in demand.

Approximately 90 percent of western water consumption is for
the irrigation of about fifty million acres.[5] As both the largest and a
relatively low-value user, irrigation is the sector most directly affected

by the changing water situtation. Nonagricultural water consumption grew twice as fast as irrigation use from 1960 to 1980. Where water has become particularly scarce and expensive, water for irrigation has started to level off or even decline. In Arizona, for example, total irrigation water consumption declined by about 6 percent from 1970 to 1980, while consumption for other uses rose by 67 percent. Only in the northern plains did the growth of water consumption for irrigation exceed the growth for other uses during the last decade.[6]

Thus, while the era of rapid water development is ending in most of the arid West, and the problem of allocating and managing a fixed supply is becoming the dominant one, the situation appears to be particularly striking in the Colorado River Basin. Expectations from the river already appear to exceed its ability to meet them. This results, at least in part, from the fact that the Colorado River Compact anticipated more water than the river can deliver on a long-term basis. As Professor Hundley has pointed out, the framers of the compact assumed the dependable yield of the river to exceed sixteen million acre-feet per year; the framers apparently believed the average flow to be close to seventeen or eighteen million acre-feet. It is now widely believed by students of the matter that the average annual yield is less, possibly considerably less, than the fifteen million acre-feet actually divided up by the compact.

The Second National Water Assessment estimated the total streamflow of the Upper Basin to be nearly fifteen million acre-feet, considerably below the amount assumed in the compact negotiations.[7] Other evidence, however, suggests that the actual flow is even lower. A particularly interesting effort to construct a very long-term hydrograph for the Colorado River was done by the staff of the Tree Ring Laboratory at the University of Arizona. Figure 1 shows a dendrohydrograph of estimated virgin flow at Lee Ferry. This hydrograph was constructed by the application of complex statistical methods to tree-ring observations in the basin and traces the estimated flow from the year 1564 to 1960. This is shown in the bottom graph. The top graph shows estimated virgin flows since 1915 past the same point based on actual streamflow observations.

Both graphs strongly suggest that streamflow information available to the framers of the compact was gathered during a period of unusually, actually uniquely, persistent high streamflow. The den-

Estimated Virgin Flow

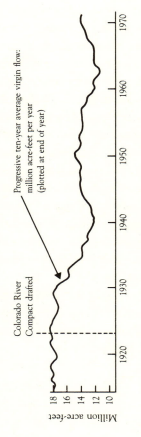

Streamflow at Lee Ferry

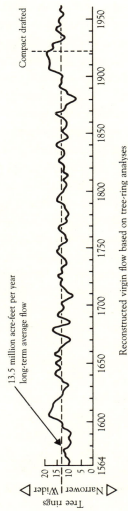

Reconstructed virgin flow based on tree-ring analyses

Source: Charles W. Stockton and Gordon C. Jacoby Jr., *Long-term Surface-Water Supply and Streamflow Trends in the Upper Colorado River Basin,* Lake Powell Research Project Bulletin No. 18, March 1976.

Figure 1.   Flow of the Colorado River

drohydrograph indicates an average long-term flow of about 13.5 million acre-feet. It also shows several periods of persistently low streamflow. We will return to those periods later when we consider the possible implications of extended drought in the Upper Basin.

Another way of looking at streamflow data is through probability analysis. Prior to the passage of the Colorado River Basin Project Act in 1968 the Lower Basin states of California, Arizona, and Nevada decided to agree on a water-supply study and make a joint presentation on water supply to the House Subcommittee on Irrigation and Reclamation. Engineers making the study agreed to do a probability study based on methods developed by Luna Leopold, formerly chief hydraulic engineer of the United States Geological Survey. In their testimony,[8] they concluded that there is a fifty-fifty chance that the supply available in the main stream will equal or be greater than the amount needed to provide: (1) 4.4 million acre-feet a year for California (this is the amount awarded California in 1963 by the decision of the Supreme Court in *Arizona v. California*); (2) water for decreed rights and existing mainstream projects in Arizona and Nevada and the southern Nevada water-supply project; (3) water for increasing demands on the Upper Basin; and (4) a full supply of 1.2 million acre-feet for the prroposed Central Arizona Project until about the end of the century, with a gradually reduced supply afterwards.

Myron Holburt, chief engineer of the Colorado River Board of California, later commented on these results. Since Mr. Holburt has been one of the chief figures in Colorado River affairs for many years, his statement is worth quoting at some length:

> Under normal circumstances, it would not be prudent to construct an elaborate and expensive water conveyance system that would serve a growing agricultural-urban civilization based upon anticipation of a water supply having only a 50 percent probability of occurrence. The special circumstances which made feasible the authorization of the Central Arizona Project, even though it was recognized that there was an inadequate long-term supply, are:
>
> 1. A pending program to bring new water into the river; the bill directed the Secretary of the Interior to develop a regional plan to supply the water needs of the region.
>
> 2. The bill gave priority to existing contractors in the Lower

Basin against the Central Arizona Project with California's protection limited to 4.4 million acre-feet per year (California now uses 5 million acre-feet per year).

3. Water from the project cannot be used to serve new lands. Service is limited to existing agricultural users in central Arizona and the expanding urban areas of Phoenix and Tucson. In the event of shortages, these users can fall back upon the alternative source of local groundwater supplies.

Thus, it is expected that any insufficient project water supplies can be overcome on a short-term basis by additional ground water pumping and can be overcome on a long-term basis by river augmentation. The interval between the completion of the Central Arizona Project and the completion of works to augment the flow of the Colorado River is the period during which there is the greatest risk of water shortage.[9]

Since the Central Arizona Project is nearly complete and since the interval between its completion and augmentation of the Colorado, at least by interbasin transfers, may well be infinitely long, we are, on this analysis, likely to have shortages. Thus, even with "normal" development there will probably be periods of more or less stress on the basin's water allocation institutions.

However, the chief purpose of this chapter is to imagine some "events" that might occur that could greatly exacerbate such stresses. We do not argue that any of them except the last (prolonged deep drought) will occur, or is necessarily likely. But it certainly is not incredible that shocks will occur even if we look only at what has already happened. For example, after the Arab oil boycott there was what seemed for a time to be a brute-force effort on the part of energy companies and the government to develop the region's energy resources. Furthermore, recent rulings in the *Sporhase* and *El Paso* cases call into question the states' previously unquestioned jurisdiction over "their" water supplies and so have already produced some cracks in the institutional structure. The hypothetical situations discussed in the following sections can serve to assist in conducting "thought experiments" to test the strength and resiliency of the Colorado's water institutions. Four situations are considered. The first three situations are discussed quite briefly but comprehensively enough that we hope to stimulate thought about them. The last situation, deep and prolonged drought in the Upper Colorado Basin, is discussed more fully because we believe it to be the most credible situation and one which could, in the foreseeable future, produce a genuine crisis for the Colorado's water allocation institutions, the current relative abundance of water supplies in the basin notwithstanding.

First Hypothetical: Renewed Disruption in International Trade and an Urgent National Need to Find and Develop Energy Resources in the Western Hemisphere

Presently there is a glut of oil in international markets. But imagine a situation in which a complete cutoff of oil from the Middle East (because of, say, an international, but contained, war in the region) damages our economy severely, both because we are still partly dependent on that region for supplies and because we have commitments to share with our allies during times of shortages. This situation would set up intense and serious pressure both to develop domestic energy supplies quickly and to help develop more secure foreign sources, most logically in Mexico. With respect to the former, as part of the Southwest Region under Stress Project we examined the water-use implications of several energy development scenarios. Scenario D was specifically designed to be a brute-force crash development scenario. The scale of development is massive but consistent with the energy resources of the region. It projects an additional 36,000 megawatts of electrical generating capacity, 10,000 million cubic feet per day of coal gasification, and $1^{1}/_{2}$ million barrels per day of oil-shale production. Such growth might be possible over the course of about two decades. This scenario, assuming some investment in water-saving technology, might require consumption in the neighborhood of one million acre-feet of water a year.[10]

Imagine further that, at the same time, as a reward for developing its petroleum reserves at a faster rate than it deems to be in its own national interest, Mexico demands the reopening of negotiations about its share of the Colorado River. Assume it obtains agreement from the United States to gradually increase its release of water to the Mexicali Valley, until after twenty years it receives an additional two million acre-feet per year.

Taking these circumstances in combination would mean that over a period of twenty years there occurs an increase in requirements for water for three million acre-feet per year over and above what would otherwise have happened. Clearly, these requirements could not be met from basin sources without disastrous effects on the region's agriculture. In this circumstance, the states in the region once more marshal all their political forces around water issues and form a coalition with northeastern states, who badly need the Mexican oil, to pressure the federal government to provide and pay for interbasin transfers to protect the region's agricultural water and to possibly increase it. In drafting the Colorado River Basin Act (which, as noted, contemplated interbasin transfers), the political representatives of the region were careful to include a provision stating that under the act the United States (not just the basin states) assumes the Mexican water treaty obligation. The international dimension, which also played a considerable role in the assumption of the cost of the Colorado Salinity Control Program by the United States,[11] plus the powerful internal political coalition provides the key to putting together the last and greatest "Christmas tree" for the traditional distributive water politics of the region, which results in a massive transfer of water from the Pacific Northwest.

Second Hypothetical: Indian Water Claims Are Quantified and the Quantities Are Large

A sword of Damocles was hung over future institutional arrangements for water allocation in the Colorado Basin in 1908 when the case of *Winters* v. *United States* was decided. The Supreme Court ruled that in land reserved for Indians water was implicitly reserved as well. These reserved, or "Winters' doctrine," rights have, for the most part, never been quantified but are potentially very large, and they, as well as other reserved rights, lie entirely outside of the prior appropriation system. As pointed out by Professor Hundley, in Chapter 2, the decision in *Arizona* v. *California* has far-reaching implications for Indian water rights; for the Colorado River tribes most directly, but by implication, for other tribes as well. As Professor Hundley observes, the Court supported the position of the federal lawyers and invoked the principle laid down in *Winters* v. *United States* that in an arid climate the reservation of land for Indians implies the reservation of water. The Court further adopted the government's position that the only feasible and fair way to determine the extent of that right is in irrigable acreage. But in a later decree, the Court held that, while the measurement of the right is irrigable acreage, the Colorado River tribes were not limited to agriculture in putting their water to use. That Indian water rights are not limited to irrigation water was recently affirmed in a state court ruling in Wyoming granting water rights to Indians (Shoshone and Arapaho) in the Big Horn River Basin.[12]

But the amount of irrigable land available is, under both the Winters' doctrine and *Arizona* v. *California,* a critical factor in determining the actual extent of the Indian water rights, and this was the subject of contention among the Colorado River Indians and interested non-Indian parties in Arizona.[13] In 1983, the Court rejected recommendations of a special master who had dealt with claims of the Colorado River tribes. This decision left the river tribes with approximately 900,000 acre-feet of water rather than the 1.2 million they wanted.

But the Colorado River tribes' water is still a large quantity from the Colorado River perspective. The claims of the Navajo, whose situation is much less clear-cut, are potentially much larger since their reservation is relatively huge—25,000 square miles—and lies entirely in the Colorado River Basin. It straddles the divide between two major tributaries, the San Juan and the Little Colorado, and its western boundary is the main stem of the Colorado. The Colorado River Basin and the Navajo reservation are shown in Figure 2.

Despite the large size of the reservation, and its potentially huge Winters' doctrine rights, it received little notice in the various agreements that have divided up the river over the last several generations.[14] The complex negotiations, described by Professor Hundley, leading to the Colorado River Compact—signed by representatives of the basin states in 1922 (except Arizona, which signed later), ratified by Congress in 1928, and proclaimed by the president in 1929—proceeded entirely without Indian participation. During the negotiations, however, Secretary of Commerce Herbert Hoover, federal delegate to the Compact Commission, requested wording designed to head off the issue of Indian rights from being raised in Congress. The resulting

96

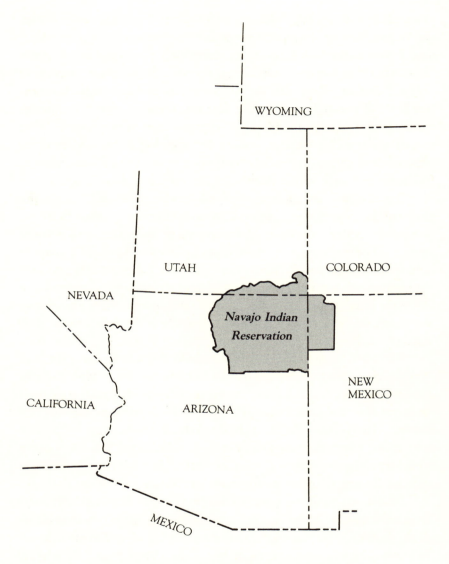

Figure 2.   The Colorado River Basin and the Navajo Indian
Reservation

brief passage simply says that nothing in the compact should be construed as affecting the obligation of the government to Indian tribes. Similar language was inserted in the Upper Colorado River Basin Compact (1948) that divided the Upper Basin allotment among the states above Lee Ferry. While it considered the question, the Upper Colorado Compact Commission decided not to attempt to quantify Navajo rights. Again, the Colorado River Storage Project Act of 1956, which was the basis for the construction of Glen Canyon Dam (Lake Powell), the main river regulation structure in the Upper Basin, avoided the issue of Navajo water rights.

The Navajo Indian Irrigation Project Act, which in 1962 authorized the Secretary of the Interior to construct the Navajo Indian Irrigation Project, obviously could not avoid the issue of water rights entirely. The Navajo Indian Irrigation Project (NIIP), which plans to irrigate 110,000 acres of Navajo land, is located in the San Juan Basin (tributary to the Colorado) in the northeastern part of the reservation. In 1957, in exchange for congressional approval of NIIP, the Navajo Nation agreed to waive its priority on the San Juan River and to share water shortages proportionately with non-Indians. The issues raised by this agreement are very complex, and its meaning in terms of Winters' doctrine rights remains unsettled. However, wording in the NIIP water delivery contract states that the tribe does not waive any reserved Winters' doctrine rights, and it is also the position of the Navajo Tribal Council that the tribe did not do so.

How large might a Navajo claim to Colorado River water rights be? As noted, *Arizona v. California* applies the irrigability test. Assuming this same test is valid for the Navajo, and assuming that only 500,000 acres or 4 percent of the total land area is *practicably* irrigable (the total Navajo irrigable land is 13 million acres), the tribal entitlement would be about 2 million acre-feet per year. Arizona's entire Lower Basin entitlement under *Arizona v. California* is only 2.8 million acre-feet. In recent years, the Navajos have employed engineers and attorneys to prepare a water rights case against the basin states and the federal government. Some outside observers of the matter believe that the suit, when and if it is filed, will be for five million acre-feet or more.[16]

Given the extent of Colorado River tribes' water rights, if such a Navajo suit were to be successful these two groups of Indians would be entitled to almost half of the total long-run yield of the river. Since such an entitlement would be quite outside the prior appropriation system, it would not, unlike rights under that system, be contingent on beneficial use. It might therefore be possible for Indians to charge non-Indian users a fee for the continued use of Indian water. Back and Taylor quote Northcutt Ely, chief counsel for California during congressional hearings on the Colorado River Storage Project in 1955, on the matter of whether Indian rights are inside or outside the compact apportionments. "If inside, and as large as claimed," Ely says, "the compact is splitting at the seams, and if outside, busted."

Third Hypothetical:
A Large-Scale Interstate Market
in Water Rights Develops

For many years, states in the Colorado Basin and elsewhere in the West have operated under the assumption that their power to regulate groundwater was complete and that their compacts dividing surface waters with other states unquestionably governed the allocation of supplies. Several recent court cases have called both of these suppositions into question. The two leading ones are the *Sporhase* case decided by the Supreme Court on July 2, 1982, and the *El Paso* case decided by the Federal District Court of New Mexico on January 17, 1983. The *El Paso* case is being appealed and may also finally go to the Supreme Court. In both cases, the courts have for the first time unequivocably proclaimed that water is an article of interstate commerce. These rulings, especially if the *El Paso* ruling is affirmed in the higher courts, may have substantial implications for the states' ability to control the interstate transfer of water. In the *Sporhase* case,[17] the appellants owned property extending across the Colorado-Nebraska boundary. From a well on the Nebraska side, they transported water to a sprinkler system in Colorado. To do this legally, the owners would have had to, but did not, obtain a permit from the Nebraska Department of Water Resources. Such a permit can be granted under Nebraska law for interstate transport of water, but only if, among other things, the state to which it is transported has granted reciprocal rights to Nebraska. Colorado law flatly prohibits interstate transportation of groundwater. Thus, had the appellants requested a permit, it would have been denied.

The attorney general of Nebraska brought suit against Sporhase and Moss et al., owners of the land, to end further transportation of water to Colorado. The district court issued an injunction prohibiting such transportation, and the Nebraska Supreme Court affirmed on the basis that groundwater is not an article of interstate commerce in Nebraska. The case was appealed to the Supreme Court of the United States.

The Court held that water is an article of commerce and therefore subject to congressional regulation. It held that the state's claim that it owned the water is a legal fiction. It held further that agricultural markets supplied by irrigated farms provide an archetypal example of commerce among the states for which the framers of the Constitution intended to authorize federal regulation. The Court held that it is specifically the reciprocity provision of the Nebraska statute that violates the Commerce Clause.

> The reciprocity requirement of the Nebraska statute violates the Commerce Clause as imposing an impermissible burden on interstate commerce. While the first three conditions set forth in the statute for granting a permit—that the withdrawal of the groundwater be reasonable, not contrary to the conservation and use of groundwater, and not otherwise detrimental to the public welfare—do not on their faces impermissibly burden interstate commerce, the reciprocity provision operates as an explicit barrier to commerce between Nebraska and its adjoining States. Nebraska therefore has the initial burden of demonstrating a close fit between the reciprocity requirement and its asserted local purpose. Such requirement, when superimposed on the first three restrictions, fails to clear this initial hurdle, since there is no evidence that it is narrowly tailored to the conservation and preservation rationale. Thus, it does not survive the "strictest scrutiny" reserved for facially discriminatory legislation.[18]

Thus, the Court recognized a state's legitimate interest in water conservation to protect the health and welfare of its population, but held that the de facto prohibition resulting from the reciprocity provision was not tightly related to such purposes. Essentially, what the

Court forbade was restrictions on water exports for the purpose of permitting or promoting economic development in the originating state.

The Court conceded, however, that "a demonstrably arid state conceivably might be able to marshall evidence to establish a close means–end relationship between even a total ban on the exportation of water and a purpose to conserve and preserve water."

That the mere fact of aridity is, however, not sufficient is underlined by the district court's ruling in the *El Paso* case. New Mexico, like Colorado and a number of other states, has a statute flatly forbidding the export of groundwater. After making its preparation to do so in secret, the city of El Paso, Texas, applied in 1981 to the New Mexico state engineer for the right to develop a large amount of unappropriated groundwater in southern New Mexico. El Paso claimed that it needed this water to meet the needs of its future population growth and economic development. Following litigation, the court held that the New Mexico statute was an illegal barrier to interstate commerce and affirmed that water is indeed an article of such commerce. Specifically, the court said: "The Court recognizes that the conservation and preservation of water is of the utmost importance to the citizens of New Mexico. . . . Nevertheless the New Mexico groundwater embargo violates the Commerce Clause of the United States Constitution, and an order will be entered herein enjoining the defendants from enforcing it."[19]

It appears that in order for states to regain control of "their" water supplies they will either have to make more persuasive "conservation" and "health and welfare" arguments, seek an act of Congress granting them power to forbid export of water, or assume actual state ownership (by purchase or condemnation) of water rights to prevent uncontrolled operation of the private market.

In this third hypothetical situation, we assume that none of these possibilities occur and that there is a rapid rise in the interstate movement of water. Water comes to be treated like any other commodity, becomes more overtly commercialized; many private water rights become transferable to the highest bidder across state lines; and interstate compacts are undercut. For example, water rights in Wyoming may become interesting to rural and urban interests in southern California

as reduced deliveries under the Colorado Compact occur and groundwater is further depleted. The physical facilities to deliver Wyoming
water to southern California already exist.

Fourth Hypothetical: Deep Sustained
Drought in the Upper Colorado Basin

Unlike the other hypothetical situations, this one is hypothetical
only in the sense that we do not know when it will occur; but we can
expect with high confidence that it will. The probability analysis
reported earlier suggested that water-supply shortfalls are likely to
happen in the future. Also, the dendrohydrograph displayed earlier
indicates that the data available to the framers of the compact reflected
the wettest period to occur in the Upper Colorado in at least several
centuries. In this hypothetical situation, we become more specific and
postulate an actual and very severe drought, but one that is consistent
with what has already occurred in history. We then try to show some
of the consequences. We focus primarily upon the ability of the Upper
Basin to meet its compact commitment in such a situation. To accomplish this, we must be more quantitative than in earlier sections;
therefore, it is necessary to burden the reader with a little arithmetic.

Let us look first at some low-flow episodes that have actually been
measured or that have been estimated from tree-ring studies. Hydro-
logical records kept by the Bureau of Reclamation can be used to look
at some low-flow episodes that have actually been recorded. The lowest
undepleted flow (that is, reconstructed virgin flow) in the Bureau's
series is for the 1934 water year (from October 1933 to September
1934) with 5.64 million acre-feet. The 1976 water year flow was near
this with 5.78 million acre-feet. But comparing annual minimum flows
to compact requirements would be misleading, of course, because the
Colorado River Compact, as already indicated, provides that the states
of the Upper Basin must deliver 75 million acre-feet at Lee's Ferry in
each successive ten-year period. Thus, deliveries do not have to equal
7.5 million acre-feet in one year. (We temporarily ignore deliveries
related to the Mexican water treaty.) More pertinent, then, are the
lowest flow intervals averaged over ten years. One of these was during
the interval from 1954 to 1963, with 11.826 million acre-feet average

Table 1.   **Selected Colorado River Reservoir Data**

Reservoir	Useable Capacity (thousand acre-feet)	Useable Storage (thousands of acre-feet)			Change in Storage	
		October 1976	May 1977	October 1977	October to May	October to October
Flaming Gorge	3,749	3,364	2,496	2,055	868	1,309
Blue Moon	829	583	337	208	246	375
Navajo	1,696	1,279	1,094	1,033	185	246
Glen Canyon	25,000	19,266	18,343	16,030	923	3,236
		Net Releases, Total			2,222	5,166

Source: U.S. Bureau of Reclamation

annual flow. In the ten-year period from 1931 to 1940, average annual flow was 11.833 million acre-feet.

The Arizona Tree Ring Laboratory's reconstructed hydrograph indicates the lowest ten-year flow occurring from 1584 to 1593, with 9.7 million acre-feet per year. Consequently, we might establish a range of expected ten-year drought flows extending from a 97-million acre-feet total to a 118-million acre-feet total for the driest ten-year periods observed or estimated. Of course, any assumed drought flows are subject to considerable uncertainty, but this range is consistent with available data.

A way to obtain an initial perspective on the potential effect of drought in the Upper Colorado Basin on its ability to deliver water to the Lower Basin is to look at reservoir release data during a previous drought. Table 1 indicates releases from four Upper Colorado River Basin reservoirs during the 1976–1977 drought, a drought which some observers labeled the "wettest drought in history" because a very dry fall and winter (1976–1977) was followed by relatively heavy precipitation in the summer of 1977. In other words, the drought was very severe, but also very short by historical standards. Table 1, which was compiled from Bureau records, shows that the net reservoir drawdown at the four largest reservoirs in the Upper Basin from October 1976 to October 1977 was over 5 million acre-feet. In comparison, initial usable storage at these four reservoirs was almost 25 million acre-feet.

Thus, the 1976–1977 drought used about 20 percent of the storage existing. Stating things mildly, we may say that if a drought of this intensity had lasted for three or four years, instead of less than one, the ability of reservoirs to sustain the river's yield would have been seriously impaired.

We now define a specific hypothetical drought of less severity but of greater duration. Our earlier discussion suggests that ten-year undepleted flows at Lee's Ferry, in a severe prolonged drought, would be perhaps 97 to 118 million acre-feet, with some individual years dipping toward the 6 to 7 million acre-feet mark. In such a situation, spot water shortages throughout the basin would be enormous; restrictions on residential water use, reduced crop yields, scrambles for sprinkler irrigation, canal lining, and drilling of new wells would all occur. As a sidelight, we may mention that a real drought would severely affect the region's ski industry; one study showed this to be Utah's most severely affected industry in the 1977 drought. Finally, as a hypothetical drought continued, reservoir storage in the Upper Colorado Basin would begin to be depleted. How serious might this depletion be and how would it affect the Upper Basin's ability to deliver water?

We will try to answer this question in four steps.

1. The Upper Basin must deliver 75 million acre-feet over a ten-year period, plus 750,000 acre-feet per year as its share of the Mexican water treaty. Another 150,000 acre-feet per year of Mexican treaty water is debatable; indeed, the 750,000 is, perhaps, debatable. But we assume the Upper Basin's obligation is 82½ million acre-feet over a ten-year period.

2. The ten-year flow will be in the range of 97 to 118 million acre-feet; we shall assume it to be 100 million acre-feet, not far below the recorded low of 118 million acre-feet in the decade from 1954 to 1963 and slightly above the lowest estimated ten-year flow.

3. To the ten-year virgin flow at Lee's Ferry, we must add water available from storage in reservoirs in the Upper Basin. The four reservoirs listed in Table 1 have usable capacity of 31.27 million acre-feet. Dracup gives an estimate of 33.8 million acre-feet of storage capacity available in the Upper Basin.[20] We assume that at the start of a ten-year drought there are 30 million acre-feet in storage in the

Table 2.   **Depletions in the Upper Colorado River**

	1972–1981	1962–1971	1952–1961
Within Basin Depletions			
Quantity	2,366	1,986	1,614
% change from previous decade	19%	23%	
Transbasin Diversions	704	508	436
Net Reservoir Evaporation Loss	609	257	0
Total			
Quantity	3,679	2,751	2,050
% change from previous decade	34%	34%	

Source: U.S. Bureau of Reclamation

Upper Basin. Thus, the undepleted ten-year runoff at Lee's Ferry would be 130 million acre-feet if all the upstream water were available for this purpose.

4. From the undepleted runoff, however, we must subtract Upper Basin depletions. Table 2 shows some compilations that we made of present Upper Basin depletions from Bureau of Reclamation data. In the last ten years, Upper Basin depletions from the Colorado River system have averaged 3.7 million acre-feet per year, including diversions to other basin and reservoir evaporation losses.

We are now ready to conclude the calculations. The hypothetical ten-year drought would leave the Upper Basin with about 130 million acre-feet of water to deliver, of which 82.5 million acre-feet are owed by compact and 37.0 million acre-feet would be depleted by present uses. Thus, the Upper Basin would have excess water of 11.5 million acre-feet over the ten-year period (130—82.5—37.0). This is about 1.1 million acre-feet per year; and we must increase this to about 1 1/2 million acre-feet because evaporation from reservoirs will decline, since we have assumed that all the reservoirs are emptied during the drought. If, then, the reservoirs are almost full at the start of the drought and are emptied, the Upper Basin could, at present, meet its obligations and maintain its water use, with about 1 1/2 million acre-feet per year to spare at Lee's Ferry.

But note that during the twenty-year period shown in Table 2 the Upper Basin depletions increased 80 percent (from 2.05 million acre-feet to 3.68 million acre-feet). We assume that no new transbasin diversions occur and that no new reservoirs are built. Thus, we consider only future increase in depletions from inbasin use. For the twenty-year period shown in Table 2, the increase in these depletions was 47 percent (from 1.61 million acre-feet to 2.37 million acre-feet). Arbitrarily, extrapolating this rate of increase for the next twenty years implies that depletions would increase by 1.1 million acre-feet; such increase would effectively use up all the water remaining during a drought. We emphasize that future water demands in the Upper Colorado could be much larger than the increase obtained by this extrapolation of past trends. See, for example, the first hypothetical situation.

Given our assumptions, we conclude that the Upper Basin could probably make good its compact commitments if a ten-year drought started tomorrow. Of course, this assumes that Upper Basin reservoirs are almost full—as indeed they presently are—when the drought starts and that authorities are willing to empty the reservoirs. If a ten-year drought begins fifteen to twenty years from now, it is unlikely that the Upper Basin can make good its compact commitments even under these extremely favorable assumptions.

In conclusion, we must reemphasize that these results are based on *very* favorable assumptions concerning the delivery of water. If the reservoir system were not to be full when the drought began, shortfalls could easily become large. The assumption that the upstream reservoirs would indeed be emptied is also a very strong one. In working out our example, we have the advantage of knowing ahead of time the length and severity of the drought. In a real situation, reservoir managers and policymakers would never have that information because the future can never be known with certainty. Thus, it might be considered extremely imprudent to continue slavishly drawing down reservoirs virtually to the last drop without any prior knowledge about when the drought will end. Moreover, public pressure not to do so would presumably be enormous, given the vast recreational value of these reservoirs. Furthermore, the extreme loss of head would have large implications for power generation, for power revenues used by the Bureau to subsidize irrigation, and for power used for pumping operations on the Bureau's projects themselves. Thus, the simple statistics we have presented about quantities of water do not reveal the tremendous conflicts that would occur among various interests and the stresses and strains that would be put on the region's water allocation institutions.

We may also add that our calculation may not include the absolute "worst case" drought. Tree-ring research completed in 1979 at Chaco Canyon in northwestern New Mexico indicates that there was an extreme drought in the area from A.D. 1130 to 1180. It was probably this drought that caused the prehistoric Anasazi people to abandon the Colorado plateau. A fifty-year drought featuring annual undepleted flows at Lee's Ferry, which are rarely above ten million acre-feet, would place incredible stress on the basin's legal and economic institutions.[21]

It is possible that a drought of the type we describe could happen in conjunction with any combination of any of the other hypothetical situations we have posited. Almost needless to say, this could greatly aggravate the stresses and strains resulting from the drought itself.

Notes

1. For further discussion of this developmental era in water development, see Gary Weatherford and Helen Ingram, "Legal-Institutional Limitations on Water for Agriculture," in Ernest A. Engelbert and Ann Foley Scheuring, eds., *Water Scarcity: Impacts on Western Agriculture* (Berkeley, 1984).

2. Calculated by Kenneth Frederick from data in the following U.S. Geological Survey circulars: 1950 data—Kenneth A. MacKichan, *Estimated Use of Water in the United States in 1950*, Circular 115 (Washington, D.C., May 1951); 1960 data—Kenneth A. MacKichan and J. C. Kammerer, *Estimated Use of Water in the United States in 1960*, Circular 456 (Washington, D.C., 1961); 1970 data—C. Richard Murray and E. Bodette Reeves, *Estimated Use of Water in the United States in 1970*, Circular 676 (Washington, D.C., 1974). The 1980 data are based on preliminary copies (provided by Ken Reid, USGS hydrologist) of tables 7 and 10 of the forthcoming U.S. Geological Survey Circular on "Estimated Use of Water in the United States in 1980." The references are to water withdrawals (the amount of water taken from a surface or groundwater source for offstream use) rather than to consumption (the portion of the water withdrawn which is not returned to a surface or groundwater source), since consumption data are not available for

1950. Subsequent references to water use will be limited to periods since 1960 and will focus on water consumption.

3. U.S. Water Resources Council, *The Nation's Water Resources, The Second National Water Assessment*, vol. 3, appx. II (Washington, D.C., 1978), table II–4.

4. Ibid., vol. 1, p. 18.

5. The range of estimates of irrigated acreage is wide. The data are examined critically in Kenneth D. Frederick, *Water for Western Agriculture* (Washington, D.C., 1982) appx. II–A. Fifty million acres is a reasonable estimate of irrigated acreage in the seventeen western states in the late 1970s.

6. Calculated from data in the U.S. Geological Survey circulars on the estimated use of water in the United States.

7. U.S. Water Resources Council, *The Nation's Water Resources: The Second National Water Assessment*, vol. 3, appx. V, p. 201.

8. Hearings before the House Subcommittee on Irrigation and Reclamation, 89th Congress, session on HR 4671 and similar bills to authorize construction, operations, and maintenance of the Lower Colorado River Basin Project, p. 532.

9. Myron B. Holburt, "What Are the Odds in Future Colorado River Flows?," meeting preprint ASCE annual meeting and national meeting on Water Resources Engineering, New Orleans, February 1969.

10. The reader interested in a fuller explanation should consult chap. 3 in Allen V. Kneese and F. Lee Brown, *The Southwest Under Stress* (Baltimore, 1981).

11. For a discussion of the politics surrounding the Salinity Control Program, see Allen V. Kneese, "Typical Cases Involving Natural Resources," in Kent Price, ed., *Regional Conflict and National Policy* (Washington, D.C., 1982).

12. "Ruling May Change Wind River Tribes," *The Denver Post*, 13 February 1983, p. 7B.

13. Norris Hundley, jr., Chapter 2 herein, pp. **–**.

14. The following discussion is based on William Douglas Back and Jeffrey S. Taylor, "Navajo Water Rights: Pulling the Plug on the Colorado River," *Natural Resources Journal* (January 1980), pp. 70–90.

15. Figures are taken from Back and Taylor.

16. Monroe Price and Gary D. Weatherford, "Indian Water Rights in Theory and Practice: Navajo Experience in the Colorado River Basin," *Law and Contemporary Problems* 40 (1976), pp. 108–31.

17. A useful discussion of the case is found in Nancy Laney, "Does

Arizona's 1980 Groundwater Management Act Violate the Commerce Clause?,"
Arizona Law Review 24 (1982), p. 202.

18. *Sporhase, et al.* v. *Nebraska,* appeal from Supreme Court of Nebraska
no. 81–613, argued 30 March 1982, decided 2 July 1982. Syllabus, p. 2.

19. The United States District Court for the District of New Mexico,
Memorandum Opinion, *The City of El Paso* v. *S.E. Reynolds,* Civ. No. 80–
730 HB, 17 January 1983.

20. John A. Dracup, "Impact on the Colorado River Basin and Southwest Water Supply," in National Research Council, *Climate Change and Water
Impact* (1977), p. 130.

21. Robert Powers, William Gillespie, and Stephen Lekson, *The Outlier
Survey, A Regional View of Settlement in the San Juan Basin,* Report no. 3
(Albuquerque, 1983).

5 Institutional Response to Prolonged Drought

Edward W. Clyde

The Colorado River has been and for awhile is destined to be a river of conflict. It is the dominant river system in the southwestern corner of the nation. The area it drains (242,000 square miles in the United States) is approximately one-twelfth of the continental United States. It begins its 1,400 mile run to the sea from two primary sources—the Green River, which originates in the Laramie range in southeastern Wyoming, and the Colorado River, which originates in the Rocky Mountains of Colorado. The two join in southeastern Utah, a short distance above Lake Powell. It is a mighty natural and an economic force, but there is not enough water to meet all of the competing demands. As the river approaches full development, the conflicts will intensify. The purpose of this paper is to examine the operation of the river in the event of prolonged drought.

The Law of the River

The key documents addressing the allocation of water and the problems we will face in the event of shortage are the Colorado River Compact negotiated in 1922, which divided the Colorado River between the Upper Basin and the Lower Basin states; a 1944 treaty between the United States and Mexico; the Upper Colorado River Basin Compact negotiated in October 1948; the apportionment made by Congress in the enactment and implementation of the Boulder Canyon Project Act of 1928, as declared by the United States Supreme

Court in *Arizona v. California*;[1] federal statutes dealing with salinity on the Colorado River and the management of the federally constructed reservoirs; the laws of the individual states, which control individual use; and the Indian reserved rights. Beyond this, we will have the continuing role of Congress, which has the constitutional authority to intervene in the river administration and water allocation.

The Colorado River Compact

The United States Supreme Court had indicated in 1907 that the waters of an interstate stream should be equitably apportioned among the interested states. It had also suggested that where a state had adopted the priority doctrine to control the use of water within the state it could not complain of the application of the same doctrine in the division of water with a sister state.[2]

The Lower Basin states, favored by a mild climate and a rapidly expanding population, were putting ever larger quantities of Colorado River water to use. Their major problems were the constant threat of floods and silt generated from the uncontrolled river. They needed a large storage reservoir, but Congress would not proceed until the waters of the river were apportioned. The Upper Basin states were not then able to use the waters of the Colorado River and its tributaries to any great extent. They feared that the Lower Basin would build up prior rights by their expanding water use. Thus, the Lower Basin, driven by the necessity for flood and silt control and the demands of an expanding population, and the Upper Basin, driven by the desire to protect against the buildup of priorities through excessive utilization of the Colorado River by the Lower Basin, were both ripe for the making of a compact. A compact between basins was negotiated in 1922. Arizona refused to ratify it, and it initially became effective as a six-state compact.[3]

The following paragraphs of Article III of this compact will play a major role in allocating the use of water during a prolonged drought.

> (a) There is hereby apportioned from the Colorado River system in perpetuity to the upper basin and to the lower basin, respectively, the exclusive beneficial consumptive use of 7,500,000 acre-feet of water per annum, which shall include

all water necessary for the supply of any rights which may now exist.

(b) In addition to the apportionment in paragraph (a), the lower basin is hereby given the right to increase its beneficial consumptive use of such waters by 1,000,000 acre-feet per annum.

(c) If, as a matter of international comity, the United States of America shall hereafter recognize in the United States of Mexico any right to the use of any waters of the Colorado River system, such waters shall be supplied first from the waters which are surplus over and above the aggregate of the quantities specified in paragraphs (a) and (b); and if such surplus shall prove insufficient for this purpose, then the burden of such deficiency shall be equally borne by the upper basin and the lower basin, and whenever necessary the States of the upper division shall deliver at Lee Ferry water to supply one-half of the deficiency so recognized in addition to that provided in paragraph (d).

(d) The States of the upper division will not cause the flow of the river at Lee Ferry to be depleted below an aggregate of 75,000,000 acre-feet for any period of 10 consecutive years reckoned in continuing progressive series beginning with the 1st day of October next succeeding the ratification of this compact.

(e) The States of the upper division shall not withhold water, and the States of the lower division shall not require the delivery of water which can not reasonably be applied to domestic and agricultural uses.

As between basins, I have concluded that the compact's allocation of the 7,500,000 acre-feet to the Lower Basin has a superior priority.[4] Paragraph III(a) of the compact does not say so, but III(d) requires the Upper Basin states not to deplete the flow of the river at Lee Ferry below an aggregate of 75,000,000 acre-feet for any period of ten consecutive years, reckoned in continuing progressive series. If this proviso is met on each ten-year basis, the Lower Basin, except for evaporation and channel losses, should have 7,500,000 acre-feet for annual consumptive use since it has carryover storage facilities. In the event of a drought, the additional one million acre-feet allocated by Article III(b) will come from the Lower Basin tributaries. This is so because during periods of low flow the Upper Basin certainly will not release more than the required amount at Lee Ferry, leaving no place for the extra one million acre-feet to come from except Lower Basin tributaries. The Mexican treaty obligation is, as noted, to be shared. The Upper Basin must look to the remainder for its allocated share.

As between the Upper and Lower basins, curtailment of use in meeting Mexican treaty obligations is governed by Article III(c) of the compact. This article expressly provides that if the United States makes a treaty with Mexico, the waters to supply the Mexican obligation shall be supplied, "first, from the waters which are surplus, over and above" the aggregate of the quantities allocated to each basin in paragraphs III(a) and (b); and if that surplus is insufficient, then the burden of such deficiency shall be equally borne by the Upper Basin and the Lower Basin. However, when it is necessary for the Upper Basin to supply water to fulfill its part of this obligation, Article III(c) requires only that the states of the Upper Basin "deliver at Lee Ferry water to supply one-half of the deficiency so recognized." The river is a losing river, and this leaves unaddressed the channel losses between Lee Ferry and Mexico.

The Article III(c) direction that all the surplus shall first be used to provide water to Mexico is on an annual basis. There will be times when the yield of the river will exceed the sixteen million acre-feet allocated by Article III(a) and III(b) and a surplus will exist to supply the water to Mexico. As noted below, this will occur this year. However, in a drought period there will be no surplus in the natural flow of the river. Its annual flow has at times been below five million acre-feet. Either basin may have placed in storage water available in a wet year which was surplus to the compact allocations and to that year's demand for the Mexican treaty. One of the issues that may develop is whether water stored in a previous wet year could be considered surplus water in terms of the obligation to Mexico. On the main-stem federal reservoirs, this has been made moot, as noted below, by federal statutes which direct the Secretary of the Interior to operate the reservoirs so as to meet the Mexican obligation. On nonfederal reservoirs constructed to enable a particular state to use its share, such stored water should not be considered to be surplus. There is not much in the language of the compact to assist in this regard, but both the compact and the treaty, and, for that matter, the general law governing the administration of streams are all on an annual basis. The priority system controls. It dictates when water can be diverted from the natural stream and either used or impounded. If at the time the water was stored the withholding of the water was legally permissible, that stored water should be treated as the private property of the one who legally withdrew and stored it. If the next year is dry, those with senior priorities should not be able to call for that stored water.

I would thus construe "surplus," as used in Article III(c), to mean water available *during a particular water year* above the fifteen million acre-feet allocated by Article III(a) and the one million acre-feet allocated by Article III(b). If there is river-flow water above that, it must be used to supply the Mexican treaty; and neither basin could store it and thus force the other basin to curtail its use of its III(a) and III(b) water to meet that year's Mexican treaty obligation. However—in my opinion—if the Mexican treaty obligation has been thus met and there is still a surplus, the Upper Basin states, against the Lower Basin states, can store all that is physically available to their reservoirs, to the extent that such storage is reasonably necessary to permit their annual allocated use and to meet their future Lee Ferry obligations.

My position is disputed by persons who rely on Article III(e), which provides that the states of the Upper Division shall not withhold water and the states of the Lower Division shall not require the delivery of water which cannot be reasonably applied to domestic and agricultural uses. However, desired overuse by the Lower Basin should not prevent diversion of water for needed carryover storage purposes. Only by so storing water can the Upper Basin states even come close to meeting their allotted annual uses and discharging their Lee Ferry obligations. Such storage is clearly a beneficial use.[5]

When we next have a period of prolonged drought and the reservoirs are empty, or nearly so, the problem of refilling them will be an even more serious one than the original filling of Lake Powell, because the Lower Basin reservoirs would also be empty or low. Most of the water originates in the Upper Basin, and as we come out of a drought, the Upper Basin reservoirs could physically be filled first. This use (storage in the Upper Basin) of all the surplus might be resisted by the Lower Basin. Still when the III(d) obligation is being met on a ten-year basis, the Lower Basin, with its own storage, can assure its own annual use of III(a) water. The III(b) water would come from the Lower Basin tributaries which are not physically available to the Upper Basin. Water for Mexico must then be met from any surplus. Then, in my opinion, the Upper Basin states clearly have the right to store the remaining surplus water to the extent needed to provide for their own allocated consumptive uses and to meet their obligations at Lee Ferry.

Many people have given their views concerning the rights of the Upper Basin to so withhold water. A difference of opinion has existed from the very beginning. For example, Mr. A. P. Davis, Commissioner of Reclamation, stated one extreme in his answer (No. 19) to a series of questions on January 30, 1923:[6]

> The Colorado River Compact provides that the Lower Basin shall be guaranteed an average of 7,500,000 acre-feet of water annually from the Upper Basin and all of the yield of the Lower Basin, and that any water not beneficially used for agricultural and domestic uses shall likewise be allowed to run down to use below. This provides for all known uses of water in the Lower Basin and a very large surplus for such uses as may develop in the future.

Opposed to this is the position taken by the state of Colorado in a resolution first introduced at a meeting of the Upper Colorado Commission at Santa Fe on September 23 and 24, 1958:

> The States of the Upper Division have the right to have impounded in Glen Canyon Reservoir all the water of the Colorado River flowing into it, except waters required by the Colorado River Compact to pass Lee Ferry for downstream domestic and agricultural purposes, not to exceed, 75,000,000 acre-feet in any consecutive ten-year period, and for such fulfillment of the Mexican Treaty obligation as may be required by the Colorado River Compact.

Herbert Hoover[7] also commented on this matter as follows:

> Question 14: Can paragraph (c) of Article III be construed to mean that the states of the upper division may withhold all except 75,000,000 acre-feet of water within any period of 10 years and thus not only secure the amount to which they are

entitled under the apportionment made in paragraph (a) but also the entire unapportioned surplus waters of the Colorado River?

No. Paragraph (a) of Article III apportions to the Upper Basin 75,000,000 acre-feet per annum. Paragraph (c) of Article III provides that the States of the upper division shall not withhold water that cannot be beneficially used. Paragraphs (f) and (g) of this article specifically leave to further apportionment water now unapportioned. There is, therefore, no possibility of construing paragraph (d) of this article as suggested.

Mr. Hoover further noted in his answer to Question 17 that probably neither basin would particularly benefit from the provisions of Article III(e), for that paragraph "applies only to an unreasonable or arbitrary withholding or demand."

Mr. Elmer Bennett, legislative counsel for the Department of the Interior,[8] noted that the compact itself refers to and contemplates the storage of water, and that storage is indispensable for the Upper Basin to use the water apportioned to it and to meet its guarantees to the Lower Basin. Reasonable storage of water for these purposes could not be considered an arbitrary or unreasonable withholding of the water. I agree.

The Lower Basin states have from time to time contended that water stored in Lake Powell is stored only for power purposes.[9] Glen Canyon Dam is located too far downstream to permit much direct diversion of water therefrom for agricultural and domestic uses in the Upper Basin; nevertheless, the water is used for these purposes by exchange. Under the exchange, water is released to meet the Upper Basin states' compact obligations (which otherwise would have to be supplied from direct flow), and in exchange therefor, direct flow water could be used from all the Upper Basin streams.

As between the basins there are a number of other conflicts. They have been discussed in detail elsewhere.[10] Curtailment within the Upper Basin to meet the Lee Ferry obligations is discussed below in connection with the Upper Basin compact.

It appears rather clear that the people who negotiated the Colorado River Compact based the allocation on a mutual mistake of fact concerning the yield of the river. Data then available suggested a bigger river than later flow measurements have demonstrated. Further, the compact itself reveals that the parties contemplated there would be a surplus above the allocated water and the water needed for Mexico and that this surplus would be divided at some future date. The actual measured flows in the river since that time indicate that there simply will not be sufficient water in the river to give each basin 7,500,000 acre-feet per year and to give the Lower Basin one million acre-feet and still meet the obligations to Mexico. Once the guarantees at Lee Ferry have been met and the Upper Basin has met its share of the Mexican treaty obligation, there simply will not be 7,500,000 acre-feet available, even with carryover storage. For example, Utah was given 23 percent of the Upper Basin allocation. Were the river to yield 7,500,000 acre-feet for the Upper Basin, Utah would receive 1,713,500 acre-feet per year. However, Utah is only planning to de-velop to a level of 1,328,000 acre-feet, or nearly 400,000 acre-feet less than was contemplated. Still, I doubt that the compact will be set aside because of a mutual mistake of fact. The states of the Upper Basin have known of this estimate for forty years, although their present development has not progressed to a point where, for the most part, they are being injured thereby. The U.S. Supreme Court recently denied the application of certain Indian tribes to reopen the *Arizona v. California* decree, largely in deference to a desire for finality.[11] The merits of a state action to be relieved from the compact guarantees, and so forth, is complex and beyond the scope of this chapter.

Finally, all of the water in the Lower Basin tributaries was not awarded to the Lower Basin by the compact. While this water is not physically available to the Upper Basin, it is a part of the Colorado River system. Water yielded by the Lower Basin tributaries is, during low-flow periods, the primary source of the one million acre-feet awarded to the Lower Basin under Article III(b), but if they produce a surplus above the III(b) one million acre-feet, this water is surplus to the compact allocations and should be used to meet the obligations of the United States to Mexico. To the extent that obligation is discharged with these "surplus" waters, the Upper Basin is proportionately relieved of its Mexican treaty obligation. Also, the water stored in the Upper Basin reservoirs is not, to that extent, called on for the Mexican obligation and thus is more firmly available to meet the Article III(d) guarantee at Lee Ferry and to support Upper Basin uses.

The Mexican Treaty

The United States concluded a treaty with Mexico dealing with the Colorado River on February 3, 1944.[12] The power of the president to enter into foreign treaties is expressly confirmed by Article II, Section 2 of the U.S. Constitution. Article VI of the Constitution provides that the laws of the United States made pursuant to the Constitution and all treaties made under the authority of the United States shall be the supreme law of the land.

Article 10(a) of the Mexican treaty provides that there shall be allocated to Mexico a guaranteed annual quantity of 1,500,000 acre-feet from any and all sources. Under Article 10(b), when the United States determines that there is water in excess of the amount necessary to supply uses in the United States and the 1,500,000 acre-feet guaranteed to Mexico, Mexico may expand its total use to a maximum of 1,700,000 acre-feet total per year, but Mexico is to acquire no rights beyond the 1,500,000 acre-feet. Finally, this article provides that in the event of extraordinary drought or a serious accident to the irrigation systems in the United States, thereby making it difficult for the United States to deliver each year the guaranteed quantity of 1,500,000 acre-feet, the water allotted to Mexico by Article 10 shall be reduced in the same proportion as consumptive uses of water in the United States are reduced. The compact does not define surplus waters, nor extraordinary drought, nor serious accident. With the large amounts of storage available, the annual use can approach the river's average yield because the surplus water in high-flow years can be stored and carried over to make up the deficiency during dry years. It is now clear, however, that the average flow of the river will not yield the amount of water which has been allocated plus the water committed to Mexico.

The first water which should be available for meeting the Mexican obligation is, as noted above, the surplus water mentioned in Article III(c) of the 1922 compact. However, in a period of prolonged drought there will be no such surplus, and this "surplus" language of Article III(c) will not come into play.

We are now in a wet cycle. In order for the large reservoirs to discharge their flood control obligations, it was announced on January 17, 1983,[13] by the Upper Colorado River Commission that during

January 1983 Hoover Dam flood control releases of 1,168,000 acre-feet would be made; whereas, downstream requirements, including water for Mexico, for January were only about 431,000 acre-feet. This results in about 737,000 acre-feet being released from Hoover Dam in excess of downstream requirements. Such releases could result in Mexico receiving substantially more water in January than it desires. We have no treaty obligation to provide storage for Mexico, and even if it was not able to use this released water, such releases should be counted against the total annual obligation, which for 1983 will be the 1,700,000 acre-feet.

There are federal statutes which specify that the required deliveries to Mexico will be supported from the reservoirs constructed by the United States. In 1968 the first of these statutes was adopted, in which Congress declared that "the satisfaction of the requirements of the Mexican Water Treaty from the Colorado River constitutes a national obligation."[14] Congress also provided that should the Secretary of the Interior determine that means are available to augment the water supply of the Colorado River system sufficiently to satisfy the Mexican water treaty, the states of the upper and lower basins would be relieved from all obligations imposed by Article III(c) of the compact. The statute directed the Secretary of the Interior to "conduct full and complete reconnaissance investigations for the purpose of developing a general plan to meet the future water needs of the Western United States."[15] In that same statute, however, he is prohibited until 1988 from studying the feasibility of transbasin diversions.

Another statute[16] directs the Secretary of the Interior to coordinate long-range operation of the storage reservoirs on the Colorado River in order to carry out the provisions of the compact, the Upper Basin compact and the Mexican treaty. However, as we approach full development of the river, a prolonged drought could well exhaust the reservoirs and require curtailment of use in the United States.

If the federal reservoirs and/or surplus flows cannot meet the obligation, we then would bring into play Article 10 of the Mexican treaty, which permits proportional reduction of required deliveries to Mexico if uses are curtailed in the United States. Next, under the terms of Article III(c) of the Colorado River Compact, the burden of meeting any Mexican deficiency is placed equally on the Upper Basin and the Lower Basin; however, as noted above, the Upper Basin is only required to deliver its one-half at Lee Ferry. There are channel losses in getting the water from Lee Ferry to the Mexican border which are not addressed. Then, curtailment of uses would be required under the individual laws of each state.

It should be specifically noted, however, that the obligation to Mexico and the allocations between basins are on an annual basis; whereas, the III(d) guarantee to the Lower Basin is on a ten-year basis. Thus, the delivery of water at Lee Ferry for the Lower Basin would not necessarily have to occur every year. So long as during each consecutive ten-year period the Upper Basin delivers seventy-five million acre-feet at Lee Ferry, its obligation is fulfilled. The Lower Basin can adjust to an overdelivery one year by storing the surplus. In any event, because of this inherent flexibility of the ten-year "continuing progressive series" in which the Upper Basin must not deplete the river below an average of seventy-five million acre-feet, the Upper Division might, in times of severe drought, try to retain a disproportionate amount of the available water for its own domestic and agricultural uses, on the assumption that the drought will end and that past overdeliveries and future rainfall will allow it within each ten-year period to meet its ten-year average requirement. At any such time, the Lower Division could have surplus water from earlier overdeliveries in storage, so that it also could maintain a higher level of current use.

During negotiation of the Upper Basin compact, it was urged that perhaps curtailment of uses within the individual states ought to be on the basis of a ten-year average, because the obligation to the Lower Basin states was on a ten-year average—in other words, a deficiency in deliveries at Lee Ferry in a particular year is not necessarily the product of overuse that year, but rather it could be the result of combined uses for the preceding ten years. Others, including myself, argued for curtailment on the basis of priority on an annual basis, and this view prevailed.

If the water users in the Upper Basin states are required to curtail their use of water under their state permits, they would not be entitled to compensation therefor. Rights under state permits are simply subject to the limitations of interstate compacts. However, curtailment of state water rights perfected before the treaty, for the purpose of meeting the obligations of the Mexican treaty, should be entitled to compensation. The difference is based on the following factors.

Initially, the federal government, as a proprietor, owned both the land and the water in the West. In addition, the federal government had its governmental or sovereign powers, including the power under the property clause to dispose of and to manage federal property. In 1866, Congress expressly recognized the right of private appropriation by following state law.[17] Where a private appropriator had proceeded in accordance with that authorization to make his appropriation, the right would vest. The Ninth Circuit Court of Appeals, in a well-reasoned opinion, expressly so held.[18] There, a right had been perfected under California law by a livestock operator to use water originating on the public lands. Thereafter, a national monument was expanded to encompass the federal lands where the water was diverted and used. The enlargement of the monument foreclosed the grazing of those lands, and the federal government took the position that this also foreclosed the use of the water. The Ninth Circuit Court of Appeals held otherwise, deciding that the livestock operator had perfected a water right; and while Congress could expand the boundaries of the monument to include addditional federal lands, it could not thereby confiscate the vested water right.[19] As Charles Meyers has noted, the taking of an existing water right may be compensable, but it is not preventable.[20]

The courts should hold that as to the unappropriated water (where the federal offer had not been accepted on February 3, 1944) the Mexican treaty was a withdrawal of that part of the 1,500,000 acre-feet not appropriated. Rights initiated thereafter would be subject thereto. Thus, where the water right was initiated after the Mexican treaty, there would, in my opinion, be no right to compensation if it is hereafter necessary to curtail use of water under that right to discharge the federal commitment to Mexico. However, on rights perfected prior to 1944, when the treaty was made, the taking of the water to meet the federal commitment to Mexico should be compensable.[21] Curtailment to meet compact commitments between states does not involve a taking. No state can issue valid permits for water belonging to a sister state under the doctrine of equitable apportionment. Thus, curtailment to meet a downstream compact commitment would not be compensable.

The Salinity Problem

Salinity becomes a problem as uses increase and the flows are decreased. The 1944 Mexican treaty did not by its express terms address the problem of the quality of the water to be delivered thereunder, but subsequent U.S.–Mexican accords have done so. Increased use and reuse of the water, coupled with inflow from sources which are naturally salty, has caused the quality of the water at the Mexican border to deteriorate seriously. The United States has, by statute,[22] as between the United States and the states, accepted the water quality responsibility. It has constructed a desalinization plant near Yuma, Arizona, and is also addressing the problems caused by inflow from sources which are unusually saline.

There is a good discussion of the problem and ongoing efforts to control it in *Environmental Defense Fund, Inc. v. Costle, et al.*,[23] which was a suit against the Environmental Protection Agency (EPA), the Department of Interior (Interior) and the Bureau of Reclamation (Reclamation). The plaintiff complained that EPA had violated Section 303(a)–(e) of the Clean Water Act;[24] that both Reclamation and Interior had violated Section 201 of the Colorado River Basin Salinity Control Act (CRBSCA);[25] and that EPA, Interior, and Reclamation had violated Section 102(2)(E) of the National Environmental Policy Act of 1969 (NEPA).[26]

The plaintiff sought an order from the district court, requiring EPA to promulgate regulations setting forth quality standards, implementation plans, and waste load allocations for salinity in the Colorado River Basin; and requiring EPA, Reclamation, and Interior to study, develop, and prescribe alternative methods for salinity control. The district court granted judgment in favor of the defendants on all claims, and the circuit court affirmed. The circuit court noted that, from a basinwide perspective, salinity is the most significant pollutant in the river. At the time of the litigation, damages to the river and its populace in the United States portion of the river system were approximately 53 million dollars annually. By the year 2000 it is estimated that these damages will reach 124 million dollars annually if control measures are not applied. Disregarding annual flow variances, the record also indicates, said the court, that salinity concentrations will increase progressively if adequate control measures are not effected. Estimates of the present value of salinity damage through the year 2000 range from 1 billion to 1.5 billion dollars. The court concluded by saying: "It is obvious that salinity in the river is a very significant problem with not only serious impact in the basin, but also indirect consequences far outside the basin." Salinity problems become worse during low flows, and if the amount of water released to Mexico is proportionately reduced because of curtailment in the United States, it will be a problem to meet the obligation to deliver water of reasonable quality with such reduced flows.

The Upper Colorado River Compact

Even though the water of the Colorado River had been apportioned between the upper and lower basins, the Bureau of Reclamation had reached a point in 1946 where, in effect, it refused to certify that there was an available water supply for large new projects in the Upper Basin. The Bureau had proceeded, pursuant to the Boulder Canyon Project Act and the Boulder Canyon Project Adjustment Act, enacted in 1940,[27] to investigate the development of the Colorado River. A report by the Department of Interior had been issued on June 7, 1946. By way of conclusion, it stated that a comprehensive plan for the development of the Colorado River Basin could not be formulated because the rights of the individual states to utilize the waters of the Colorado River system had not been determined. It noted that water supplies for proposed projects could be assured by a compact among the states of the separate basins, by appropriate court action, or through congressional action. It encouraged the states of both the Upper Basin and the Lower Basin to proceed expeditiously to determine their respective rights. The Upper Basin states so proceeded and the Upper Colorado River Basin Compact was signed on October 11, 1948, in Santa Fe, New Mexico.

This compact did not try to determine the precise amount of water each Upper Basin state would receive. Rather, it apportioned the water allocated to the Upper Basin by the 1922 compact on a percentage basis. Arizona, with relatively small acreage in the Upper Basin, was allotted its consumptive use of fifty thousand acre-feet of water per annum. The allocations to the other states were made on a percentage basis: to Colorado, 51.75 percent; to New Mexico, 11.25 percent; to Utah, 23 percent; to Wyoming, 14 percent.

In essence, the apportionment among the individual states gives the rights to deplete the river at Lee Ferry. Article VI provides that the commission shall determine the quantity of consumptive use by "the inflow, outflow method in terms of man-made depletions of the virgin flow at Lee Ferry, unless the commission by unanimous action shall adopt a different method of determination." The commission is thus told by Article VI to measure the effect that a manmade depletion by any state will have on the flow at Lee Ferry. In addition to return flow, it is possible that a diversion of water will cut down evaporation losses or channel losses, will stop the river from flooding over its banks, or will dry up a swamp. The Upper Basin seeks to take advantage of all water so salvaged and to be charged only with net depletions of the river at Lee Ferry. In my opinion, the Upper Basin states will never voluntarily agree that "exclusive beneficial consumptive use," as that term is used in the 1922 compact, means the amount diverted without such credits. Water returned to the stream has not been consumed.

I attended all of the sessions resulting in the drafting and final execution of the Upper Basin compact and have heretofore analyzed it in depth.[28]

One of the major problems encountered was the protection of a downstream state against an upstream state concentrating diversions of its compact allocation from a particular stream. Wyoming is, and Utah might be, dependent primarily upon the Green River. A study of the Engineering Advisory Committee indicated that in normal periods of runoff this combined demand would not cause a problem, nor would it do so on the basis of a long-time average. However, during extreme drought conditions continuing for a period of years, if Wyoming diverted and used its full entitlement and also insisted upon filling empty reservoirs it could prevent Utah from getting its allotted share during that year. Utah insisted that language be placed in the compact which would prohibit combined uses and diversion into storage in any one year in excess of Wyoming's 14 percent, if the effect of that excess use (storage and consumption) would deprive Utah of the opportunity to get its apportioned share that year.

To me, the definition of "apportionment" as being an apportionment of manmade depletions means that there would be charged against Wyoming's 14 percent all waters diverted that year either for direct flow use or into storage. Either diversion would deplete the river that year at Lee Ferry. It was important that the right of consumptive use, even if so defined, be on a per-annum basis. Express language was placed in the compact to the effect that each state was entitled to a total consumptive use "per annum." This per-annum apportionment was then defined to be the apportionment of "all man-made depletions."

A similar problem developed in regard to the use by Colorado of water from the Yampa River, and this was compromised by language in Article XIII, which contains a guarantee by the state of Colorado that it will not cause the flow of the Yampa at the Maybell gauging station to be depleted below an aggregate of five million acre-feet for any period of ten consecutive years. At that time Utah hoped for construction of the Echo Park Reservoir, which was downstream from the point where the Yampa enters the Green River. Ultimately, Echo Park was abandoned because of environmental objections. Instead, storage was constructed at Flaming Gorge, which is upstream from the Yampa, so that this guarantee may not function as intended.

An embryo dispute may be developing between Colorado and Utah over the use of the water from the White River. The compact does not address the White River, and the extent to which the waters of the White River are yet to be apportioned to each state is unknown. Both states plan to develop the White River for oil-shale production, and the stream will need to be apportioned. The December 1982 decision of *Colorado* v. *New Mexico*[29] is of considerable interest here. In its decision, the U.S. Supreme Court recognized that each state on an interstate stream has a federal common-law right to its equitable share of the water. Past decisions of the U.S. Supreme Court have placed emphasis on the priority of existing rights where the contesting states themselves had each adopted the priority system. New Mexico established that its citizens had already appropriated all of the water of the stream in question and, under the doctrine of prior rights, should be protected in their use. Under *Hinderlider* v. *LaPlata River & Cherry Creek Ditch Co.*[30] (not cited in this recent case), the Supreme Court had made it crystal clear that state appropriations could not exceed that state's equitable share of the river. If any state had granted

permits which purported to allocate more than its equitable share, the
excess permits would have to yield to the rights of the sister state, as
they are ultimately fixed by compact, by Congress, or by court decision.
The U.S. Supreme Court described the equitable apportionment doctrine and stated that even between states, both of which follow the
prior appropriation doctrine, prior rights are not to be the sole test.
The Special Master had found that the appropriators in New Mexico
were using water wastefully. The U.S. Supreme Court sent the case
back for more definitive findings on these wasteful uses, but in doing
so it indicated that the prior appropriation of all of the water by New
Mexico's users will not be permitted to deprive Colorado of an equitable share.

There are other clauses of the Upper Basin compact which address
the problems of particular tributaries. These, too, will come into play
in the event of a prolonged drought.[31]

The Upper Basin compact deals in some detail with the problems
of meeting the Upper Basin's obligation to deliver 75,000,000 acre-
feet during each consecutive ten-year period. With the river fluctuating
between 4,400,000 and 21,900,000 acre-feet per annum, it was obvious that in addition to carryover storage, it might be necessary during
drought years to curtail use of water in the Upper Basin to assure that
the Colorado River at Lee Ferry would not be depleted below the ten-
year minimum thus guaranteed by the states of the Upper Division.
Therefore, it was necessary, or at least desirable, to write into the
compact language to govern the curtailment of use, and this was done.

Article IV provides that if any state (or states) of the Upper
Division, in the ten years immediately preceding the year in which
curtailment was necessary, shall have consumptively used more water
than it was (or they were) entitled to use under the apportionment
made by the compact, then those states would replace this overdraft
to the extent necessary to meet the Lee Ferry obligations before other
states were called upon to curtail. If the replacement of the overdraft,
if any, were not sufficient to assure deliveries, then Article IV(c)
provides that the states of the Upper Division will curtail their use of
water on a prorated basis according to the water actually used during
the water year immediately preceding the year in which the curtailment became necessary. However, in computing the amount of water
used, all uses of water under rights perfected prior to November 24,

1922 (the date of the signing of the original compact) are to be eliminated. The Upper Colorado Commission was authorized to determine when such curtailment should be made, and the amount thereof.

At the final session in Santa Fe, where the compact was being finalized, two points were made: first, that curtailment of uses in the Upper Basin would only occur when the reservoirs were empty, or nearly empty; and, second, that the water stored in the reservoirs was not held there for the account of any state, but was held in common. In explaining the draft to the negotiating commission, the following occurred:

> Mr. Clyde: . . . there are four essential parts of this article. . . . The first one is that this will only apply after the reservoirs are empty and there is still a shortage at Lee Ferry. If the reservoirs are taking care of it this won't come into operation at all. Second, if curtailment is necessary because reservoirs are empty, then the curtailment is allocated to the states based upon the use that they are making of the water . . . rather than on the allocation to the state.

> In taking those uses the uses prior to 1922 are excluded.

> And the last thing is the penalty provision that if any state has used more than its allocated share, then it must make it up by returning to the source, the excess it has used during the previous 10-year period. (pp. 76–77)

> .   •   •

> The Chairman: It seems to the Chairman that this article in some way assumes that a state is going to overuse its allotment by failing to contribute to the main stem reservoirs. . . .

> Mr. Clyde: I think this article will only come into operation when the reservoirs are empty.

> The Chairman: Not necessarily, sir. I don't think you are correct.

> Mr. Clyde: Or so low that they can't make up the obligation at Lee Ferry.

> Mr. Riter: Yes, Mr. Clyde is absolutely right. You operate the reservoirs when the flow approaches the minimum; you start releasing water.[32]

A question was then asked as to whether or not an accounting should be kept of the water bypassed by each state into the large main-stem reservoirs. The answer was that there would be no such accounting, but rather the water in those reservoirs would be owned in common. The following is taken from the record of proceedings:

> *The Chairman:* This assumes then that some state has not been contributing to the main stem reservoirs in accordance with the provisions of the compact?

> *Mr. Breitenstein:* . . . I think the water is going to be owned in the reservoirs in common and you are not going to attempt to keep track of what each state contributes to the reservoir. . . .[33]

Allocation in the Lower Basin

In 1963 the United States Supreme Court held that the waters of the Lower Basin had been allocated among the individual states by Congress,[34] although I do not believe that Congress ever intended to do so.[35]

Insofar as that allocation is concerned it will suffice here to note that the Court held that Congress had provided for the allocation. As a condition to having the compact become effective as a six-state compact, California had adopted on March 4, 1929, what is usually referred to as the California Limitation Act.[36] By the terms of the act and for the express benefit of the other six states (including Arizona), California "irrevocably and unconditionally agreed" that the aggregate annual consumptive use of Colorado River water in California should not exceed 4,400,000 acre-feet of the water apportioned to the Lower Basin states by the compact, plus not more than one-half of any surplus. "Consumptive use" was defined in a parenthetical expression as "diversions less returns to the river." This fixed a limitation on California's share. Nevada had never argued for more than 300,000 acre-feet and the other states always appeared to agree. Of course, this left 2,800,000 acre-feet which the Court said had been allocated to Arizona. The Lower Basin tributaries were also awarded to Arizona. The fact that Utah has some Lower Basin streams and lands was not addressed.

The Special Master had determined that shortages should be shared on the basis of the basic allocation, but the Court disagreed.

The Court said that prorating shortages on the basis of each state's allocation might be reasonable, but discretion was left by Congress with the Secretary, and the Court should not bind the Secretary to any particular formula. The Secretary must follow the standards in the act, but otherwise he is free to choose among recognized methods to be determined by him. The Court noted that the reservoirs had functions to perform other than to provide water for irrigation. It noted flood control and the intent of Congress to improve navigation, to regulate stream flows, and to provide for the generation and distribution of power. While both the equitable apportionment of the stream and the priority of existing rights may provide guidelines for allocating shortages, they are not binding, except to the extent that the Secretary is directed to protect rights perfected as of the date of the act. The Court said it saw no particular problems with the Secretary's broad discretion to prorate shortages because Congress itself still has broad powers and can intervene. Congress subsequently did so in the 1968 Colorado River Basin Act when it provided that the Central Arizona Project would be subordinate to present perfected rightholders in the Lower Basin in the event of shortage.[37] This elevated California's 4.4 million acre-feet above Arizona's prized project, recapturing for California some of what it lost in the 1963 Supreme Court decision. When shortages do occur, the allocations and prorations among Lower Basin states will be made by the Secretary of the Interior, within the guidelines provided in the 1928 and 1968 legislation, and/or by Congress, through new enactments.

The Curtailment and Administration Within Each State

Within its allocated share, each state has, under its own laws, permitted the appropriation of water. If curtailment of use within the individual states becomes necessary, it is my opinion that the entire Colorado River system within that state—which includes the river itself, all of its tributaries to the outer reaches of the watershed, and the underground water which is tributary thereto—should be administered as one system. In six of the states, state law follows a priority system. California has a mixed priority and riparian system. Each state, if called upon to curtail, would do so under its own state system. Also, since much of the water in the Lower Basin will be used under Bureau contracts rather than under state appropriations, the terms of the contracts will be important. To some extent, water is used under Bureau contracts in the Upper Basin, but there we usually have the Bureau water rights themselves dependent upon a state permit secured by the Bureau under state law. Under *California* v. *United States*,[38] such filings by the Bureau are mandatory.

On Lake Mead and Lake Powell there are no such filings. I assume that the Bureau disregarded Section 8 of the 1902 Reclamation Act, on the theory that it was superseded by specific authorization for the construction of Boulder Dam and Glen Canyon Dam. Since there are no state filings for either of these projects, there could be a problem in administering the impoundment of water in harmony with the priority system of state law. Also, Boulder Dam is partly in Nevada and partly in Arizona, and with no state filings it is more likely that Congress could be required to intervene—not to control individual water use (this will be controlled by contract) but in regard to filling the reservoir in competition with other storage and other uses. Where there are such state filings by the Bureau, they, of course, have their priority under state law. The need to administer the river and its tributaries, including underground water, as a single system was suggested by the Utah Supreme Court in *Richlands Irr. Co.* v. *West View Irr. Co.*[39] The court there noted that the entire watershed, to its uttermost confines covering thousands of square miles out to the crests of the divides which separate the river from its adjacent watershed, is the generating source from which the water of the river comes or accumulates in its channels. Rains and snows falling on this vast area sink into the soil and find their way, by surface or underground flow, and this entire watershed or water table constitutes the river. Any appropriator of water from the channel is entitled to rely and depend upon all of the sources which feed his source of diversion.[40]

Indian Water

The water reserved for the Indians under the Winters Doctrine encompasses a very large block of water.

In Utah we expect that we will be able to proceed to develop to a level of about 1,328,000 acre-feet a year under Utah's 23 percent allocation. However, this is not the quantity to be diverted, but is the depletion at Lee Ferry. Utah has negotiated a draft compact with the Ute Indian tribe, which, if finally executed and approved, will allocate to that Indian tribe approximately 480,000 acre-feet of water to be diverted to irrigate Indian land with a net depletion at Lee Ferry of about 50 percent. The water is on the headwaters of the tributaries to the Green River in Utah, and if used there it would be available for reuse; but the tribe is relatively small, something like 1,800 members, and they are not going to be able to irrigate or tend the land that would be required for such use. The return flow from any such use would be high, and thus the net depletion at Lee Ferry will not be substantial for a very long time from on-reservation uses. Like other tribes, the Ute Indian tribe desires to market some of this unused water for off-reservation use by non-Indians. The law is not clear as to their ability to do so. Justice Brennan, in the recent (March 1983) *Arizona* v. *California* decision cited above, said:

> The Tribes can *probably* lease their rights to others with the consent of the United States, but they have not explored this option extensively. See Cohen 592–593; Meyers 71; cf. 2 Ops. Solicitor of the Dept. of the Interior Relating to Indian Affairs 1917–1974, at 1930 (Feb. 1, 1964) . . . [emphasis added]

The statement is dicta and is in a dissenting opinion. If the consent of the United States were given by Congress, it would be clear that such a sale could be made, but I seriously doubt that under existing laws such a sale could be made without the consent of Congress.

There are two cases in which the U.S. Supreme Court has made statements which indicate that the water for the Indians is to be charged to the allocation made to the state in which the Indian use is made. Those cases are *Arizona* v. *California*[41] and *United States* v. *California*.[42] The statements are probably dicta. Article VII of the Upper Basin compact expressly so provides.

Even though under *Hinderlider* v. *LaPlata and Cherry Creek Ditch Co.*[43] the power of the states to bind their own citizens with a interstate water compact is affirmed, it is equally clear that the state cannot bind the Indian tribes. The states do not have jurisdiction over Indian water or Indian property except as Congress grants such jurisdiction to them. Further, the compacts expressly state that they do not purport to affect the rights of the Indians to receive water. Congress has the power to deal with Indian water rights, although the reserved rights are held in trust and if Congress were to do something to take or to impair those rights for the Mexican treaty, or otherwise, it should be compensable. Congress, of course, did consent to the compacts, but it appears clear under the adjudicated cases that Congress, in giving that consent, does not relinquish any federal interest.[44]

Thus, the compacts do not bind the Indian tribes, but it is probable that the Indian use within a state will be charged against that state's allocated share. Insofar as the state's resource base is concerned, it really does not matter whether we process a ton of coal or grow a bushel of wheat with Indian water, with Bureau of Reclamation project water, or with water obtained under a state permit. The coal and the wheat become part of our economic resources. Because the Indian reservations were created at such an early date, it is unlikely, under proper river administration, that we will ever curtail uses to such an extent that we will need to reach the issue of curtailment of Indian water use under their priority to meet downstream obligations. If we do, it seems clear to me that the United States, under its treaty-making power, could curtail Indian uses as it can curtail non-Indian uses to make the required deliveries to Mexico; but since the Indian rights vested before the Mexican treaty was made, the taking should be compensable. The commitment by the Upper Basin states to deliver 75,000,000 acre-feet of water at Lee Ferry should not be binding on the Indians, and although we have a priority ascribed to the Indian water right, which would control in local administration, the Indians did not agree to the compact and they have no compact obligation at Lee Ferry.

I do not think the states can obligate the Indians by an interstate compact, even though consented to by Congress. They were given the land and the water to meet the needs of those lands which were susceptible of irrigation, as of the time the reservation was created. The priority is the date the reservation was created. At that time the states had a common-law right to an equitable share of an interstate stream; and while the extent of that right only becomes quantified by a compact, by a court decision, or by congressional apportionment, the right itself predates the actual quantification. In many cases, however, the Indian reservations even predate statehood. Thus, there is a hiatus in the law as to how curtailment of use required by the compacts will affect Indian water, if at all. It is, however, likely to remain moot because of the following factors: The Upper Basin states are going to level off their development within the now apparent limits of the available water supply; the enormous amounts of water in storage provide carryover water to meet these downstream obligations in times of drought; the Secretary of the Interior is directed to operate those reservoirs so as to meet these obligations; and the Upper Basin Commission is to supervise instate use so that these obligations can be met.

Powers of Congress

The United States holds rights, under the reserved rights doctrine, as a proprietary owner, and it has many other sovereign interests. The United States acquired these western lands primarily through the Louisiana Purchase (1803), the Oregon Compromise (1846), the Mexican cession by the Treaty of Guadalupe Hidalgo (1848), the boundary settlement with Texas (1850), and the Gadsden Purchase (1853). The power of Congress to control these public lands and the unappropriated waters thereon is inherent in Article IV, Section 3, Clause 2 of the Constitution, which vests in Congress the power "to dispose of and make all needful rules and regulations respecting . . . property belonging to the United States." This grant of power has been construed repeatedly by the U.S. Supreme Court as giving Congress the right to deal with these lands precisely as an ordinary individual may deal with his farming property. Congress may sell them or withhold them from sale and make all needful rules and regulations respecting them. The power thus entrusted to Congress is without limitation.[45]

The federal sovereign powers include the right to control navigation in interstate streams.[46] Article II, Section 2 of the United States Constitution grants to the United States the exclusive right to make treaties, and under Article VI treaties once made "shall be the supreme law of the land; and judges in every state shall be bound thereby." The United States has the power to develop water resources to provide for the general welfare.[47] Congress has the power to apportion the waters of an interstate stream,[48] and this has been extended to interstate underground basins.[49] It also has the ultimate power to regulate the use of the large quantities of water reserved for the Indians. By consenting to the two Colorado River compacts, the United States did not relinquish or restrict its own sovereign powers.[50]

Conclusion

In the final analysis, it probably will be necessary and perhaps even desirable to have Congress intervene in the solution of the unsolved problems on the Colorado River. There will be many problems arising in the future which are administrative or legislative (policy-making) in nature. They cannot be readily resolved by resorting to litigation in the United States Supreme Court. By nature, they require change as conditions change, and they should not be controlled with the rigidity of a judgment under principles of *res judicata.*

It is also evident that the other traditional method for settling interstate disputes (by compact) has its limitations. In nearly half a century Arizona and California were unable to reach an agreement on the division of the waters of the Colorado River. When the problems are of an interstate or regional nature, the individual state, by itself, cannot solve them. There is a void if the affected states fail to reach an agreement, and the federal government must act if the problem is to be solved. The Supreme Court has clearly stated in *Arizona v. California,*[51] and echoed in *Sporhase et al. v. Nebraska,*[52] that Congress has the constitutional power to resolve these problems by direct legislative action. The Upper Basin states have, under their compact,[53] created a commission to constantly work toward the solution of their problems, and if they solve them in this fashion Congress may not need to intervene. However, development of the river should not again be delayed because of an impasse among the states.

Today, Hoover and the other nine dams on the Colorado, plus fourteen on tributaries, can store 61.4 million acre-feet of water. Other dams will be constructed in the future. This available storage will permit development to proceed in the Upper Basin to approximately the actual average flow of the river. The key to the Upper Basin states not being required to curtail use by their farms, cities, and industries is for them to stop development within that limit. If, for example, Utah will forego development of 1,713,500 acre-feet of water (which is 23 percent of the Upper Basin allocation) and will curtail development at approximately 1,325,000 acre-feet (which is 23 percent of the longtime average which will be available to the Upper Basin), the users within that development level should have a dependable supply. If development goes beyond that, there will be the hardship and the conflict caused by the need for curtailment.

Notes

1. 373 U.S. 546 (1963).

2. *Kansas v. Colorado,* 206 U.S. 46 (1907); see also *Hinderlider v. LaPlata and Cherry Creek Ditch Co.,* 304 U.S. 92 (1938); but see *Colorado v. New Mexico,* 103 S. Ct. 539 (1982).

3. Boulder Canyon Project Act, 45 Stat. 1057. Edward W. Clyde, "Legal Aspects of the Development of the Colorado River," *Utah Law Review* 1 (1949), p. 26.

4. Edward W. Clyde, *Conflicts Between the Upper and Lower Basins on the Colorado River* (Western Resources Conference Resource Development for Research, 1960).

5. In 2 S. C. Kinney, *Irrigation and Water Rights,* 2d ed. (San Francisco, 1912), the rule is stated as follows: "not only may a valid appropriation of the water from a natural stream be made for immediate use, but the water may be saved up and stored in times of plenty and thus saved for the ultimate purpose of using the same in times of scarcity for irrigation, or any other useful purpose." See, also, Robert Emmet Clark, *Water and Water Rights* (Indianapolis, 1972); 1 Wells Hutchins, *Water Rights Laws in the Nineteen Western States* (Washington, D.C., 1971); Joseph Ragland Long, *Irrigation,* Sec. 276, 2d ed. (Denver, 1916); 1 Samuel Charles Weil, *Water Rights in the Western States* 10, 3d ed. (San Francisco, 1911); *Edwards v. City of Cheyenne,* 19 Wyo. 110, 114 P. 611 (1911); *Van Tassel Real Estate & Livestock Co. v. City of Cheyenne,* 54 P. 2d 906 (Wyoming, 1936); *A–B Cattle Co. v. U.S.,* 589 P. 2d 57 (Colorado, 1979); *Friends of the Earth v. Armstrong,* 485 F. 2d 1, 10 Cir. (1973); *East Side Canal Irr. Co. v. U.S.,* 76 F. Supp. 836 (Ct. Cl. 1948), *cert. denied,* 339 U.S. 978 (1950).

6. *Congressional Record* (30 January 1923), pp. 2713–17.

7. Extract from the *Congressional Record* (30 January 1923), pp. 2710–13.

8. In a hearing on S. 500, 84th Cong., 1st sess., before the Subcommittee on Irrigation and Reclamation of the Committee on Interior and Insular Affairs.

9. See Senate Doc. 96, 85th Cong., 1 May 1978. See, also, Clyde, *Conflicts Between the Upper and Lower Basins on the Colorado River.*

10. Ward Bannister, "The Colorado River Compact," *Cornell Law Quarterly* 9 (1923–24); Jean S. Breitenstein, "Water Administration Under the Proposed Treaty with Mexico," *American Bar Association Journal* 31 (1945), p. 67; Julius M. Friedrich, "The Settlement of Disputes Between States Concerning Rights to the Water of Interstate Streams," *Iowa Law Review* 32 (1947), p. 244; Clyde, "Legal Aspects of the Development of the Colorado River"; C. H. Stone, "Interstate Water Compacts," *Rocky Mountain Law Review* 24 (1951–52); Clyde, "Current Developments in Water Law," *Northwestern Law Review* 53, no. 6 (1959), p. 725; Frank Trelease, "Federal Limitations and State Water Law," *Buffalo Law Review* 10 (1960), p. 399; Clyde, "Present Conflicts on the Colorado River," *Rocky Mountain Law Review* 534 (1960); Clyde, *Conflicts Between the Upper and Lower Basins on the Colorado River;* Clyde, "The Colorado River Decision–1963," *Utah Law Review* 8 (1963–64), p. 299; Charles Meyers, "The Colorado River," *Stanford Law Review* 19 (1966), p. 1; W. D. Back and S. S. Taylor, "Navajo Water Rights: Pulling the Plug on the Colorado River?," *Natural Resources Journal* 20 (January 1980), p. 71.

11. *Arizona v. California* (30 March 1983), Law Week Extra Edition no. 2.

12. Act. of 3 February 1944, 59 Stat. 1219.

13. **Table 3.   Scheduled Water Deliveries to Mexico in Calendar Years 1981, 1982, and 1983**

Month	Scheduled 1981 Delivery	Scheduled 1982 Delivery	Anticipated 1983 Scheduled Delivery	Col. (4) Minus Col. (3)
(1)	(2)	(3)	(4)	(5)
Jan.	55,370	126,192	64,057	−29,594
Feb.	81,731	121,653	107,506	−6,039
Mar.	211,991	217,827	234,436	16,609
Apr.	241,042	230,990	262,057	31,068
May	155,617	114,202	132,133	13,877
June	178,542	105,669	153,054	35,195
July	220,798	133,612	203,670	61,952
Aug.	234,825	140,714	218,931	70,110
Sept.	105,522	89,308	96,084	2,722

Table 3 (continued)

Month	Scheduled 1981 Delivery	Scheduled 1982 Delivery	Anticipated 1983 Scheduled Delivery	Col. (4) Minus Col. (3)
(1)	(2)	(3)	(4)	(5)
Oct.	57,209	56,398	56,750	351
Nov.	54,519	55,857	56,750	892
Dec.	102,834	107,548	114,572	2,857
Total	1,700,000	1,500,000	1,700,000	200,000

The above was taken from an Upper Colorado River Commission memorandum of January 17, 1983.

14. 43 U.S.C.A. Sec. 1512.

15. 43 U.S.C.A. Sec. 1511.

16. 43 U.S.C.A. Sec. 1552.

17. Act of 6 July 1866, Chap. 262, 14 Stat. 251.

18. *Hunter v. United States*, 388 F. 2d 148, C.A. 9, Cal. 1967.

19. Meyers, "The Colorado River," *Stanford Law Review* 19 (1966), p. 1.

20. This concept that appropriated water would have to yield to the obligations of the Mexican treaty is discussed in some detail in Meyers "The Colorado River."

21. *Prevost v. Greenaux*, 19 How. 1, 15 L. Ed. 572 (1857).

22. 43 U.S.C. Sec. 1512.

23. 657 F. 2d 275 (1981). See also, Richard Hennig and Janice Olson, "The Colorado River Salinity Problem—Old Approaches to a New Issue," *Land and Water Review* 11 (1976), p. 459; N. A. Evans, "Salt Problem in the Colorado River," *Natural Resources Journal* 15 (1975), p. 55.

24. 33 U.S.C. Secs. 1313(a)–(e) (1976 Supp. III 1979).

25. 43 U.S.C. Sec. 1591 (1976 and Supp. III 1979).

26. 42 U.S.C. Sec. 4332(2)(E) (1976 and Supp. III 1979).

27. 54 Stat. 774.

28. Clyde "Legal Aspects of the Colorado River," p. 26.

29. 103 S. Ct. 539 (1982).

30. 304 U.S. 92 (1938).

31. A series of articles deal with such peculiar problems which relate to only part of the states. Article X recognizes the La Plata River Compact, entered into between the states of Colorado and New Mexico in 1922. Article

XI deals with the waters of the Little Snake River, which was a problem relating exclusively to Colorado and Wyoming. Article XII relates to the consumptive use of water from Henry's Fork, Beaver Creek, Burnt Fork, Birch Creek, Sheep Creek, and their tributaries. These are of concern to Wyoming and Utah. Articles X, XI, and XII all provide that water used from the particular tributaries named shall be charged against the states under the apportionment made by Article III.

32. *Upper Colorado River Basin Compact Commission Record*, vol. 2, pp. 76 and 80.

33. Ibid., p. 80.

34. Meyers, "The Colorado River," p. 1.

35. Edward W. Clyde, "The Colorado River Decision—1963," p. 299. See, also, Frank J. Trelease "*Arizona v. California*: Allocation of Water Resources to People, States, and the Nation," *The Supreme Court Review* (1963), p. 158.

36. Cal. Stat. 1929, chap. 15, p. 67.

37. 43 U.S.C.A. Sec. 1521(b).

38. 438 U.S. 645 (1978).

39. 96 Utah 403, 80 P. 2d 454 (1938).

40. See also *Spanish Fork West Field Irr. Co. v. District Court*, 99 Utah 527, 104 P. 2d 353 (1940).

41. 373 U.S. 546 (1963).

42. 438 U.S. 645 (1978).

43. 304 U.S. 92 (1938).

44. Clyde, *Conflicts Between the Upper and Lower Basins on the Colorado River.*

45. *Alabama v. Texas*, 347 U.S. 272, 273, 98 L. Ed. 689, 693, 74 Sup. Ct. 481 (1954), reh. den. 347 U.S. 950, 98 L. Ed. 1097, 74 Sup. Ct. 674 (1954). See also *United States v. City and County of San Francisco*, 310 U.S. 16, 84 L. Ed. 1050, 60 Sup. Ct. 749 (1940); *Ivanhoe Irrig. Dist. v. McCracken*, 357 U.S. 275, 2 L. Ed. 2d 1313, 78 Sup. Ct. 1174 (1958).

46. *United States v. Gerlach*, 339 U.S. 725 (1950); *F.P.C. v. Niagara Mohawk Power Co.*, 347 U.S. 239.

47. See *Ivanhoe Irr. Co. v. McCracken*, 357 U.S. 275 (1958); *United States v. Public Utility Comm.*, 355 U.S. 534 (1958).

48. *Arizona v. California*, 373 U.S. 546 (1963).

49. *Sporhase v. Nebraska*, 102 S. Ct. 3456 (1982).

50. See Felix Frankfurter and James Landis, "The Compact Clause of the Constitution—A Study in Interstate Adjustments," *Yale Law Journal* 34 (1925), p. 685; Clyde, *Conflicts Between the Basins of the Colorado River; State*

of Pennsylvania v. *Wheeling & Belmont Bridge,* 18 How. 421, 433 (1856); Stone, "Interstate Water Compacts," *Rocky Mountain Law Review* 24 (1951– 52), p. 141.

51. 373 U.S. 546 (1963).

52. 102 S. Ct. 3456 (1982).

53. Upper Colorado River Basin Compact, ch. 48, 63 Stat. 31 (1949).

6 Law of the River: A Critique of an Extraordinary Legal System

Paul L. Bloom

The "Law of the River" cannot be found in any single set of statutes, codes, or compilations. Instead, it is an odd composite of state, federal, and international laws and decisions.[1] Nowhere are its perimeters explicitly defined. They must be discovered and applied from case to case. This is not surprising. Natural resource law in the West has been generally a uniquely empirical system, evolving out of a political-legal tradition of ad hoc problem resolution.

In the law of the river, compacts generally attempt to cover broad subject matter, but since they represent severely limited political compromises they leave unsettled problems like Indian water rights. Court decisions, on the other hand, tend to deal with relatively narrow fact situations, but sometimes they produce broad rules of revolutionary impact, such as the Winters Doctrine or the doctrine of equitable apportionment. The constant tension between the relatively limited compact "solutions," created to paper over broad problems, and the relatively broad-gauged judicial decisions that "solve" specific problems with wide-ranging precedents has characterized the history of the Colorado River in the twentieth century, creating many of the more curious features in the law of the river. The 1922 compact itself represented an extraordinary agreement among basin states to recognize a mutual interest in establishing a predictable legal environment in which their respective rights could be developed, while responding to each state's understandably parochial need to maximize its own water share and development opportunities, thus yielding the smallest possible advantage to its sister states.

Over many years, voices have been raised in criticizing the law of the river as unresponsive, inflexible, anachronistic, and excessively parochial. At the same time, the evolution of the law of the river unquestionably has served the people of the region and the nation by creating over time a body of ad hoc rules, definitions, and decisions that have facilitated the development of water and power resources, thus enabling the states of the basin to enjoy unprecedented growth and prosperity in the twentieth century.

Still, it must be conceded that the law of the river has been painfully slow in recognizing, let alone solving, certain water resource-related problems, including some of great importance that remain troublesome today. Important examples of problems that have escaped firm resolution in the law of the river include Indian tribal water rights; the relationship of rightful new development in the states vis-à-vis federal water-quality legislation; and the definition of the respective obligations of the upper and lower basins for the Mexican treaty burden under the Colorado River Compact.

Let us turn to some illustrations of how the law of the river has worked and has not worked, preparatory to considering some improvements that could be made in it.

Success: Operating Criteria
for River Management

One of the most important successes of the law of the river lies in the ability of the upper and lower basin states, acting in consultation with the Secretary of the Interior, to fashion workable criteria[2] for the potentially traumatic problem of filling and operating upstream storage facilities. The balancing of water supply, power generation, and other interests of the two basins, without litigation, during this critical transition period demonstrates the strength of the Colorado River's legal mechanisms. It should be remembered that the Glen Canyon Dam was sought for many years by Upper Basin interests, and eventually it was constructed under federal auspices in order to provide to the Upper Basin the major storage facility essential for that basin's ability to store surplus waters in high runoff years. This regulation of the river over time allows compliance with the compact delivery obligations while optimizing the Upper Basin's ability to increase its consumptive uses.

The Upper Basin states had long entertained suspicions that the hostility of Lower Basin interests to the Upper Basin's new consumptive-use projects dependent on Lake Powell would tempt the Lower Basin to obstruct the filling and operation of Lake Powell. The Colorado River Basin Project Act of 1968 was an ideal vehicle for finally resolving these fears and concerns conjunctively because in it the representatives of the two basins were making reciprocal concessions and agreements in order to solve some of the major problems on the river.

The act was necessary to permit Arizona to obtain the authorization for the construction of the massive Central Arizona Project to export the Colorado mainstream to the Phoenix-Tucson areas, which were already experiencing severe drops in groundwater. Certain Upper Basin interests were insisting that, as the price for the support of this major new project, Arizona and other Lower Basin interests should reciprocally support authorization of additional projects in the Upper Basin, and, in at least one case,[3] agree to a congressional modification of a Supreme Court decree apportioning a Colorado tributary between two states. In this framework of sometimes confrontational but ultimately successful compromise, the joint achievement of a simultaneous authorization for the CAP and Upper Basin projects, as well as the establishment of a mechanism for creation of criteria for balanced management of upstream and downstream reservoirs, illustrated the pragmatism and statesmanship of basin representatives both in the state capitols and in Congress.

On the debit side of this accounting, it should be noted that the horse trading and logrolling that accompanied this exercise in statesmanship had to be worked out in and around the committee rooms of the U.S. Congress. It would surely have benefited the basin if some institutional mechanism had existed that permitted the basin states to work out their policy and legal problems on a regional basis and then to take a unanimous "Colorado River" position to the Congress. Because the 1922 compact did not create a continuing compact commission, the ability of the Colorado River system states to achieve political agreement and present a united front in Congress is certainly handicapped, and it is necessary for the states to flex their political muscles before major steps forward can be taken in legislation.

Failure: Unresolved Federal and Indian Water Rights

For most of the twentieth century the reclamation program, the process of resolving interstate water claims by equitable apportionment or compact, and the evolution of Indian water claims have proceeded apace, generally without common planning or consultation and with unsettling and confusing results in stream systems like the Colorado.

As dozens of Indian tribes occupy lands within the Colorado River system and can make Winters Doctrine claims, these represent, in the aggregate, a massively destabilizing collection of unresolved claims. These generally early-priority and potentially large-magnitude rights will, when adjudicated, at least cloud and perhaps eventually preempt many water rights under which non-Indian users have invested untold millions of dollars and on which their lives and livelihoods depend.

An objective observer would probably express astonishment that scores of federally financed projects have been constructed in such western streams as the Colorado, under contracts requiring local water-user reimbursements to the U.S. Treasury by an agency of the same U.S. Department of the Interior that is charged by law with executing the fiduciary responsibility of the United States to the Indian tribes, which are known to have inchoate interests in those streams under the Winters Doctrine.

In other words, while the states and their water users were struggling among themselves in a series of intrastate and interstate disputes to resolve apportionment problems in the Colorado River, so that eventual political consensus could be achieved to allow the construction of reclamation projects, the relevant reclamation project acts, interstate compacts, and, to a large extent, the interstate judicial allocations, ignored or only tangentially dealt with the unresolved federal and Indian claims to the waters of the same stream systems.

The consequence of this collective failure is illustrated in the growing number of pending suits involving state, federal, and private disputes over Indian water rights claims, including some directly affecting federal projects, such as those of the Pyramid Lake Paiutes against the users of the Truckee-Carson Irrigation District; the conflicting claims of the Indian and non-Indian communities to the waters of the San Juan River in New Mexico (including waters impounded in Navajo Dam); the well-known conflicts between Indian and non-Indian claimants to Arizona's mainstream waters under the Central Arizona Project; and Indian claims to waters involved in the massive Central Utah Project. In such cases, Indian tribes are not only making destabilizing claims to water supplies committed to non-Indian projects and uses, but the tribes are also aggressively litigating claims of "conflict of interest" resulting from the "adversity" between the proprietary and reclamation interests of the U.S. Government, on the one hand, and the interests of the tribes themselves in the same waters. The oral arguments and briefs in the *Pyramid Lake*[4] and *San Carlos Apache*[5] cases before the U.S. Supreme Court prominently featured this issue.

A Call for a New
Federal-Interstate Compact

There have been noble efforts to improvise informal governmental mechanisms[6] to fill the vacuum created by the absence of a seven-state Colorado River compact commission. In my mind, however, the time has come for a basinwide compact commission to be established through a new federal-interstate compact.

A fresh look should be taken at the interstate compact as a vehicle for the resolution of Colorado River and analogous water resource problems. In particular, I believe that Congress has the means, and should now have the will, to eliminate the difficulties that have obstructed effective use of the interstate compact in the past by enacting legislation that thoroughly respects the primary role of the states in water resource planning and management, while recognizing the interests of the American people in certain critically important water resources as well as the proprietary and fiduciary obligations of the United States. This proposal is fully applicable, I believe, to already compacted streams like the Colorado.

The compact clause of the U.S. Constitution (Article I, Section 10, Paragraph 3) authorizes states, with the consent of Congress, to negotiate and implement interstate agreements. These agreements have ranged from colonial boundary agreements in the days of the Articles of Confederation, through interstate stream allocation agreements, and more recently, interstate agreements for river basin planning, the control and abatement of water pollution, the operation of interstate port facilities, and the return of runaway juveniles. Although the interstate compact has demonstrated its usefulness over the entire life of the United States, it has over the last two decades proved ineffective as a tool for resolving the increasingly complex disputes among states and the United States over water resources. Prudent action by Congress can rescue the interstate compact from its moribund condition and permit it to facilitate regional and local water resource solutions that respect the authority of the states while permitting the protection of the national interests of the United States in such areas as navigation, interstate commerce, federal proprietary rights, and the rights of Indian tribes. At the same time, Congress may be able to move toward resolution of the frustrating problem of the final determination of federal proprietary rights in water, particularly rights held on behalf of Indian tribes. The Indian water rights problem has clouded economic development in several states, and it has pitted state and local interests against tribal and federal interests in an array of expensive, time-consuming, and divisive lawsuits.

In their 1924 study of interstate compacts, Professors Felix Frankfurter and James Landis of Harvard Law School observed:

> The overwhelming difficulties confronting modern society must not be at the mercy of the false antithesis embodied in the shibboleths "States Rights" and "National Supremacy." We must not deny ourselves new or unfamiliar modes in realizing the national ideals. Our regions are realities. Political thinkers must respond to these realities. Instead of leading to parochialism, it will bring a fresh ferment of political thoughts whereby national aims may be achieved through various forms of political adjustments.[7]

In the last twenty-five years, the interstate compact has been used only fitfully as a tool to solve water resource problems, and when used, it has been employed principally to seek solutions to water-quality and flood-control problems rather than interstate water allocation.

The probable reasons for this include, first of all, the heavy preoccupation of Congress, and thus necessarily of the states, with the massive national effort to clean up polluted stream systems, causing a very large redirection of effort among water resource managers in the 1960s and 1970s. The struggles among the states and the United States over the proper governmental roles of the Environmental Protection Agency, the Corps of Engineers, state water-management and water-quality officials (as well as the struggles of municipalities and water-using industries to cope with a rapidly changing regime of effluent controls, stream standards, and federal and state permits) have forcibly preempted the central attention of water managers from allocation to water quality. In a related way, those states, principally western, that have been most acutely involved in federal-state water resource development, have also had to face the problem of a drought in the supply of funds for new federal projects constructed by the Bureau of Reclamation and, to a lesser extent, by the U.S. Army Corps of Engineers. Because many of the western states with the most acutely sensitive concern over water resources still have priority lists of water resource projects for which federal construction assistance is considered indispensable, and because congressional funding for them has largely dried up since the mid-1960s, they have been distracted from the unfinished business of interstate water allocation.

Nonetheless, the critical problems surrounding the failure of the states and the U.S. to solve interstate water allocation problems have left many of the principal streams of the nation in legal and institutional chaos. Indian tribes, western states, and private water users have engaged in bitterly contested struggles over the forum for adjudication of federal (and other) rights, as between state court and federal court jurisdictions and over the substance of those rights.

Disputes over the application of the McCarran Amendment[8] of 1952 have now burdened the courts for thirty years. Despite earlier decisions that appeared to settle the issue, last year a federal appeals court held that state courts lacked jurisdiction over federal claims to "Indian water rights" in Arizona and Montana. The mere observation that, more than thirty years after its enactment, the McCarran Amendment (which did not even deal with the substantive problem of water allocation between the United States and the western states, or among those states) has still not produced definitive rules for the jurisdictions of federal and state courts in adjudicating stream systems that include federal claims illustrates how extremely unwise Congress has been in legislating on an ad hoc basis rather than seeking to address the critical underlying problems themselves.

There are presently pending, in federal and state courts in the West, dozens of slow and expensive stream adjudication suits involving federal and Indian claims, and private claims, in stream segments within particular states. Other disputes over water resources are also troublesome, such as *Sporhase*[9] and *City of El Paso* v. *New Mexico;*[10] the congressional moratorium on Bureau of Reclamation studies of imports into the Colorado system; the litigation over the Southern Dakota coal pipeline water sale to ETSI; the general congressional concern over the coal-slurry problem including proposals for "sister-state signoff" compacts limiting pipeline water exports; and the growing concern of Great Lakes States' Representatives over possible water export plans. They illustrate the broad spectrum of unsettled water allocation issues that have unfortunately escaped resolution well into the third century of the nation's existence.

Does the interstate compact represent a valuable tool in the resolution of such water resource problems? To answer this question, it is necessary first to look at the political environment in which water resource decision making has occurred in the United States.

First, it should be observed that there is an interesting disparity between the treatment of water allocation and management, on one side, and the protection of water quality, on the other. In the former area, the states have traditionally played a dominant and almost comprehensive governmental role, limited only by their occasional collisions with the national interest in protecting navigation and commerce on interstate streams and protecting the treaty power with foreign nations. The Supreme Court has often ruled that Congress, through the acts of 1866 and 1870, the Desert Land Act of 1877, the Reclamation Act of 1902, and many other water-related acts, has delegated to the states an extensive power to supervise the development of rights in waters, including waters arising on the public domain of the United States. Although the Court has said that this very broad power does not permit state interference with navigation or with the power to authorize power generation dam sites on navigable streams, to authorize statutes impermissibly burdening interstate commerce in water, or to eliminate the proprietary claims of the United States for water to satisfy the purposes for which its own reservations of land were made from the public domain, the Court has also recognized that the states have a very broad authority over water development and use.

Obviously, each state's authority must stop at its own borders, and it must respect the right of coriparian states in an interstate stream. For this purpose, interstate compacts and the Supreme Court's decisions in original actions provide problem resolution. The Supreme Court has itself frequently recognized the superiority of the interstate compact as a device for resolving interstate stream problems. This recognition makes only more painful the failure of the states and the United States to negotiate compacts for major interstate surface and groundwater systems.

While the Supreme Court has often noted that Congress has supreme constitutional authority to legislate in the area of interstate water control, including allocation, Congress has left to the regimes established by fifty different states the resolution of water resource management problems, except where interstate compacts or Supreme Court decisions must supplement state management in critical local situations. The unmistakable result of decades of this laissez-faire policy has been the deep institutional confusion discussed above. The interstate compact may represent an underutilized resource for the regional—as opposed to the federal—resolution of these problems, because the compact is a uniquely flexible device for reconciling those disputes in which conflicting interests can be adjusted at the local level. It permits not only congressional review of interstate agreements, but also a more dynamic federal agency participation.

The failure to use compacts effectively in recent years derives from the understandable tendency of state, local, and federal interests to defer painful concessions in water resource allocation. Indecision persists as long as there is no absolute requirement that problems be solved. For example, the large number of interstate stream compacts (including those on the Colorado system) that involved federal participation in negotiation and consent from the Congress, without producing definition of the nature, extent, and priority of federal rights, must represent in historical terms a significant lost opportunity. It is very probable that the federal agencies faced with the necessity of making politically sensitive water-need inventories, and formulating claims for a variety of controversial federal proprietary rights (like

Indian rights), will not take these actions unless mandated to do so by the Congress or the courts.

The National Water Commission studied at length the Delaware River Compact, and pointed out its usefulness as a possible model for what the Commission called "federal-interstate compacts." While the Delaware River Compact itself does not constitute a paradigm of federal-state problem solving, it does contain the seeds of a creative solution for the major water resource management problems discussed above. It was negotiated principally to coordinate the water resource planning activities of Pennsylvania, New York, Delaware, and New Jersey, along with those of federal agencies. (One of the reasons that a compact was possible at all was because the most acute water allocation problems within the Delaware Basin had already been resolved by federal court decisions which had reviewed and approved such sensitive questions as New York City's diversions from the Delaware.) However, the compact itself is a valuable model in the sense that it involves Congress on behalf of the United States *as a fully participating substantive partner along with the riparian states of the basin,* and thus creates a federal-interstate agreement differing materially from the conventional western interstate stream compacts. The latter typically allocated waters of a disputed stream among the riparian states, recognized that the compact did not apply to certain federal functions (such as navigation, international treaties, and Indian rights), and then merely obtained federal consent to the compact. Although the Upper Colorado River Compact of 1948 allows the federal compact commissioner to vote along with state members, that compact does not establish a federal-interstate compact because the United States merely consented to it and did not join as a compacting party. The federal-interstate compact enables the full participation of the United States in the negotiating and enforcement of the compact, and the involvement of federal water agencies in the planning work of the compact commission.

Of course, it is far easier to develop a federal-interstate compact when the focus is on interstate and state-federal coordinated water resource planning rather than on the more painful subject of competing water claims. Nevertheless, the successful integration of the United States as a full participating member of the Delaware River Compact Commission arguably represents an important policy departure.

Setting Deadlines for Settlement

Congress has not provided a system of incentives for states or the involved federal agencies to induce them to resolve outstanding interstate water resource problems on a basis of compromise. The federal agencies will probably offer to contribute to such problem solving, but they will point out, correctly, that the states are themselves hypersensitive to federal interference in water resource matters and that the federal agencies are chronically starved of expert personnel and financial resources to accomplish such an arduous and expensive process. The states will correctly observe that they are legally and politically unable to solve their major outstanding water resource disputes (witness the frustrating experience between California and Nevada over the Truckee River) until the federal government becomes more supportive and conciliatory in establishing its claims. The Interior Department will correctly observe that it has statutory obligations, in such areas as the fiduciary protection of Indian interests, which prevent it from "bargaining away" the water resources owned by the United States for the benefit of its Indian wards. Likewise, the states will correctly observe that until federal proprietary claims, particularly for Indian tribes, are resolved either in court or by compromise, interstate compacts will be largely ineffective because they will leave unsettled many of the most divisive and destabilizing claims in important river systems or reservoirs. This is particularly true if, as some scholars contend, federal-Indian rights are not even limited by conventional compacts.

As of today, the lack of interstate water allocation formulas merely burdens all parties with substantial uncertainty in planning, developing, and managing resources. Interstate stream litigation, which usually must be brought in the U.S. Supreme Court, is slow moving and dangerously unpredictable, and often it cannot proceed without the joinder of the United States Government as a party. The appropriate legislative action to right the situation is that Congress should legislate a time certain, after which the failure to reach good-faith compromises among the states and the United States will result in mandated apportionment litigation or legislative resolution of the various problems.

In order to accomplish this, and thus motivate the states and federal agencies to accelerated negotiations, Congress must do several things. First, it will be necessary to order the relevant federal agencies, after full consultation with the states, to publish a list of those stream systems in which a failure to produce federal-interstate compacts (or judicial adjudications) resolving interstate and state-federal problems is preventing necessary planning and development of water resources. The president should be required to produce a priority list of such streams within $1\frac{1}{2}$ years of the enactment of the statutes.

The legislation should further provide that upon the publication of this priority list the Congress, unless it modifies the list within six months of publication, gives its consent to the negotiation of federal-interstate compacts for the resolution of all claims in these stream systems. In all negotiations involving streams on the priority list, the Secretary will be mandated by Congress to provide maximum financial assistance (federally financed cooperative studies of the water resources to quantify present and probable future demands against those resources) and to invite affected states to open compact negotiations. In addition, the president will be required to complete, within not more than two additional years, the quantification of all federal proprietary claims made by the United States for its own agencies, and for its Indian wards, in any of the stream systems on the priority list if the states involved have accepted the invitation of the United States to enter federal-interstate compact negotiations. To reflect appropriate sensitivity to the issue of federal "conflicts of interest" between proprietary and fiduciary federal claims, the president should be required to appoint a special representative to quantify and advocate Indian claims, independent of other federal interests.

These provisions are designed to create strongly positive incentives for the states as well as for federal agencies involved. First, the states should recognize that the deadlines contained in the statute create an altered water policy environment. They will no longer be able to prefer the uncertainty of the status quo to the painful necessity of making political concessions to other states and to federal agencies; on the contrary, they will understand that the failure to achieve agreements will surely subject these streams to allocation by the courts or by Congress.

In this connection, it is recommended that the bill also provide that, as to any stream system on the published priority list, if all of the riparian states have not formally accepted the federal invitation to open negotiations toward a federal-interstate stream compact within one year, the president will be required to report that fact to the "jurisdictional committees" of both houses of Congress. Unless both of those committees resolve (within ninety days after receipt of such notice) to initiate a direct legislative settlement of the water allocation problems on the identified system, the president, through the attorney general, will be required to file suit in the Supreme Court for the resolution of all outstanding water allocation problems on any such stream. The absolute certainty that failure to produce a regional-federal solution to the problem will result in either federal allocation legislation, or a Supreme Court apportionment decision, will focus the minds of state and federal agency personnel on the necessity of making the political compromises necessary to effect a solution.

Another important incentive to the states will be the requirement that the federal agencies quantify all federal claims in the priority stream systems within two years after the states undertake compact negotiations. In order to avoid the taking of unrealistic or exaggerated claims by federal agencies, which could obstruct prompt compact negotiations, it is suggested that the federal agencies be required, within a specified time, to submit their quantified claims to the oversight committees of Congress. Then, if these committees do not object to or modify the claims, after such hearings as the committees may deem necessary, the United States will have the strengthened weight of congressional opinion behind its claims. If the committees do modify or order the affected federal agency to reconsider their claims, then the negotiations may be more likely to produce agreements.

The states will recognize that they will, jointly and severally, have a political opportunity to rewrite this priority list on its submission to Congress, as each state will have a chance to make a showing that the federal determination is erroneous or unreasonable. They will also view with favor the provision that federal proprietary claims, including claims for Indian tribes, must be quantified within a sharply limited period, and that these claims must then be submitted for review by the jurisdictional committees of Congress. The states will understand that they are thereby being given another opportunity to argue the case that specific federal claims are unreasonable. If they are successful in doing so, negotiations will proceed on the basis of less extensive federal claims, and if they are unsuccessful at least all parties will know that Congress stands behind the claims as presented.

As the states obviously believe very strongly in their right to speak with a dominant voice in the area of water allocation, they may be willing to take significant steps to avoid the necessity of either a congressionally imposed or a judicially imposed solution on a stream that cannot be settled by compact. In any event, they will understand that the alternative of an indefinite extension of the status quo, with a cloud of lawsuits and unpredictable ad hoc interventions by the Congress, cannot continue.

The federal agencies will hopefully see in this proposal several positive features. Congress will be expected to appropriate sufficient funds to the agencies to enable them to make the expedited studies and reports mandated by the statute. Because the president will be inviting the states to enter into federal-interstate compact negotiations, the federal government and its agencies will in each case be playing an enhanced role in the negotiations, eventually serving as a fully participating compact member. The framework created by the statute would enable the federal agencies to cut through long-standing problems that have long stood in the way of effective federal-state water resource planning and development.

It has often been noted by states and legal commentators that one of the drawbacks of the interstate compact is that, on the basis of Supreme Court decision, Congress can modify or terminate compacts by enacting subsequent inconsistent legislation, thus accomplishing a partial or total repeal. In order to ensure that the very large efforts intended to be made by state and federal agencies in resolving long-standing water problems not be held hostage to the political vagaries of every session of Congress, it is suggested, as the National Water Commission Study Report recommended, that each federal-interstate compact should be approved for a specified number of years—no less than twenty-five years—so that an effective contract between and among the states and the United States for a fixed period will exist, one upon which private and governmental interests can rely with greater security for planning and investment.

Conclusion

These ideas for the promotion of interstate compact negotiations to settle western allocation problems are submitted in the hope that they might contribute to the resolution of an array of painful contemporaneous water-related problems at relatively small cost to the United States or to individual states. With such divisive and unsettled problems resolved, the law of the river on the Colorado and other streams will serve for many future decades as a reliable and comprehensive legal environment for harmony and progress.

Notes

1. The principal constituents of the "Law of the River" are well known. They are the 1922 compact (which actually took effect only in 1929), dividing the river between the upper and lower basins; the Upper Colorado River Basin Compact of 1948, apportioning shares of the Upper Basin supply; the U.S.–Mexican Water Treaty of 1944; the Supreme Court's decision in *Arizona v. California,* fixing the lower basin states' mainstream shares and adjudicating the rights of mainstream Indian tribes; the Boulder Canyon Project Act of 1929; the Colorado River Storage Project of 1956; and the Colorado River Basin Project Act of 1968. In addition, of course, the water users of the basin states are often directly affected by specific federal statutes governing storage and use of "project" water, by the water laws and decisions of their respective states, as well as by the decrees of state and federal courts adjudicating the nature, priority, and extent of water rights. While one could pursue endless scholastic debates over the ultimate definition of the Colorado River's "Law of the River," it is only necessary to observe here that it is a remarkable amalgam of legal institutions that must be studied in its entirety, with its parts interpreted conjunctively, in order to produce an informed opinion on the rights and duties of persons involved in disputes over Colorado River waters.

2. The criteria for filling were officially promulgated on 19 July 1962, 27 Fed. Reg. 6851.

3. P.L. 90–537, Sec. 304(f)(1) and (2).

4. *Pyramid Paiute Tribe of Indians v. Truckee-Carson Irrigation District,* 103 S. Ct. 2906 (1983).

5. *Arizona v. San Carlos Apache Tribe,* 103 S. Ct. 3201 (1983).

6. The creation and later resurrection of the "Committee of Fourteen" illustrates a tendency to develop ad hoc consultative mechanisms to coor-

Paul L. Bloom

dinate seven-state policies where possible. Particularly in the painful triangular negotiations with the U.S. State Department and Mexico over Colorado River salinity, the Committee of Fourteen performed distinguished service in coordinating and protecting domestic water interests in the Colorado River states. The Colorado River Salinity Forum, created on an ad hoc basis to cope with the problems resulting from enactment of stringent national water-quality control laws, represents another generally successful effort of basin state water-management officials to deal coherently with federal agencies and public interest groups whose activities were threatening to interfere with water resource development plans. The courts generally upheld this collegial and balanced management against environmental attack. *E.D.F., Inc.* v. *Costle, et al.*, 657 F. 2d 274 (1981).

7. In 1971, the National Water Commission, in its legal study no. 14 attached to the final report, examined interstate water compacts, quoted with approval the observation of Professors Frankfurter and Landis, noted subsequent decisions recognizing the authority of the federal government in the area of interstate waters, and went on to make a number of thoughtful recommendations to Congress and the states. Unfortunately, these recommendations have not been incorporated in legislation or followed up in constructive action by the states and the United States.

8. 43 U.S.C. 666(a).

9. *Sporhase* v. *Nebraska*, 102 S. Ct. 3456 (1982).

10. *City of El Paso* v. *Reynolds, et al.*, U.S.D.C., N.Y., 17 January 1983, Bratton, J.

7 The Untried Market Approach to Water Allocation

B. Delworth Gardner

In the American West, water is generally the most limiting of all factors that influence the production of goods and services. This is especially true in irrigated agriculture, where most of the water is consumptively used. Therefore, the key to the economic development of the region has been the harnessing of water supplies and their application to activities such as mining, agriculture, and recreation. Because water availability at an "affordable" price was almost always a necessary (but seldom sufficient) condition for development, its control largely determined the distribution of the wealth created by primary economic activity in the region.

Thus, during the region's developmental phase, a critical need existed for institutions that would encourage water development and use. Prospective users must have reliable supplies available, and there must be as little ambiguity as possible about the terms on which it would be supplied. At the same time, because water is essential to life itself, and is a fugitive resource that moves from place to place, before, during, and after use, it has always been regarded as a "public" resource. The water itself was not subject to private ownership. Rather, the ownership of water would reside with the "public" or with the state, and use entitlement would be acquired by "right," contingent on demonstration of beneficial use. Under the riparian doctrine in California, location on the water course determined eligibility for acquiring the right. Under the more prevalent appropriation doctrine, those who filed first received rights that had to be satisfied before more "junior" rights could be considered. Since the granting of rights was reserved by the states, conflicts between states had to be settled by interstate compacts, court adjudications, and legislative statutes. Water disputes between nations have required resolution by international treaties.

So long as water was plentiful and cheap these institutions were quite effective in promoting a stable, secure environment in which a high rate of development could and did occur.

The primary thesis of this chapter, however, is that these allocative institutions became inefficient as competition for water increased, as water became steadily more valuable, and as the cost of developing new supplies grew substantially. In this new era in which we now live, a new and more efficient set of institutions is required if the economic output that can be produced with water and other scarce resources is to approach the maximum possible.

The next section of this chapter will describe more fully the existing institutions that currently allocate water in the Colorado River Basin and establish why they are economically inefficient. The third section will discuss market allocation and why, in principle, it is so promising as an allocative vehicle. The final substantive section will review some empirical studies of water markets that estimate the magnitudes of the economic gains that can be expected if market allocation is utilized. A few closing comments will conclude.

The Existing Allocative Institutions

Norris Hundley's fascinating chronicle[1] of the Colorado River's allocative history conclusively demonstrates that political and legal rather than economic criteria were utilized to decide the allocation of the region's liquid gold. Political and legal criteria would allocate water on the basis of constitutional right, history of use, political power of conflicting parties, standards of equity, legislative intent, and so on. By contrast, economic criteria would have directed water allocation to the highest valued uses. From the time that Arthur Powell Davis attempted to implement his dream of developing the river, Hundley's history is replete with power brokering, intrigue, negotiations, compromise, shifting federal-state relations, congressional and judiciary appeals, and interstate and international agreements. From the perspective of an economist, the entire focus seems to have been on who would be permitted to capture whatever economic benefits resulted from water use, while scarcely any attention at all was given to efficient water allocation that would maximize the magnitude of the net benefits created. Given the allocation criteria utilized, it is small wonder that with the passage of time the resulting allocation has been wasteful in the sense that large net benefits have been forfeited. Hundley's litany of allocative settlements—the Upper and Lower Basin Compact, the California–Arizona Supreme Court ruling, the intrabasin agreements among states, the quantity and quality treaties with Mexico, and the recognition of Indian claims—are all examples of legal and political fixes that probably misallocate water.

For example, consider water use in irrigated agriculture in the upper and lower Colorado basins. Per acre-foot of water diverted, the value of water for producing native hay on the high meadows of Wyoming or northwestern Colorado, must be less than ten dollars, whereas on the highly valued crops in Arizona and southern California water is worth ten times as much.[2] The Colorado River Compact, however, pays no attention whatever to this disparity in water values. It simply imposes a rigid allocation to the upper and lower basins. In the process society, as a whole, foregoes the difference in the net benefits between the highest valued prospective use and the lower valued actual use. Economists call this "misallocation" or "economic inefficiency."

Let me now be even more explicit about the definition of economic efficiency before proceeding to a more explicit evaluation of current institutions. Economic allocative efficiency results when resources are employed in production such that the net economic product resulting from the production process is maximized. This outcome is identical with the maximization of new income (revenues from output sales minus the sum of all costs incurred). Usually high per capita net incomes are associated both with high standards of living and with saving that results in net capital formation and increases in asset wealth.

Economic efficiency has spatial and temporal dimensions. In terms of spatial allocation, efficiency requires that resources be allocated among current users at different locations such that the net value of the resource at the margin be equal for every user. For example, suppose

water is worth 100 dollars per acre-foot at the margin in use A and
110 dollars in use B, and the cost of moving it from A to B is 10
dollars per acre-foot. Efficiency has been achieved in the given allocation since the net marginal values are equal. Moving the last unit
of water to B created a net benefit of 100 dollars (110 − 10 dollars),
exactly the same net benefit as the marginal value in use A.

Optimal temporal allocative efficiency for those resources that
may be stored and used in the future requires that the discounted
present marginal values for a resource for all future time periods of use
be equal. Future values must be discounted to the present to be com-
parable because an alternative to future use is present use and the
revenues from present use could be loaned out at interest. Some thorny
problems exist in the selection of a discount rate for calculating these
present values, but they are beyond the scope of this paper. In principle, however, the temporal efficiency problem is straightforward. For
example, if the marginal value of water in a reservoir has a current
use value of 100 dollars per acre-foot and the expected value five years
from now is 200 dollars per acre-foot after allowances for storage and
risk costs, there is temporal misallocation providing the relevant discount rate is less than 12.94 percent. In this case, 200 dollars discounted at 12.94 percent for five years has a present value of 100
dollars. If the discount rate were 10 percent, the present value of
$200.00 received five years hence is $124.18, exceeding water's current
worth of $100.00. Water should be stored and used five years hence
if efficient temporal allocation is to be realized. Both spatial and temporal examples imply that the movement of water from lower to higher
valued use is needed to reach an efficient equilibrium.[3]

Thus, the efficiency of current allocative institutions can be assessed by estimating the marginal values of water in existing allocations. If spatial and temporal disparities are large, the gains from
reallocations that are efficient will be large. Later in the chapter I will
refer to some empirical estimates of the current misallocation in some
situations that have been studied.

Let me now discuss existing institutions in the context of economic efficiency. The legal doctrines establishing water rights as implemented in the West are themselves inimical to efficient exchanges
of water. The riparian right, in vogue in some areas of California,
entitles water use only on land contiguous to a water source. The

quantity of water entitlement is limited only by the necessity of demonstrating reasonable and beneficial use and of not jeopardizing the rights of other riparian users. No filing requirement to obtain a right is imposed. As a result, there is little information on the quantity of riparian water that is actually used, and obviously there is no opportunity to transfer it to nonriparian lands, regardless of the economic incentive to do so.

Appropriation rights, as administered in most western states, are somewhat more flexible. The right usually specifies the quantity that may be diverted from a watercourse and the location of the diversion, although recent practice in some states measures the right by its "consumptive" use. The reason for this will become clear in later discussion. The intended use must be defined as "beneficial," and usually a requirement is imposed that the right will revert to the state if water is not used in the quantity and type of use specified. This "use it or lose it" requirement often leads to excessive use as water users have tried to protect themselves against loss of their rights.

Still, some states have been quite flexible in allowing shifts in the point of diversion. *Allowing* is the correct term. All states have some agency that has discretionary authority to approve or disapprove proposed transfers. In most states this authority is a state engineer; in California it is the State Water Resources Control Board; and in Colorado it is the courts. Presumably, the purpose of this authority which allows or disallows transfers is to protect the "public interest," whatever that is. Water transfers sometimes injure third parties, who can appeal to the authority that must approve the transfer. My experience in California leads me to believe that usually the appeal will successfully block the transfer, regardless of the economic merit. One celebrated example involved a proposal to sell Sacramento Valley groundwater to the San Joaquin Valley during the recent California drought. The proposal was denied by the control board. It has been reported that in other states side-payments have been made as compensation to injured third parties, thus reducing the likelihood of transfer-blocking appeals; but I know of no systematic study of these transactions.

In the case of mutual irrigation companies and some water-supply districts, it is not the individual water users who hold the rights but the supplying company or district. A proposal to transfer water outside the unit usually requires approval from a majority of the voting stock. Sometimes the votes are proportional to the acreage held or the acre-feet in the water entitlement; thus, the voting stock is concentrated in a few hands. These factors may make it very difficult to transfer water to higher valued uses if those who have the votes do not wish it to be done.

Due to the growth of federal and state involvement in water development, the federal and state administrative agencies, quite apart from the water rights regulatory agencies, have become increasingly influential in allocative decisions. Hundley[4] discusses the Supreme Court ruling in the *California* v. *Arizona* dispute, which gives the Secretary of the Interior the prerogative of interstate allocations of water generated by federal projects. This is only a start. In California, and presumably in some other states, proposed transfers in federal and state projects must be approved by the relevant administrative agency, the Bureau of Reclamation (BR) or the California Department of Water Resources (DWR). Technically, in California these agencies are permittees of the State Water Resources Control Board, but they effectively hold the rights and allocate water to contractors—usually to a public district,[5] which then sells it to final users.

In the case of the state water project, any changes in either the contracts or points of diversion must be approved by the director of DWR. Once again, a reading of history of proposed transfers shows that this approval is very difficult to obtain. In the approval process, losers from changes in the status quo are more influential than gainers, since it is widely interpreted that the purpose of approval is to protect potential losers. If transfers were restricted to historical consumptive use, then much of these third-party losses would disappear. In any case, given that DWR usually contracts with water districts which sell to final users, the latter are powerless to recontract exchanges. The most they can do is simply forfeit their use of contracted water, and the state then reallocates it. But what is the incentive for the original contractor to do so since it must pay for the contracted quantity? At the very most, it may be able to escape paying the marginal transport cost. The resulting use is inefficient in the sense that water is used where it is valued below what it would be worth if transferred.

Transfer policy is no more conducive to efficient exchanges in the Bureau of Reclamation. Its allocation policy is dominated by a perceived need to contract out available water supplies. Since projects are immense and often prematurely built, finding contractors is a severe problem. The best evidence for this allegation is found in the need to weaken repayment obligations imposed on water users through time in order to sell available water. In the case of irrigators, interest costs have been waived, repayment periods have been substantially lengthened, and the proportion of total project costs assigned to irrigators for repayment has been reduced. Even these significant concessions have not often been sufficient to generate enough water demand, and the BR has had to fall back on an "ability-to-pay" rule that has established water prices far below supply costs.

With all this as a backdrop, it is not difficult to understand the Bureau's transfer policy, which prevents any contractor from purchasing BR water from any other contractor unless the former is taking the maximum quantity established in their BR contract. If a noncontractor wants BR water, he cannot purchase it from another contractor but must deal directly with the Bureau. Also, under present law, all contractors must meet the acreage-limitation restrictions. All these rules serve to increase the quantity of contracted water with the BR and weaken the potential for efficient exchanges or transfers among contractors.

The Colorado River Basin has a tremendous variety of competing water uses: municipal and industrial; agricultural; recreational; and energy development and transport, particularly in the Upper Basin. In fact, most of the recent controversy about the adequacy of water has surfaced because of the anticipation that large quantities of water will be demanded for development of coal, oil shale, tar sands, and petroleum resources. Demands for the traditional uses have slowly grown over a half century, but the interest in energy during the past ten years has provided a real shock to the economic system in the Upper Basin states.

Marie Leigh Livingston[6] has analyzed a situation in the state of Colorado that provides a useful example even though the area is outside the Colorado River drainage. A pipeline known as the San Marcos has been proposed to carry coal from the coal fields in south-central Colorado near Walsenburg to Houston, Texas, nearly nine hundred miles away. The slurry requires about 12,000 acre-feet of water to transport approximately 15 million tons of coal per year. The company has applied for a water right to utilize groundwater which might be needed for agriculture sometime in the future.

Livingston cites a study by ICF Corporation[7] that estimates that moving the coal by the slurry pipeline would be from $1.29 to $8.75 per ton cheaper than transporting it by rail, the apparently cheapest alternative. That translates into cost savings ranging from about 20 million dollars to 130 million dollars per year. If the water were used in agriculture, budgets for representative San Luis Valley farmers reveal that the annual profits generated would be about 600,000 dollars per year.

Several points seem relevant. Even though the water appears to be thirty to two hundred times as valuable for the pipeline than if used in farming, it is by no means clear that the pipeline company will be able to obtain the rights to use it. This is all the more remarkable because the groundwater is not presently being utilized in agriculture. Of course, the prospective agricultural water users and the railroad coal haulers could be expected to oppose the granting of the right, and they will no doubt get their chance since presumably the right must be approved by the courts in Colorado. As has actually occurred in other states, it is conceivable that pressures could be brought on the state legislature to pass a law prohibiting the use of water in the pipeline. This is a clear example of how political influence could be brought to bear in a number of ways to thwart an economically efficient allocation of water.

It has been argued persuasively in other contexts that political allocations are not necessarily economically efficient.[8] Consider the water transfer approval decisions made by federal or state agency officials discussed earlier. The public choice theorists[9] have postulated that these officials can be expected to make decisions consistent with their own self-interest. The success of an individual in a bureaucracy is largely determined by his role in the success of the bureau itself, defined in terms of its size, budget, power, and influence. A political decision maker is seldom in a position to benefit personally from reducing agency cost or by selling a product to those who value it most highly, both of which are essential in producing efficient allocations.

It is useful to think of political water allocations by federal and state congressional mandate, administrative discretion, or even by judicial review as a "commons" to be influenced by political currency—

votes, campaign contributions, influence peddling, and even public demonstrations, recall threats, and so forth. Those who stand to benefit most from inefficient allocations, such as those receiving subsidized water or being granted a new water right, know who they are, tend to be relatively few in number, and know well their financial interest in the decision. They serve their self-interest by mobilizing, investing heavily in lobbying, campaign contributions, and hiring the best lawyers. They also invest in propaganda to attempt to convince the public that the decision should be made in their favor. On the other side, those who would gain from efficient transfers or who bear the cost of subsidies (for example, consumers of food or taxpayers) are generally much more numerous as individuals and have a small stake in the decision; and since they are *prospective* beneficiaries, they may not even know who they are. It should be obvious which side will usually win in the political arena. We should not be surprised, therefore, to find evidence of inefficient political allocations all around us, and, of course, we do.

There has to be a better way to allocate water. And there is! It is that same "old mule" that we utilize to allocate most other scarce resources. It is the free and voluntary exchanges of rights and resource entitlements called the "market." I will first discuss the advantages of market allocation in a general way, after which some empirical water market studies will be reviewed. A couple of these involve the Colorado River Basin.

Market Allocation of Water

During the past ten years several students of water allocation have strongly advocated implementation of market processes.[10] Let us consider what the minimal requirements would be for market formation, and why a water market would be both efficient and equitable. We must also consider some objections that are likely to be raised in opposition to water markets, and determine how serious they are likely to be.

What are some of the prerequisites for an efficient market? First of all, the property right in water must be well defined so that negotiating parties know precisely what is being considered for trade. Are there any proscriptions on use? Is an annual rental or a permanent

right transfer being contemplated? The entitlement must be quantifiable either as a number of acre-feet or as a fraction of the water
course, so that at least a probability function of alternative quantities
can be calculated. If there are water quality problems, then even the
quality may have to be specified. A transport system must be available
to move the water from seller to buyer, and it must be clear who will
pay the transport costs. Any attenuation of rights such as being a
junior appropriator, for example, must be clearly specified.

The incentives for efficient transfers will be most conducive if
the individual water user holds the transfer rights. It is only he who
knows what the use value is compared to the offer price being considered. Exactly opposite to the "use it or lose it" rule of current
doctrine, the opportunity to transfer water at prices above use value
would provide incentives for investing in water-efficient technology,
more careful water-saving irrigation practices, and more water-efficient
cropping patterns. These incentives for transfer would be greatly weakened if, as presently, it is the water district or the mutual irrigation
company which holds the rights.[11]

Transfer prices convey tremendously useful information about
water values. Presumably, buyers would be willing to pay up to their
marginal values for water and sellers would be unwilling to accept less
than theirs. In free competitive markets, therefore, price would be
expected to reach equilibrium where the net marginal value of water
(the value to the buyer, with the net of transfer cost) would be equal
to the marginal value to the seller. Allocation would be efficient. In
addition, the allocation would be equitable in the sense that both
buyer and seller benefit from the exchange, *ex ante*. If both did not
expect to gain, the transfer would not be negotiated. This is the great
advantage of market transactions: All parties think they will benefit
from the process of reaching an efficient allocation.

So far, our discussion has been rather abstract. How well do our
current allocative institutions meet the criteria required for implementing efficient water markets?

Appropriative rights are much better suited than riparian rights
since the former usually specify quantities and the point of diversion.
Riparian rights do neither, so if markets are to work either they must
be quantified or replaced by appropriative rights. Since market allocation provides ample incentives for efficient use, the requirement of

beneficial use is redundant and should be abolished. Rights to water should be upgraded to the level accorded to land or any other real property.

Because of its "common property" character, groundwater use is especially troublesome in the matter of right definition.[12] Some of the states using Colorado River water have statutory regulations governing groundwater extraction. California does not. Just as in the case of riparian rights, groundwater entitlements must be quantified, both in terms of current and future use, if the entitlement is to be successfully marketed.

The water contracts of the big federal and state agencies seem to present no great obstacles to market allocation, providing administrative rules are accommodative.[13] Of course, the buyer and seller would negotiate an agreement of their own. The agencies would need to be informed of any transfer so that deliveries could be made at the appropriate place and water charges could be collected. Most federal and state projects have user charges specified in repayment schedules. The question of liability in case of payment default would need to be settled. A reasonable arrangement might be to make the original contractor responsible for collecting the water fee from the transferee and passing it on to the agency as required in the original contract. Suppose, for example, that farmer A in the Imperial Valley contracts to take one thousand acre-feet of water per year from the Bureau of Reclamation at three dollars per acre-foot. Subsequently, farmer A recontracts five hundred acre-feet to farmer B at ten dollars per acre-foot. Farmer A would continue to pay the Bureau three thousand dollars per year until the contract expires. If additional delivery costs are incurred by the Bureau, those should also be the responsibility of farmer A, so he would take them into account in negotiating a price with farmer B. Perhaps more satisfactory arrangements to accommodate transfers could be implemented than those proposed here. I see no problems that could not be easily surmounted except the return-flow externality problem that I shall discuss shortly.

The fixed allocations of the interstate compacts and the international treaty with Mexico present real problems for a water market. Interstate differences in the marginal values of water are no doubt substantial, even for a given use. It is highly probable that, within agriculture, most of the water used in the Upper Basin has a marginal value of less than ten dollars per acre-foot. In California and Arizona the marginal value on average is several times higher.[14] As argued earlier, it is this disparity that makes the economic gains from transfer in a water market so large. But what if the farmers in Arizona and Wyoming negotiated a transfer that would benefit both groups. This type of reallocation, however, would require changes in the compact. In fact, a well-functioning water market would obviate the need for any political allocation such as the Colorado River Compact. This is its great virtue. So much for a half century of political wrangling!

Potentially, the market could also be utilized to allocate water between the U.S. and Mexico. However, the market transactions costs would be higher because of language differences and the restrictions on international movements of people that are needed for efficient negotiations. The monitoring and enforcement of contracts would also be more costly.

Let me now anticipate some arguments that will be made against water markets and give you my views as to their merit.

Because water is a fugitive resource it would be difficult to bring all those affected by a market decision into the negotiations. Economists call these third-party impacts, "externalities." There are several categories. The spillover impacts which are most serious and difficult to cope with are those that are protected by right. In the process of use, the quantity of water diverted is never physically used up, even in agriculture. Because of the laws of thermodynamics, this is an obvious and trivial point. Use may change water's form and location and even result in the addition of sediment and chemicals which change its quality. But water continues to exist to be recycled. What is of utmost concern here is that much of the diversion returns to a potential water-supply source, where it becomes subject to the right of another user. A transfer of an entire diversion would deprive this user of the return flow which is his right. Of course, in the area of new use, return flows would be created that could become the source of new rights. I believe it is this problem, more than any other, that has led to the discretionary approval process that in one form or another exists in all western states. It is these affected third parties that can and do block most proposed transfers.

It seems to me that most of these return-flow externalities could be avoided by limiting transfers to the historical consumptive use of the transferring party.[15] The quantity of return flow would thus remain in the water source and the rights of third parties would be minimally affected. This policy would also give water users an incentive to improve water-use efficiency since it would allow them to transfer a larger quantity if their irrigation efficiency improved. Unfortunately, some arbiter (the state engineer in most western states) would be needed to decide what is historical consumptive use, and thus not all bureaucratic costs could be eliminated by implementation of water markets.

Other external effects are not protected by rights. For example, if irrigation declines in one area because of water sales to another, other parties in the economy are affected, some positively and some negatively. Even though economic activity in aggregate will increase due to more efficient use of water and other resources, its distribution will shift and some may be hurt. I see little that can or should be done about this problem beyond the existing programs to redistribute income such as unemployment compensation and welfare. In a free and dynamic economy these kinds of resource shifts are ubiquitous anyway as resource owners search for and find more productive opportunities. In fact, this resource mobility is the source of much of our economic growth and the origin of improvements in our standard of living.

What about the noneconomic, nonmarket values that are affected by transfer negotiations? If there are such values, and they affect the well-being of the negotiating parties, they will be incorporated in the decision if the transaction costs are not prohibitive. If they are broad, public goods, such as open space,[16] they may not be. There may be circumstances where public goods are significant, but in most cases in water allocation my sense is that they are not very important.

Is a water market likely to be inimical to resource conservation? To the contrary, I believe a water market will provide incentives that will greatly improve conservation, which is usually defined as protecting water quantity and quality for future use. By definition, market allocation results in the flow of resources to those who value them highest. Water rights will be owned by those who are most optimistic about their future value; thus, water will be bid away from those less optimistic. These optimists who see a profitable future will provide for it by making sure that the resources are preserved and productive when needed. Water-saving investments will stretch the available supplies as far as economically feasible. If conservation is transforming current assets into future assets, what more reliable and more efficient mechanism for conservation could be found than the profit motive of these optimistic entrepreneurs?

One of the problems inherent in political allocation is that each user group portrays itself as inappropriately treated and deprived of resources. Instream water users utilizing water for fishing recreation, transport, and power argue that the law and administrative allocation rules focus on diversions and consumptive use and therefore discriminate against them. It is true that it has been difficult for them to qualify for water rights as traditionally defined in most states; thus, they have lobbied hard for legislated minimum-flow standards. How would they fare in a market situation? Probably very much better. They could buy up all the rights that their user beneficiaries would be willing to pay for, thus meeting the same legitimate test for all other efficient water users. I can see no compelling reason to legally exclude them from purchasing rights which would allow them to preempt diversions. The water could be put to its highest use, and the instream users could still strike bargains with other types of users if consumptive use were physically and economically feasible.

I will summarize by stating my perception that the costs in terms of anticipated problems seem to be small in comparison to the benefits of efficient market allocation.

Let us now review some empirical studies of water markets and see if the prospective economic gains described above are supported by the data.

Some Empirical Results of Market Studies

Most studies analyze the *prospective* gains that our theory postulates would be captured if markets operated in place of current allocative institutions. Our study[17] of the water market in the lower Sevier River in Utah is significant because it identifies the *actual* gains in economic efficiency that were reaped by the removal of exchange restrictions. Before 1948, only intracompany transfers of irrigation water were permitted in four mutual irrigation companies in the Delta area of Utah. In 1948, by agreement of all four companies, it became possible to transfer water between companies as well as within each company. For more than thirty years before and after 1948, water market rentals were recorded and an office was established to broker water exchanges. Hundreds of transfers occurred, and in one year after 1948 more than 30 percent of the irrigation water supplied to the area was transferred among users. This was not an isolated exchange of water here and there, but a full-blown active market.

Recorded real rental prices were assumed to fully reflect the value of the irrigation water in use. The average real rental price in the peirod after free intercompany exchanges was more than three times that in the exchange restricted period. Water availability per acre accounted for some of the year-to-year variation in rental prices but not for much of the big difference between the averages of the before and after intercompany transfer periods.

Since the crops and livestock enterprises were largely the same before and after intercompany exchanges, what could cause the value of water to more than triple? First, permitting intercompany transfers increased the market area by about four times. Given the variation in the management expertise of farmers and the inherent differences in soils, the expansion of the water market permitted the water to go to higher valued applications. Second, knowing that water would be available for rent on an established and reliable basis reduced an important element of risk. Efficient farmers could produce high-value and high-water-using crops; others would save water in order to rent it out. Finally, two of the companies had reservoir storage while two did not and had to rely on more unreliable surface flow. Before intercompany transfers, water deliveries based on rights varied greatly among companies and inefficient use must have occurred as a result. The transfer flexibility made the stored water available to all and improved the allocation among users as well as among years of fluctuating supplies. This case study is a clear example of why water markets work to increase the economic productivity of an irrigated region.

Several studies indicate the misallocation of water produced by institutional impediments to water mobility that water markets would remove. They do this by showing disparities in the marginal value of water in proximate uses which would be reduced or eliminated in a water market of the type just described in Utah. The results of three recent studies in California will be presented.

Yolo County, in the southwest corner of the Sacramento Valley, is a region in which conjunctive use of groundwater and surface water has evolved without any direction. Several water agencies have their own surface-water supplies or pump from a common aquifer, and they manage these supplies with the goal of maximizing the private benefits of their water customers. The use values of irrigation water in six contiguous subbasins of the county were estimated.[18] Linear programming was utilized to estimate "shadow" prices of water, or their marginal values in use. In the six subbasins these varied from $2.44 per acre-foot near the Sacrament River, where water is plentiful and groundwater is pumped from only a few feet, to $61.13 per acre-foot where water is pumped from depths of over one hundred feet. The distance between these two areas is less than twenty miles.

Because they pump from a common aquifer and there are no restrictions on pumping in California, farmers impose costs on each other that are not accounted for in their individual decisions. Pumping a unit of water from a groundwater reservoir reduces the water table, other factors being the same, and increases the future costs of pumping by all who use the aquifer. A technique known as optimal control permitted us to estimate these so-called user costs: the per acre-foot cost to the pumper for removing an acre-foot of water from the aquifer plus the increased costs borne by others resulting from this action. These varied from $12.23 per acre-foot to over $150.00. The tremendous variability in these estimates of marginal values and user costs give some idea of the economic gains that could be realized if water markets were permitted to reallocate water until these marginal values were equated.

Perhaps the most definitive analysis of the gains to be captured from free market allocation of water is that of Howitt, Mann, and Vaux.[19] They utilized a computer model to assess water allocation in California under three scenarios: (1) existing water institutions are assumed to remain largely unchanged over the next forty years; (2) the conditions are identical to scenario 1, except that new supplies of water could be provided if they were fully paid for by water users; and (3) changes in water institutions and policies occur that would permit the use of a limited market system for transferring water between areas of the state and sectors of the economy.

The state was divided into three agricultural sectors: (1) the north; (2) the south, with the boundary between north and south at the thirty-sixth parallel, about thirty miles south of Fresno; and (3) the Imperial Valley, which gets the bulk of its irrigation water from the Colorado River. There were two municipal and industrial (M and I) sectors, north and south. Supply and demand functions for water were estimated for each sector for 1980, 1995, and 2020. Demands were assumed to grow through time with expected growth of population. Supply functions were assumed to shift through time in response to estimated changes in energy cost.

Under scenario 1, between 1980 and 1995 the price of water could be expected to rise substantially in all areas and regions. In real terms, this increase was expected to be one-third to one-half of the 1980 price. The price increase would induce a decline in the quantity demanded of 2.9 million acre-feet in aggregate, approximately 10 percent of 1980 use. Approximately two-thirds of this reduction would be in agricultural and one-third in M and I use.

As expected, the model results for scenario 2 are quite similar to those of scenario 1, with the difference being new supplies of about 500,000 acre-feet delivered to the urban sectors. Only urban uses could afford to cover the costs of new supplies. This quantity of new water somewhat buffers the expected decline in total use, but the effect is modest. Agricultural sectors are largely unaffected.

It is under scenario 3 that interesting things begin to happen. Any sector and/or region can buy from any other so long as it pays the market price and transport cost. In 1980, compared to scenario 1, Imperial Valley agriculture would have sold about 1.17 million acre-feet to M and I south, and northern agriculture would have sold about 0.74 million acre-feet to northern M and I. In the south, agriculture would have sold about 0.65 million acre-feet to southern M and I.

A commonly expressed fear of such transfers is that market prices to the low-value agricultural use would increase to a prohibitive level. This did not occur. The price in northern agriculture in 1980 would have increased modestly from where it actually was in 1980 (from 21 to 23 dollars per acre-foot). The price to farmers in southern agriculture would have increased from $31 to $32.50, also a very modest rise. In the Imperial Valley, however, the price of agricultural water would have been about 32 dollars in 1980 compared to the actual price of 6 dollars.

Of course, the market could be expected to narrow the difference between agricultural and urban prices, and this is what the model results show. In 1980, the northern M and I price would have been 56 dollars instead of 139 dollars, and the southern M and I price 102 dollars instead of 173 dollars per acre-foot. Naturally, the lower prices would have induced the higher quantities demanded in urban areas that were transferred from agriculture.

By estimating net gains to farmers *and* urban users, the model results indicate the direct "social" or aggregate net benefits from the water market. These annual gains from trade would have amounted to 70 million dollars in 1980, and would grow to 83 million dollars per year by 2020.

In 1980, almost two million acre-feet of water would have been saved, primarily by a very modest reduction in agricultural acreage and increases in water-use efficiency. Both the water saving and the aggregate net benefits of the water market are no doubt significantly understated, however, because only exchanges among these gross regions and sectors are included. All the intraregional and intrasectoral gains that would accompany a full-fledged water market are entirely neglected in this analysis.

It is intuitively clear that water markets among states and among sectors in the Colorado River Basin would produce large gains in economic efficiency that would leave everyone better off. It should be obvious that disparities in water values in current political and judicial allocations are very large, implying foregone economic benefits of large magnitudes. In fact, it is interesting that the political allocations seem to have encouraged transfers out of the basin so that the individual states could more efficiently utilize their allotments. The transmountain transfer from western Colorado in the Colorado River Basin to the eastern slope of the Rockies outside the basin, the Central Utah Project which transfers water from Utah's portion of the Colorado River Basin into the Great Basin, and the transfer of water outside the basin to southern California are all cases in point. All have required heavy investment costs to effectuate transfers to higher valued uses.

A very recent study[20] by the Environmental Defense Fund (EDF) in California proposed that the Metropolitan Water District of southern California (MWD) finance water conservation investments for the Imperial Irrigation District (IID) in the Colorado River Basin. Briefly, these investments would increase water-use efficiency and the newly available "conserved" water could be transferred to MWD through the Colorado River Aqueduct. This water could be more than adequate to replace the "lost" Colorado River water due to implementation of the Central Arizona project in the late 1980s.

The EDF study quotes a 1981 Department of Water Resources analysis which showed that up to 500,000 acre-feet could be conserved by employing conservation practices.[21] Including the costs of conservation in the valley, the costs of energy generation foregone at IID hydroelectric facilities, the costs of energy generation foregone lower on the Colorado River, the cost of the consequent increase in energy demand in the MWD service area, and the cost of increased salinity in blended water throughout the MWD service area, the marginal costs of the proposed transfer were still less than the marginal costs of expanding the state water project as proposed by Proposition 9 in 1982.

The EDF study concludes that the transfer could be highly beneficial to both IID and MWD and that agriculture in the valley would not be impaired. Of course, policy in IID, MWD, the Bureau of Reclamation, and the state of California must be conducive to transfer, but it is clear that political and economic gains would be substantial.

Concluding Comments

It has been shown that our current water allocations are extremely economically inefficient. They may have been well suited for another time when water was plentiful and cheap and when economic development depended on its capture and security of tenure. That time has long since passed. If costly development of new supplies is to be avoided and growth is to continue, more flexible water-allocating institutions must be found. It will no longer suffice to lock water up in certain uses and in specific geographic areas as is done by our water law, transfer approval rules, and interstate and international treaties.

Water markets provide a solution to our allocation problems, regardless of whether new water is developed. Both economic efficiency and equity would be well served by allowing market transfers of consumptive use. Some government participation would be useful in deciding historical consumptive use. Because federal and state governments own or control most of the water transport facilities, they must be parties to transfer agreements since they are not likely to be willing to divest themselves of these facilities. Little additional institutional baggage is required to implement water markets. Governments might even be useful as brokers to facilitate exchanges until private institutions arise to do so, such as occurred in Utah's Sevier Valley.

Water rights should be held by direct water users rather than by water districts or irrigation companies. This would greatly facilitate efficient transfers.

No doubt the greatest impediment to the development of a regional water market on the Colorado River would be the reluctance to give up the political and legal agreements that have been difficult and costly to forge for nearly a century. That is too bad! But sunk costs are gone forever and should not be relevant to the decisions before us now. We must look ahead, not behind us. Water markets can be our salvation as we look forward to a vigorous and growing economy in the Colorado River Basin.

Notes

1. See Norris Hundley, jr., Chapter 2 herein.

2. For more discussion of these issues, see B. Delworth Gardner, "Water Pricing and Rent Seeking in California Agriculture" (paper prepared for a forthcoming book to be published by the Pacific Institute for Public Policy Research).

3. Both the achievement of spatial and temporal efficiency depend on the "principle of diminishing returns." As water is moved spatially from use A to use B, its marginal value in use B is assumed to decline and in use A to increase. Likewise, as water is stored to be used in year 5 as opposed to being used in year 1, its marginal value in year 1 is assumed to increase and its marginal value in year 5 to decrease. The principle of diminishing returns is one of the most ancient and most celebrated in economic theory.

4. See Hundley, Chapter 2, p. **

5. See Gardner, "Water Pricing and Rent Seeking in California Agriculture."

6. Marie Leigh Livingston, "Competition for Water: Criteria for Decisionmaking," *State Government* (Winter 1982).

7. See ibid., p. 2.

8. See Richard L. Stroup, "In Defense of Asset Management: The Pri-

vatization Component" (paper presented to the Senate Subcommittee on Public Lands and Reserved Water Committee on Energy and Resources, Workshop on Land Protection and Management, 24 June 1982); Richard L. Stroup and John Baden, "Externality, Property Rights, and the Management of Our National Forests," *The Journal of Law and Economics* 16, no. 2 (October 1973); and Thomas Sowell, *Knowledge and Decisions* (New York, 1980), especially chaps. 5 and 10.

9. William A. Niskanen, *Bureaucracy and Representative Government* (Chicago, 1971); James M. Buchanan and Gordon Tullock, *The Calculus of Consent: Logical Foundations of Constitutional Democracy* (Ann Arbor, Mich., 1962).

10. For example, see: Paul Gitschlag, "Interview with Del Gardner: An Agricultural Economist Proposes a Controversial Solution to the West's Impending Water Crisis," *PSA Magazine* (February 1980), pp. 83–92; Lee Brown, Brian McDonald, John Tyselling, and Charles duMars, "Market Reallocation, Market Proficiency, and Conflicting Social Values," in Gary D. Weatherford, ed., *Water and Agriculture in the Western U.S.: Conservation, Reallocation and Markets* (Boulder, 1982); Sotories Angelides and Eugene Bardoch, *Water Banking: How to Stop Wasting Agricultural Water* (San Francisco, 1978); and Charles E. Phelps, Nancy Y. Moore, and Marlie H. Graubard, *Efficient Water Use in California: Water Rights, Water Districts, and Water Transfers* (Santa Monica, Calif., 1978).

11. See ibid.

12. See B. Delworth Gardner, "Economic Issues of Groundwater Management," *Proceedings of the Twelfth Biennial Conference on Groundwater*, Report no. 45 (Davis, Calif., 1978), pp. 163–69.

13. For a thorough discussion of the prospects for market allocation by the state water project in California, see Madelene Mary Curie, "The California State Water Project: Analytical Description of Water Allocation, Water Pricing; Conditions for Market Formation and Market Activity" (Ph.D. diss., University of California, Davis, 1982).

14. See B. Delworth Gardner, Raymond H. Coppock, Curtis D. Lynn, D. William Rains, Robert S. Loomis, and J. Herbert Snyder, "Agriculture," in *Competition for California Water*, ed. Ernest A. Engelbert (Berkeley, 1982), pp. 18–23.

15. This issue is competently discussed in Ronald N. Johnson, Micha Gisser, and Michael Werner, "The Definition of a Surface Water Right and Transferability," *Journal of Law and Economics* 24 (October 1981), pp. 273–88.

16. See B. Delworth Gardner, "The Economics of Agricultural Land

Preservation," *American Journal of Agricultural Economics* 59, no. 5 (December 1977), pp. 1025–36.

17. B. Delworth Gardner and Herbert H. Fullerton, "Transfer Restrictions and Misallocation of Irrigation Water," *American Journal of Agricultural Economics* 50, no. 3 (August 1969), pp. 556–71.

18. Jay E. Noel, B. Delworth Gardner, and Charles V. Moore, "Optimal Regional Conjunctive Water Management," *American Journal of Agricultural Economics* 62, no. 3 (August 1980), pp. 489–98.

19. Richard E. Howitt, Dean E. Mann, and H. J. Vaux, Jr., "The Economics of Water Allocation," in *Competition for California Water*, pp. 136–62.

20. Robert Stavins, *Trading Conservation Investments for Water* (Berkeley, March 1983).

21. Ibid., pp. 45–46.

8 Replacing Confusion with Equity: Alternatives for Water Policy in the Colorado River Basin

Helen M. Ingram, Lawrence A. Scaff, and Leslie Silko

From its beginning the fate of civilization has been tied to water and the management of water resources. Regional development, shifts in population, the growth of trade, and the ebb and flow of cultural influence have all depended in important ways on water transportation routes, sophisticated irrigation works, and uncontaminated supplies for consumption. In the semiarid American West we hardly need to be reminded of these universal facts of experience. Our landscapes are dotted with the ruins of ancient cultures—the Hohokam, the Anasazi—forced to surrender to nature's privations. Theirs is a history we do not want to repeat.

Nevertheless, memories can be surprisingly short. We are quick to assume that modern society, supported by new technologies, will readily avoid past errors. But, as the twentieth century comes to a close, some of our more comfortable assumptions have been badly eroded. It has become naive to hope that we can continue to muddle through, merely reacting to crises as they arise, or to expect that over the long run the maximum demands of all interests can be fully accommodated. There is increasing awareness that the destiny of people in arid lands depends far less upon technical understanding and physical structures than upon institutions and an appreciation of the *kinds* of political choices available to us as well as the contrasting consequences of those choices. For instance, in concluding a comparative study of six irrigation communities in Spain and the American West,

Maass and Anderson point out that their observations about water policy "relate to the justice of institutions—to the relations in irrigation communities among popular control, distributive shares, economic growth, and farmers' concepts of fairness."[1] Significantly, the precise nature of these crucial relationships is not specified by the authors; they suggest that the "challenge remains" to find an acceptable "model" for justice, fairness, or equity with respect to water distribution and management. A similar plea has been entered recently by Norris Hundley, jr., based upon his searching review of the checkered legal and political history of water rights in the West, especially in light of controversies flowing from the Winters decision of 1908. We must "find a way of replacing confused law," Hundley says, "with clear and reasonable principles." "The challenge," he also concludes, "is to replace confusion with equity."[2]

Of course, the concern for "equity" in the disposition of water resources is hardly a new issue, particularly in the Colorado River Basin. To examine the record of "dividing the waters" in this century is to encounter constant appeals from all sides to principles of "reciprocity," "rights," and "equity." This is as true of officials in the western states and the Supreme Court, which defended its decision in *Wyoming v. Colorado* as "consonant with the principles of right and equity,"[3] as it is of those communities, like the Indians and Mexicans, who have generally been excluded from the decision-making process. Today, however, it is the perception of persistent inequalities and the attempt to assert "water rights," advanced especially by Indians, which is "the sword of Damocles that hangs over the West." In Philip Fradkin's words, "It threatens, like nothing else, to sever the complex web of laws, agreements, regulations, quiet understandings, and court decisions that, collectively known as the Law of the River, constitute the major determinant in the growth of the West—the white man's West, that is, since the Colorado is essentially a white man's river."[4] This may be strong language, but it only states what we know: In the West, water has gone to those with political power, legal skills, technical knowledge, and sheer tenacity; others have been excluded. In light of this record and our common reliance on legal adjudication, the complex and troubling question of "equity" will surely not disappear; for coming generations it poses questions that will have to be confronted, whether we like it or not.

We are presented, then, with a double challenge: confusion and uncertainty of principles matched by controversy over "water rights" within the social order. In these circumstances, nothing could be more timely than the articulation of a principled understanding of what has come to be called the "equity perspective." Such an understanding does not yet exist, at least not with respect to the special domain of water distribution, use, and management. Our aim is to develop a rational defense of "equity," calling upon both the general theoretical discussions of "distributive justice" and the particular circumstances and history of water policy in the West. The task is to identify and clarify those points of contact at the intersection between the general and the particular. In order to accomplish this aim we propose to start with observations about two aspects of the problem: the nature of water as a special kind of resource, as a "social good"; and the nature of the American "democratic" political process and the principles and expectations associated with it.

Water as a Social Good

The fundamental social significance of water was acknowledged at the inception of our civilization. In fact, the earliest discussions of water as a special human resource emerged as part of a series of comments on the conditions appropriate to a "just" political community, to its health, defense, beauty, and legal arrangements. Thus, in several passages in *The Laws*, Plato sought to show that of all resources and necessities of life, water, because of its basic importance for human well-being and its vulnerability to "doctoring, diverting, or intercepting the supply," must always be subject to public regulation. Time-honored practices recognized "priority rights," but such rights were qualified by norms of "reciprocity" that were publicly enforced.[5] The same ideas recur in Aristotle's *Politics*, with the added reminder that despite its all-too-obvious importance for the "self-sufficiency" of a polis the public management of water "is a matter which ought not to be treated lightly."[6] And a less familiar figure, Pausanias, writing in Roman times, scornfully dismissed the civic aspirations of a small town merely by noting that it has "no government buildings, no theater, no town square, no water conducted to a fountain." As if to underline the human consequences of such deprivation, he observed that "the people live in hovels like mountain cabins on the edge of a ravine."[7] The absence of visible water works and water institutions was a sure sign of the lack of public life and civilization itself.

As citizens of semiarid lands, writers from Plato to Pausanias were well aware of how capricious nature could be: Droughts were inevitable, rainfall came during the wrong season, irrigation was a necessity. Scarcity raised basic questions about resource use and distribution, questions that could only be answered by institutionalizing a set of arrangements that would produce socially sanctioned decisions. Distributive problems were no less compelling for urban communities than for rural peoples. Everywhere water was caught up in a web of social interdependencies, and this meant that like other "social goods" it could be considered under the heading of "distributive justice."

To adopt the long-standing conception of water as a "social good" is certainly not to suggest that water should never be considered as a natural resource. Of course, it is *also* a natural resource; and it is this double identity which can create considerable perplexity. Our understanding suggests minimally that water should not be seen simply as an economic commodity, subject to the usual market laws of supply and demand and to calculations of efficiency, but, rather, that it should be viewed as a fundamental necessity that society chooses (for good reasons) to treat differently from other resources. Historically, the conception that "water is different" has often prevailed. In fact, Spanish water law, from which much of our present water law in the West is derived, went to great lengths to protect the public interest in the resolution of water disputes by limiting private water rights, even ones based on prior appropriation.[8]

In the contemporary setting, Maass and Anderson capture the essence of the issue when they state that in actual experience the goal of "economic growth" often conflicts with other community objectives, so much so "that farmers typically refuse to treat water as a regular economic good, like fertilizer, for example." "It is," they say, "a special product and should be removed from ordinary market transactions so that farmers can control conflict, maintain popular influence and control, and realize equity and social justice."[9] If water is indeed different, as seems to be the case, then it is closer in its most signficant aspects to being a social good than an economic good; it is more like basic education or basic health care than fertilizer. It may seem surprising to speak of water in this way. Yet it should seem neither surprising nor irrational to realize that communities show considerable reluctance to surrender to the "market mechanism" decisions so closely tied to the collective well-being as are those surrounding water distribution.

Three important consequences follow from this distinction understanding of water as a social good: a definition of government's role, a characterization of the function of "public interest" in relation to water rights, and an identification of the kind of "public ownership" that applies to water.

The Role of Government

Political communities are formed in order to provide certain basic services and to protect certain basic rights that citizens could not secure by acting alone. We suggest that together with providing for the common defense, the security of life and property, and the enforcement of law one of the most basic tasks of a political community, acting through its government, is to oversee the maintenance and distribution of water supplies. There is a crucial sense in which government and its agents must function as "trustees," as the institutional locus of accountability. Attempts to shift accountability to individuals, private interests, or a market's "invisible hand" will, in our judgment, tend to fragment this role and to exacerbate conflict. The tendency increases in arid and semiarid environments where questions over water distribution among competing users are inherently divisive and continually test the community's capacity to institutionalize negotiation and compromise. After all, as we have seen again and again in the West, a threat to the system for allocating water is perceived as a threat to a community's well-being or way of life. It may be a slight exaggeration to suggest (borrowing a page from Hobbes) that in the settlement of the West disputes over water rights made life "solitary, poor, nasty, brutish and short."[10] But we have it on the authority of Elwood Mead, an early observer of western irrigation practices, that until public institutions for adjudicating disputes were developed "there was either murder or suicide in the heart of every member" of the irrigation communities.[11] In short, there was a clear interest in channeling private grievances into public institutions.

Public Interest

If government is to be assigned an activist role, then the category appropriate to its decision making is "public interest" (which, like many political concepts, is open to partisan abuse). However difficult it may be to decide what the pubic interest *is* in actual cases, there is no acceptable alternative to undertaking that task. The public interest is to be found in certain primary values of the American political community, especially in those which state a belief in the inherent fairness of "open" and "democratic" political processes. The "public interest" attaches to process itself, not to a specific constellation of "right results." Where a "social good" such as water is the subject of such a process, particular interests are subordinated to general interests, and individual interests become secondary to common interests. Accordingly, with respect to water, people are expected to act in ways that serve primarily a collective public interest as opposed to isolated self-interest. The grounds for this expectation must be sought in the notion of "equity" itself, discussed below.

Public Ownership

It follows from this notion of "social good" that if water resources are to be viewed as "property" they must be considered as being owned by everyone—or by no one. In short, water is at best owned by the public, acting through its authorized political agents and institutions. When government grants or recognizes claims for water rights, it acknowledges a right for *use*, not ownership. There are no natural, innate, fixed, or absolute rights to the ownership of water, but, rather, there are rights to use it that are contingent upon an implicit conception of "public interest" as developed by the political process. Water and its "status" as a "good" seems to be radically conditioned, once again, by social and political arrangements.

Politics as a Democratic Process

Having developed a perspective on water as a social good, we need to turn directly to our second theme, to the political context within which considerations of "equity" have become prominent. This context is profoundly shaped by certain deeply ingrained assumptions about that much-abused term, *democratic politics*. Stated in a bold form, the enlightened experiment that we call American democracy is based on two assumptions (at least): first, our respect for legal or constitutional rules and procedures arrived at in an "impartial" and "fair" manner, and, second, our commitment to the notion that power should be shared by members of a community organized as participants having equal access to the law, to social goods, and to political positions. The first idea expresses a procedural norm, the second a participatory norm; democracy in the first sense is a form of decision making, and in the second sense it is a mode of association.[12] When taken literally, both are ideals which we can at best be approximated only in partial and limited ways. Nevertheless (or perhaps for this reason), these ideals have provided the motive force behind the appeal for equity.

Both the procedural and participatory conceptions of democracy have assumed that the democratic public is essentially an association of individuals in whose collective interest policies are to be set. After all, in order for such policies to meet with approval, most would agree that democracy as a form of rule should operate for the benefit of individuals. But, as a condition for securing potential benefits, it becomes necessary for individuals to have certain rights protected. One normally thinks of First Amendment rights in this connection, but of course there are other kinds of "rights," such as water rights, which may be just as controversial as their standard counterparts. In any case, the exercise of all rights, a hallmark of the democratic process, tends to produce two results. First, rights come into conflict, individual is set against individual, one part of the political community pitted against another part. Second, inequalities are created which affect the ability of individuals to exercise rights.

Interestingly, the two otherwise satisfactory norms of democratic politics—impartial rules and power sharing—appear to lead to a point at which inequalities in power, participation, and the practice of rights threaten to undo the norms themselves. Our conceptions of democratic politics seem to say one thing; our practices seem to say another. The democratic process is marked by unavoidable tension.

Controversies over water rights and the use and distribution of water invariably face this tension: current distributive practices are attacked in the name of principle, and principles are criticized in view of existing practices for distributing water. The problem of the democratic process relative to water policy, then, poses a series of questions. How do we keep the political community functioning in a situation of severe conflict? How do we decide which inequalities are acceptable and for which categories of users? What principles can be proposed for correcting unacceptable inequalities? Are there any principles at all, consistent with our democratic expectations, that can establish once and for all the meaning of distributive justice with respect to water, allowing us "to replace confusion with equity?"

To raise these questions is to move toward the heart of the problem posed by the equity perspective. We need to see whether general notions of democratic politics can illuminate the meaning and application of equity.

The Problem of Equity

In the language of politics, "equity" is dependent for its meaning on conceptions of equality that are rooted in general theories of distributive justice. Over the last decade, following upon the heels of John Rawls's well-known work,[13] we have seen an avalanche of such general philosophical theories and models of rational choice. These efforts have sought to answer questions like "what is justice?" or "what is equity?" by identifying principles and decision rules that are abstract, hypothetical, invariant, universal, and applicable to whole societies. However, because of these characteristics, the general theories of justice have had difficulty in coping with areas of public policy, such as water policy, where all of the serious problems are of a different order, where the context of policy is established by relationships that are concrete, historically specific, changeable, particular, and applicable only in restricted settings.[14] Often, it seems as though the relationship between "theory" and "policy" has remained about where Pausanias left it.

If we are to move toward a coherent understanding of "equity" in water policy, then two new assumptions seem to offer the greatest promise. First, it strikes us as reasonable to categorize the issues of water resources and water rights as occupying a "sphere of justice," that is, a particular area of policy and decision where society acknowledges the relevance of certain questions having to do with distribution and equity.[15] This "sphere" may have a family resemblance to other spheres, such as welfare, security, education, and the like, but the rules and history shaping its policies are different in important ways. What equity can mean in this sphere, then, will depend importantly on the particular and even unique conditions characterizing water policy in the Colorado Basin. It follows, secondly, that what the equity perspective requires is an identification and logical ordering of practical principles that will fit the unique circumstances of water. There are no general postulates or theories of equity that will clarify policy in this sphere, and it is pointless to look for them. What we need are "middle-range" generalizations, and not grand theories that might provide some practical guidance through this labyrinthine sphere of compacts, rights, laws, claims, and interests.

Now, it is unfortunate but true that equity (or equality) has long been recognized as a protean and paradoxical concept, which is hardly the most reliable instrument. As suggested above, the problem is this: To affirm equity in one of its many forms—equality of rights, for example—is, in fact, to affirm inequality of results. That is, arguments for equity always end up at some point as rationalizations for "acceptable" levels and types of inequality among different categories of persons. In *The Promise of American Life* (1909), Herbert Croly complained that "in so far as the equal rights are freely exercised, they are bound to result in inequalities; and these inequalities are bound to make for their own perpetuation, and so to provoke still further discrimination. Wherever the principle has been allowed to mean what it seems to mean, it has determined and encouraged its own violation."[16]

In the messy and clouded political world, where things are often not as they seem, equity taken literally as an arithmetical relation of identity is simply a myth. Any defense of equity must therefore be "complex." When inequalities arise or when differences emerge in the criteria used for resource allocation for given categories of users, we need to be able to defend them as "reasonable" or "fair." Although the equity perspective is usually composed of implicit claims about reasonableness and fairness, let us attempt to make some of those claims explicit.

Five Principles of Equity

An acceptable "equity doctrine" can be explicitly formulated around five distributive principles: reciprocity, value-pluralism, participation, promises, and responsibility. These principles are offered as a statement of "necessary and sufficient" conditions for equity, and in this sense they may serve as a "test" for equity in water policy.

Principle 1

"Reciprocity" captures one sense of equity, namely, the notion that *distributive advantages and costs should be shared by all members of the relevant community.* The difficult problem here is to decide how costs related to the protection, development, and use of water resources should be apportioned. Reciprocity suggests some minimally applicable rules. First, everyone should share in the burdens of a water system, as occurs on a small scale in northern New Mexico where each spring the *mayordomo* enlists all able-bodied men for servicing the *acequia madre,* the main irrigation ditch, and for repairing diversion dams.[17] Also, as a general rule, those emerging users who overburden the resource and strain the existing allocation system must find ways to ameliorate or to avoid those results. Furthermore, in the case of water allocation those who use more should expect to have to sacrifice more under conditions of scarcity.

Reciprocity is sufficiently complicated to deserve a brief comment. As used here, it is actually a "balancing" principle that acknowledges the doctrine of prior appropriation ("first in time, first in right"), but it is also committed to frugality and protection of third-party rights. The difficulty here stems from prior appropriation, which was invoked initially as a fair rule for protecting stability of allocation, security of investment, and reciprocity in the treatment of users. When pushed to an extreme, however, it can have negative effects. One of the most justifiable criticisms of western states' water law is that in practice it often encourages waste (or penalizes those who postpone resource use) through operation of the "use it or lose it" formula, which is the flip side of the doctrine of prior appropriation.[18] For example, we end up with the Navajo Indian Irrigation Project, which received tribal support not because a consensus formed in favor of using Winters Doctrine rights for a marginal (arguably, ill-advised) irrigation project, but rather because Navajos believed that if others successfully claimed and used the water, while they did not, their opportunity to use their water would be lost forever. As one councilman mused, "We will never see the water again if it goes over the mountain."[19] Just as prior appropriation needs to be modified by frugality, then, it also needs to be modified by third-party rights. In this respect, the record in the West is more promising. In the case of purchases of senior water rights by energy companies, for example, courts have often (and appropriately) invoked a doctrine of no injury to third parties.[20] It seems consistent with the principle of reciprocity to expect costs for this kind of growth— rapid expansion of energy development in coal and oil shale that places additional demands on Colorado Basin water resources—to be borne by the agents of growth.

Principle 2

Our second equity principle, value-pluralism, holds that *users' rights to employ water to pursue whatever values they consider legitimate should be respected, provided use does not degrade the resource or harm others.* This typically "liberal" assertion is important,[21] because like all complex human environments, the Colorado River Basin includes political communities with very different value orientations toward fundamental social goods, such as work, leisure, recreation, education, welfare, health, and water. The equity perspective is consistent with the view that different communities should be able to decide independently about such fundamental matters, including water resources use and development, assuming that conditions of "no degradation" and "no harm to others" are satisfied. Few would deny that such "negative" conditions may become quite restrictive, in which case value-pluralism is necessarily counterbalanced by the principle of reciprocity. Like the scales of justice, our first two principles exist in tension and must, in fact, be weighed against each other. On the positive side, however, our second principle has implications both for low income rural communities, which should be able to pursue their own "values" without fearing arbitrary loss of access to water as a social good, and for the relative autonomy of the western states. In its recent *Sporhase* v. *Nebraska* decision (1982), the Supreme Court appears to have adopted a contradictory position on this important aspect of equity. As noted below, we think it unlikely that such a position can be maintained.

Principle 3

The third principle of equity is derived from our statements about the participatory aspects of politics within democratic communities. Due to water's fundamental importance, *members of society having claims consistent with other stated values should always be accommodated in re-source allocation and in the decision process.* To have a share in water resources is a legitimate right of every member of society, and government has an obligation to protect that right. Similarly, to take part in allocative decisions is a right that should not be infringed. It does not seem equitable, then, to attempt either to limit community membership by restricting access to water or to decrease the probability of technically "inefficient" decisions by restricting the circle of participants. Exclusionist policies of both kinds invite destabilizing conflict and further accusations of inequity. Accommodating a variety of claims will render the decision process more confused and tempestuous than under "authoritarian" conditions attributed to "hydraulic societies,"[22] but such inconveniences necessarily accompany equity and are less damaging to public interest than the alternatives.

Principle 4

As a fourth principle, we suggest that equity assumes the *obligation to obey promises agreed to in good faith in the course of negotiation and compromise.* In a sense, the politics of the Colorado River Basin is nothing more than a fabric of promises, incurred at different times, under different conditions, and often for different purposes. Despite such differences, promises express shared social understanding of the meaning of water. In the basin as a whole, there appears to be a consensus that promises do matter precisely because they are the underlying metaphorical "social contract" binding members, communities, and government together in a common fate.[23] This is a controversial principle, however, because promises come into conflict with each other and because the circumstances under which promises are made later change. Unfortunately, there is no single, unambiguous rule of equity for solving the dilemmas posed by long-standing promises. Instead, emphasis should be placed on the need for flexibility and adaptation. We must be able to accept a built-in ambiguity in water decisions. Renegotiation of contracts is always possible, but (and this is our main contention) only on the condition that the other four equity principles apply. Promises are inviolable, to be sure, but when "dilemmas" appear they may be qualified by the other principles we have proposed.

Principle 5

Finally, the equity perspective includes the viewpoint that *the present use of water resources should take account of future generations.* It is important that use of a basic resource and social good like water not be part of a "Faustian bargain" which sacrifices future well-being to momentary pleasure. We need a kind of "ethic of responsibility" that will encourage attention to consequences, especially to long-term costs of short-term benefits. Of course, it is not always clear how the welfare of future generations might best be served. Economists have argued that among the finest gifts to be handed on by society are knowledge, technical advancement, and economic prosperity, and that these achievements may well depend upon the exploitation of resources.[24] Could such reasoning support the allowing of toxic pollution of groundwater supplied today in hopes that future users will have developed the technology to clean up aquifers, to cure cancer, or to find a substitute water supply? We think not. Equity is also an ethical idea which restrains the undertaking of large risks bearing on the fate, social good, and well-being of future humans.

These five principles serve as a concise summation of what has come to be called the "equity perspective." As should now be apparent, that perspective is not unitary, but consists instead of a variety of competing yet internally consistent principles that must be considered together and weighed against each other. Approached in this way, the five principles can be effectively used to analyze and assess Colorado River Basin water policy.

Application and Discussion

Difficult water reallocation decisions are facing the Colorado River Basin. Rising demands are placing pressure upon dwindling supplies.

Long-standing interests whose use of water had been deferred are now pursuing their claims. New interests whose use yields relatively higher rates of return are demanding preferential treatment. Present water users are resisting any sacrifices. At the same time, the strategies currently being chosen to deal with these conflicts tend to be insensitive to the politics and principles of equity. Pricing schemes, market mechanisms, and quantification of water rights are placing high value on efficiency, permanence, and security at the expense of equity. Yet the unintended result of these strategies may well be to perpetuate and amplify inequities, thus unleashing further conflict instead of subduing it.

Consider the issue of treating water as a market commodity. In accord with a preference for unfettered interstate trade, courts have recently declared water an "article of commerce" and have held as unconstitutional the state anti-export statutes that place an undue burden on interstate commerce.[25] Such decisions depart from precedents where courts recognized the special status of water as a social good. For instance, in a 1908 opinion written by Justice Oliver Wendell Holmes, the Supreme Court found that "few public interests are more obvious, indisputable and independent of particular theory than the interest of the public of a State to maintain the rivers that are wholly within it substantially undiminished, except for such drafts upon them as the guardians of the public welfare may permit for the purpose of turning them to more perfect use."[26] Furthermore, the "article of commerce" designation is not entirely consistent with the Court's own language in *Sporhase* v. *Nebraska.* In representing the majority, Justice Stevens noted that the Court was "reluctant to condemn as unreasonable measures taken by a State to conserve and preserve for its own citizens this vital resource in times of severe shortage," and he cited four specific grounds for such reluctance.[27] Justices Rehnquist and O'Conner dissented on the grounds that "'commerce' cannot exist in a natural resource that cannot be sold, rented, traded, or transferred, but only *used.*"

The treatment of water as an article of commerce erodes the value-pluralism principle of equity and places a special burden upon states that have chosen to husband resources and to develop economically at a slower pace. It has been long assumed that states could follow the wishes of their own citizens in allocating water. The states' power to protect their citizens' value in regard to water is no longer secure.

The circumstances surrounding the anti-export statute recently struck down by a United States district court, in the case of *El Paso v. Reynolds,* illustrates the equity problem. New Mexico, in contrast to Texas, has closely regulated groundwater pumping in order to control overdrafts and to conserve for the future. The city of El Paso, Texas, seeks to import groundwater from New Mexico. El Paso is the fifth fastest growing city in the West, and currently residents use two hundred gallons per capita per day. In the words of the *Albuquerque Journal,*

> El Paso has the problem and succeeded in making New
> Mexico's scarce and diminishing water resources the solution.
> That in turn has given New Mexico an even bigger problem—
> protecting its ability to govern its own resources. Quite simply
> New Mexico's border has been breached. Theoretically, outside
> municipalities or states—or anybody—can now apply to claim
> every unappropriated drop of New Mexico water. It is ironic
> because New Mexico has carefully guarded and conserved its
> water resources, only to lose a lawsuit to a city and state that
> take far less care of the resources.[28]

Claims of equity should not be allowed to protect mere hoarding of water resources, and laws that discriminate solely against out-of-state users cannot be justified. At the same time, it is consistent with respect for pluralism and the Court's long-standing recognition of water as a social good for states to be permitted to deny permits to pump water for export on bona fide, reasonable grounds of water conservation.[29]

The issue of Indian water rights is subject to enormous conflict and confusion. Legal and historical scholarship has had only limited success in clarifying the issue. It would serve little purpose here to tally the injustices committed on what has been called "dark and bloody ground."[30] More useful, we believe, is a discussion of how present and future application of equity principles can help sort out Indian rights. In our view, equity is weighing less heavily than it should in contemporary decision making, and unless equity is served, decisions made in the name of finality are likely to be ephemeral.[31]

By any reasonable hierarchy of promises made about water in the Colorado River Basin, those made to Indian people must be placed near the top. Nineteenth-century pledges given to Indians guaranteeing their water rights have been frequently repeated. The obligation as stated in the Winters decision is sufficiently clear: When Indian lands were reserved, so were the rights of Indians to the use of water. These rights were described by the Court as paramount and continuing to exist, even though unused, against federal and state governments and all others granted subsequent rights.[32] Indians were also promised flexibility in accommodating their needs, which might expand in the future. The Court, in another case, stated:

> What amount of water will be required . . . may not be
> determined with absolute accuracy at this time; but the policy
> of the government to reserve whatever water . . . may be
> reasonably necessary, not only for the present uses, but for
> future requirements is clearly within the terms of the Treaties
> as construed by the Supreme Court in the Winters case.[33]

However uncomfortable it may be to other users of water in the Colorado River Basin, Indians have been promised that lack of water will not be allowed to hamper their future opportunities. We have promised to tolerate uncertainties in all water rights subsequent to the Indians' paramount rights. Is this to mean that all development that has taken place in the basin is vulnerable to the whims of Indian people who may decide to reclaim use of water? Certainly not, since Indians are bound by the same rules of equity as others: they have been promised what is "reasonably necessary." Reasonable necessity must be determined in the light of circumstances. The political influence of non-Indians constrain the exercise of Indian water rights. Paramount Indian water rights are not potent enough to make up for injustices in other realms, such as health, education, or general economic welfare.

Had the principle of full and fair participation in allocation decisions been followed in the past, many of the most troublesome issues faced today in Indian water rights would have been avoided. Indians have seldom been at the negotiating table when decisions crucial to their water interest were being made. Of course, the federal government itself agreed to represent Indians as a "trustee" (Chief Justice Marshall called Indian tribes domestically dependent nations and said that their relationship to the United States resembled that of a ward to a guardian).[34] Once having accepted this responsibility, the federal government was obliged to protect Indian interests, a job often poorly performed. To take only one instance, there is widespread agreement that in the 1920s the federal government badly neglected its obligation to protect the Paiutes' water rights in Pyramid Lake. Sixty years later, the Justice Department was correct in trying to expand the Paiutes' decreed water right,[35] although its effort failed.[36] No lasting settlement of water allocations at Pyramid Lake or on the Colorado is likely to be built upon perpetuated inequity.

Lack of full and fair participation has also deprived our relations with Mexico over the Colorado of the blessings of equity. The United States has had the decided advantage of being upstream and of controlling dams and canals. It has also had superior information and expertise about the river and the implications of decisions. Bargaining from weakness understandably leaves the Mexicans dissatisfied with the equity of decisions and anxious to exploit whatever international situation might provide an opportunity to reopen issues. Rather than take advantage of Mexican weakness, western states need to seek ways to empower Mexican negotiators with better information and more meaningful choices.

As the largest users of the river, western states need to shoulder the burden for the welfare of the river, including its salinity, and for satisfying the Mexican treaty obligation. For instance, the Colorado River Basin Project Act of 1968 makes the supply of water guaranteed by the Mexican water treaty an obligation of the national government. The provision was the product of Byzantine congressional politics and a common motivation among basin states to relieve themselves of delivering to Mexico its share of the river.[37] The provision implied that the United States would supply an additional quantity of water beyond that already allocated by the Colorado River Compact. Forcing the nation to seek water sources outside the basin, from the Columbia Basin perhaps, has set the stage for further conflict and further perceptions of inequities. In the same vein, basin states later shifted the burden for salinity control, causing the federal government to fund inefficient and environmentally damaging projects.[38] The conflict over the responsibility to deliver water of reasonable quality to the Mexicans is almost certainly only temporarily dormant.

The development of the Colorado River Basin has been enormously uneven. Upper Basin states have lagged behind the Lower

Basin, and within the Lower Basin the city of Los Angeles and the Imperial Valley have consumed vast quantities of water. This growth was made possible in part through the consent of upstream users who believed that they would eventually have a turn in line for federally funded water development. The case of the state of Colorado in the Upper Basin was recently systematically laid out:

> Colorado's position consists of several elements: (1) that over a span of more than 60 years this State has cooperated generously with other states and with the Federal Government in fabricating a "Law of the River"; (2) that through this carefully, although not flawlessly, crafted system of compacts and Federal statutes Colorado is entitled to make beneficial use of more than 3 million acre-feet of water from the river system; (3) that Congress registered its unequivocal intent in every major act concerning the Colorado River to develop completely—that is to treat the entire basin as an integrated hydro-climatic system, not as merely a conveniently contrived collection of State development plans; (4) that as part of this overall plan, the Federal Government had explicitly committed itself to construct and operate dams and reclamation projects in Colorado (by the terms of various acts); (5) that realistically Colorado's full compact share of the river system could only be made available to the people of the State if and when the Federal Government completed the promised projects at Federal expense; (6) consequently the Federal Government and the other compact States have not only a statutory commitment but a moral/historic obligation to support Federal development of water projects.[39]

What is the continuing obligation to the Upper Basin for promises made? We have already suggested that promises sometimes conflict and that renegotiation of promises is always possible. But the conditions of equity must apply. It is patently unfair for the claimants who have yet to develop to carry their entire burden for previous decisions overestimating the amount of water in the river and underestimating claims of Indians and Mexicans and the possible adverse environmental consequences of overbuilding on the river. The obligation for satisfying all legitimate claims that exist on the river belong especially to the Lower Basin users whose interests have been for so long so well served.

Conclusion

In this paper, we have attempted to show that a coherent rationale for the "equity perspective" must rest on an understanding of water as a social good and on an appreciation of the democratic aspirations at work in the political process. Our practically oriented principles of equity have, in fact, led us to embrace an open-ended distributive norm: As a social good, water should *not* be distributed to persons who possess some other kind of good (such as wealth) merely *because* they possess that other good and without respect to the meaning of water as a *social* good.[40] And what is this meaning? As we have seen, water represents satisfaction of a socially defined and legitimated "need," but it also represents security and it represents opportunity. All of these meanings are complex, but it is perhaps opportunity that is most intriguing, for as a password to potential economic and social development it is closest to the core of the concern for equity. As far back as the Winters decision of 1908 we have heard of water as a means "to practice the arts of civilization." Unfortunately one group's opportunity to practice this art is not necessarily compatible with another group's security of investment, as the latest round of Supreme Court cases are demonstrating once again. Socially defined needs conflict and change under new circumstances; meanings clash. But, from the perspective of equity, security must not be allowed to displace opportunity, and the uncertainties which result must be shared equitably.

Thus, our argument at the level of principles has implication for water policy and water institutions. Water is a social good and for that reason a public trust; private ownership of it is not desirable. "Public interest" must be protected by government, especially if water becomes part of a market exchange. But to treat water as a commodity is a mistake in our view. In addition, the use of "efficiency" alone is a poor rule for evaluation of water projects and for water allocation. Finally, quantification of water rights in the basin, a temporary expedient to settle immediate conflicts among users, can be considered final only so long as the broad public interest is served. Equity claims will be with us for generations, and we will need to learn the democratic virtues of flexibility, toleration of differences, and compromise.

In sum, any solution to the problems in the Colorado Basin which attempts to deny equity will increase already existing tensions and generate new forms of opposition. At the least, it will breed piecemeal special interest legislation and more costly and protracted litigation, all of which will interfere with attempts at sound, long-range planning for river management and regional development. Or, in the worst-case scenario, it will lead to a kind of regional "Milagro Bean Field War" and a highly emotional and politicized environment. Time is running out. In present circumstances, the "equity perspective" on Colorado River Basin issues is not just high-flown rhetoric or unworkable idealism. It is simply the assertion of common sense.

Notes

1. Arthur Maass and Raymond L. Anderson, *And the Desert Shall Rejoice: Conflict, Growth, and Justice in Arid Environments* (Cambridge, Mass., 1978), p. 395.

2. Norris Hundley, jr., "The Dark and Bloody Ground of Indian Water Rights: Confusion Elevated to Principle," *Western Historical Quarterly* 9 (October 1978), p. 482.

3. Quoted in Norris Hundley, jr, *Water and the West* (Berkeley, 1975), p. 178.

4. Philip Fradkin, *A River No More* (New York, 1981), p. 155.

5. Plato, *The Laws* 844a–845e.

6. Aristotle, *Politics* 1330a–b.

7. Quoted in M. I. Finley, *Economy and Society in Ancient Greece* (London, 1981), p. 3.

8. See Michael Meyer, *'Til the Wells Run Dry: Water and Water Law in the Hispanic Southwest* (book manuscript, 1983), chap. 8.

9. Maass and Anderson, *And the Desert Shall Rejoice*, p. 5.

10. Thomas Hobbes, *Leviathan*, I, 13.

11. Maass and Anderson, *And the Desert Shall Rejoice*, p. 2.

12. The phrase is from John Dewey, *The Public and Its Problems* (Denver, 1927), p. 149. In Dewey's more complete statement, the democratic idea "consists in having a responsible share according to capacity in forming and directing the activities of the groups to which one belongs and in participating according to need in the values which the groups sustain" (p. 147). Like our second conception, this definition might be said to represent the "Jeffersonian" tradition in America. But in order to achieve a comprehensive understanding, this tradition must be combined with the "Madisonian" emphasis on constitutional rules.

13. John Rawls, *A Theory of Justice* (Cambridge, Mass., 1971).

14. Not surprisingly, therefore, in the burgeoning philosophical literature on areas of public policy there is not a single discussion of water policy, nor even examples drawn from the numerous water rights controversies of the twentieth century. In policy discussions dealing with water, on the other hand, despite numerous casual references to "equity," there is not a single successful application of any of the general theories of distributive justice. From both points of view these failures seem extraordinary in light of the undeniable social importance of the water issue. The fault does not lie in the subject matter, we would suggest, but rather in the assumptions that have governed inferences drawn from the theory of justice.

15. Michael Walzer, *Spheres of Justice: A Defense of Pluralism and Equality* (New York, 1983), especially chap. 1.

16. *The Promise of American Life,* ed. Arthur M. Schlesinger (Cambridge, Mass., 1965), p. 189.

17. Sue-Ellen Jacobs, "'Top-Down Planning': Analysis of Obstacles to Community Development in an Economically Poor Region of the Southwestern United States," *Human Organization* 37 (Fall 1978), p. 248.

18. Traditional Spanish water law, for example, clearly recognized that prior appropriation did not include a right to waste, even in the case of spring or well water originating on private property. Instead, when considering disputes, a conception of a socially defined need was often invoked; in the words of a Santa Fe decree of 1720, water judges should "divide the water always verifying the greatest need . . . , and giving to each one that which he needs" (Meyer, *'Til the Wells Run Dry,* chap. 8, p. 6).

19. Quoted in Monroe E. Price and Gary D. Weatherford, "Indian Water Rights in Theory and Practice: Navajo Experience in the Colorado Basin," *Law and Contemporary Problems* (Winter 1976), p. 121.

20. See Gary D. Weatherford and Gordon C. Jacoby, "Impact of Energy Development on the Law of the Colorado River," *Natural Resources Journal* 15 (January 1975), pp. 199–200; Gary Weatherford et al., eds., *Acquiring Water for Energy: Institutional Aspects* (Littleton, Colo., 1982), pp. 65–66.

21. The classic expression of a similar principle is found in the first chapter of John Stuart Mill's *On Liberty* (1859).

22. Karl A. Wittfogel, *Oriental Despotism: A Comparative Study of Total Power* (New Haven, 1957).

23. This idea is found not only in the basin but in an authoritative tradition within political theory. For example, David Hume remarks that "the principal object of government is to constrain men to observe the laws of nature. In this respect, however, that law of nature concerning the performance of promises, is only comprised along with the rest; and its exact observance is to be considered as an effect of the institution of government,

and not the obedience to government as an effect of the obligation of a promise" (*A Treatise of Human Nature*, III, ii, 8).

24. See, for example, Harold Barnett and Chandler Morse, *Scarcity and Growth: The Economics of Natural Resource Availability* (Baltimore, 1963).

25. See *Sporhase v. Nebraska*, 458 U.S. 941 (1982), and the report on *El Paso v. Reynolds*, "Judge Rejects New Mexico Ban on Water Exports," *Albuquerque Journal*, 18 January 1983, pp. 1–2.

26. *Hudson County Water Co. v. McCarter*, 209 U.S. 349 (1908).

27. "Our reluctance stems from the 'confluence of several realities,'" Stevens continued. "First, a State's power to regulate the use of water in times and places of shortage for the purpose of protecting the health of its citizens—and not simply the health of its economy—is at the core of its police power. . . . Second, the legal expectation that under certain circumstances each State may restrict water within its borders has been fostered over the years not only by our equitable apportionment decrees . . . but also by the negotiation and enforcement of interstate compacts. Our law therefore has recognized the relevance of state boundaries in the allocation of scarce water resources. Third, although appellee's claim to public ownership of Nebraska ground water cannot justify a total denial of federal regulatory power, it may support a limited preference for its own citizens in the utilization of the resource. . . . Finally, given appellee's conservation efforts, the continuing availability of ground water in Nebraska is not simply happen-stance; the natural source has some indicia of a good publicly produced and owned in which a state may favor its own citizens in times of shortage."

28. *Albuquerque Journal*, 21 January 1983, p. 4.

29. Michael D. White, "Reasonable State Regulation of the Inter-State Transfer of Percolating Water," *Natural Resources Lawyer* 2 (September 1969), pp. 383–406.

30. Hundley, "The Dark and Bloody Ground of Indian Water Rights."

31. See, for example, the recent ruling of the Supreme Court in the continuance of *Arizona v. California et al.*, reported in *The Washington Post*, 31 March 1983, pp. 1, 11.

32. Norris Hundley, jr., "The 'Winters' Decision and Indian Water Rights: A Mystery Reexamined," *Western Historical Quarterly* 13 (January 1982), pp. 17–42.

33. *Conrad Investment Co. v. U.S.*, 161 Fed. 831, 835 (1908).

34. *Cherokee Nation v. Georgia*, 30 U.S. 16 (1831).

35. Charles R. Babcock, "Indian Tribes Discover Friends in Court," *The Washington Post*, 13 April 1983, p. 23.

36. *Pyramid Paiute Tribe of Indians v. Truckee-Carson Irrigation District*, 1053 S. Ct. 2906 (1983).

37. Dean E. Mann, "Politics in the United States and the Salinity Problems of the Colorado River," *Natural Resources Journal* 15 (January 1975), p. 117.

38. Ibid.

39. Conrad L. McBride, "Colorado Water Resources Development Politics" (paper presented at the annual convention of the Western Political Science Association, Seattle, 24–26 March 1983).

40. Adapted from Walzer, *Spheres of Justice*, p. 20.

9 Wilderness Values and the Colorado River

Roderick Nash

Swirling together down the Colorado's "colored river," fact and myth mix uneasily. Some things are fixed, definable, and quantifiable about the Colorado—like the length of the river and the number of square miles in its upper and lower basins. Terms like *acre-foot* and *kilowatt-hour* ring with reality. They can be counted, stored, allocated, and no matter how people may fight over them everybody agrees on the meaning of the terms.

Not so in regard to wilderness. Here, there is no consensus. Wilderness issues launch us down the heavy rapids of relativism. We encounter myth—what people believe to be the case. Wilderness, after all, is a state of mind.[1] It has more to do with psychology than geography. The depth of a canyon can be measured and its miles from the nearest Coke machine calculated, but whether someone calls the place "wild" is unpredictable.

So it is that Ken Sleight, who began guiding in the canyon lands of the Colorado in the 1940s, can say "there's no wilderness left, just scenery."[2] But for a tourist from Philadelphia who has never camped out, a trip today through the Grand Canyon can be a wilderness experience of extraordinary power. And, to complete the spectrum, John Wesley Powell would have chuckled in amusement at Sleight's conceit in finding wilderness as late as the 1940s. It is all a matter of

perspective, and the subjective element complicates the task of identifying and protecting environmental values.

One consequent axiom seems to be that the more civilized our
point of view the less strict our requirements for wilderness. We learn
to make do with less. Perhaps this is a fortunate adaptation to the
shrinking quantity and quality of wildness in the world. It is the
beginning of a cultural process of accommodation that allows, for
example, some Japanese to find wilderness in tea gardens.

The problem of defining wildness—or even naturalness—is particularly complicated on the Colorado River. Knowledge in this case
can be dangerous. Consider a first-time visitor to Grand Canyon National Park who, at this very moment, could well be resting on the
right bank of the Colorado at a popular stop for river travelers called
Nankoweap, fifty-two miles below Lee's Ferry. Let's explore this situation. The park visitor is sitting in the feathery shade of a low tree
he has just learned to call "tamarisk" or salt cedar. He (or she) is
watching the point at which a six-pound test monofilament line slips
into the clean, blue water of the Colorado. The river is cold, about
forty-six degrees Fahrenheit, and is reputed to contain trophy-size
rainbow trout. But the fishing is difficult. Over the course of an hour,
the fisherperson is obliged to shift position several times as the Colorado rises rapidly a distance of six vertical feet. The sky, however, is
hard cobalt blue, and the visitor assumes that it must be raining heavily
somewhere upstream. Later, gathered for the evening around the romantic sputtering of a propane stove, our tourist compares notes with
the other river runners about how smoothly the float trip began two
days before. It's good, he muses, that people can simply drive up to
Lee's Ferry, launch their boats, and escape the harassments of civilization into what, for him, is pristine wilderness.

But now consider the way someone familiar with the ecological
and political realities of the Colorado, say a boatman on the first-
timer's trip, perceives the same scene. The tamarisk, he knows, is an
"exotic"—a plant native to the Mediterranean Basin that has achieved
a dominant position in the riparian ecosystem of the Colorado only
in the last century. Powell never saw a tamarisk.[3] Does its presence
compromise the wilderness qualities of the canyon? Only, apparently,
if you know the full story and even then, perhaps not much. Wilderness
is in the eye of the beholder. As for the trout, almost a symbol of

wilderness conditions in many rivers, they only arrived at Mile 52 in the late 1960s. The 1963 closing of Glen Canyon Dam, upstream from the Grand Canyon, totally changed the temperature and quality of the water moving down the Colorado. Previously lukewarm, heavily silted flow supported only nongame species like the humpback chub and the squawfish. But after Glen Canyon Dam the silt dropped out in Lake Powell, and the water, drawn from the cool depths of the reservoir, made prime trout habitat. Fish and game folks planted the trout near Lee's Ferry. They thrived, and in a few years spread out upstream to the base of the Glen Canyon Dam and downstream almost to the next reservoir, Lake Mead.

The impact of Glen Canyon Dam on the Colorado River in Grand Canyon is also evident, to the knowledgeable river traveler, in what boatmen call "tides." The cause of the rapid rise in the river that startled the tourist has nothing to do with upstream cloudbursts. Air conditioners and electric toothbrushes are closer to the truth. Every day, the Bureau of Reclamation releases water through the turbines of Glen Canyon Dam to meet the power demands of an awakening Southwest. The releases move, like pulses, down the river. Experienced river runners know when to expect the rising and falling phases, and they time their trip to reach difficult rapids at optimum flow levels. Indeed several Grand Canyon rapids are virtually unrunnable at the lowest point in the Glen Canyon Dam tide.

The upstream dam has, of course, other effects on the predam ecosystem in Grand Canyon. That propane stove is a direct consequence of the disappearance of driftwood that used to move down into the canyon lands from the mountains at the Colorado's source. So did sand and silt that now accumulates in the bottom of Lake Powell. The "pristine" beaches at Mile 52 are, in fact, relics. As they erode and wash downstream there is little or no replacement. Luna Leopold and other geologists have found that the dam-controlled flow produces similar "unnatural" changes in the contour of the bed of the Colorado.[4]

But what is "natural"? The Colorado still flows through the Grand Canyon. The rapids still dance in the sunshine and tie boatmen's stomachs into tight knots. There are no condominiums and shopping malls. And, to be fair, the Glen Canyon Dam has done something to create the modern river industry by evening out the Colorado's flow. In Powell's time, high or low water made the river unrunnable for months on end. Still, what nags at the back of the boatman's mind is that the Colorado River is *controlled*. It's a push-button river now, responsive, as Philip Fradkin reminds us so well,[5] to the needs of civilized man rather than to the rhythms of the natural world. Indeed, most of the time the Colorado never reaches the Gulf of California; the feeble trickle that survives fourteen hundred miles of human demands sinks into the Mexican sands some twenty miles from the ocean. In the extraordinarily wet winter of 1982–83, Colorado water did reach the gulf, but the biologically rich delta, the "green lagoons" that Aldo Leopold described in *A Sand County Almanac,* are long gone. And so, presumably, is the ecological regime in the gulf that depended on nutrients and sediments carried down the predam river.

The Colorado is controlled in other ways as well. Outdoor recreation is no longer a good that is free for the taking. Consider the perception of our first-time river runner that the orderly launching of boats at Lee's Ferry for two weeks in the wilderness represents a pleasant alternative to the rules and regulations of civilization. It is a fine thing, he thinks, that freedom survives in the American West. But, again, the experienced river traveler knows this is an illusion. He is aware of the fierce competition for "user days" among the twenty-odd commercial river outfitters operating in the Grand Canyon. As an occasional noncommercial or "private" river runner, the boatman knows that a permit to lead a flat trip down the Colorado through the Grand Canyon presently necessitates a twelve-year wait and a mountain of paperwork. The days when a group of friends could, on impulse, drive to Lee's Ferry, rig out their boats, and shove off into the current ended in the late 1960s. Computers allocate wilderness now. The result may be orderly, but it is hardly uncontrolled.[6]

But for all its problems, for all the compromises with civilization, the push-button, computerized river and its watershed is still one of the great reservoirs of wilderness values remaining in the western United States. There are several ways to understand this. The view to the southwest from the deck of my cabin at the seven-thousand-foot level of the La Sal Mountains near Moab, Utah, extends a hundred miles to the Henry Mountains. It is a sun-dappled expanse of mesas, buttes, and slickrock canyons. The Colorado River runs approximately through the center of the scene. On any given afternoon, when it's Miller time and I prop my boots on the railing of the deck, it is probable that there is *nobody* in my line of sight. The exception would be the occupants of a vehicle on Route 163, near Moab, or on Route 95 in the vicinity of Hanksville. There might be a hiker in Canyonlands National Park or a group of river runners on the Colorado. But these are all ephemeral presences, swallowed up by an immensity of unmodified space through which the spirit can soar. Call this "wilderness" or not, it is, in 1983, extraordinary.

For another perspective, consider accessibility. There are two ways to drive a vehicle across the river in the vicinity of Needles, California. Important since the Spanish frontier, the old ford is now the scene of Interstate 40's bridge. After its completion in 1935, the top of Hoover Dam, 80 miles away, offered the next upstream crossing. From there, it is a full 350 lake and river miles to the next possible crossings: Navajo Bridge and the bridge just below Glen Canyon Dam. In the entire 280 miles of the Grand Canyon it is possible to reach the Colorado with a wheeled vehicle in only one place (the mouth of Diamond Creek), and there is no bridge. Continuing up the Colorado, across Lake Powell, one finds no crossing for another 160 miles or until Utah Route 95's bridge at Hite. Then, it is back into the canyons for 109 river miles to the bridge at Moab or, if you follow the Green River, 166 miles to Green River, Utah, and the Interstate 70 crossing. Continuing upstream on the Green River, it is 128 miles to the Ouray crossing and 54 more to Jensen and the U.S. Route 40 bridge. Flaming Gorge Dam, almost on the Wyoming border, is another 90 miles away. In sum, between Flaming Gorge and Needles, a distance of just over a thousand river and lake miles, there are just six places to cross the Colorado in a car. The old saw about "you can't get there from here" still has some meaning in this wide-open country.

The point is that today, right now, there are quite unique geographical characteristics in the canyon lands that have to do with spaciousness and wildness. Get off what few beaten tracks there are, and the mark humans have made is still relatively faint. In the eastern United States, by way of comparison, wildness exists in bits and pieces, surrounded by a matrix of civilization.[7] In the Colorado watershed it is the other way around. Wilderness is the matrix; civilization thinly distributed.

As a final illustration of what is special about the Colorado River Basin, consider confluences—the places where major rivers come together. In most parts of the world, these are the sites of major cities. But the major confluence in the Southwest, that between the Green and Colorado rivers, is fifty miles from the nearest video game and in the heart of the national park. Indeed, there is no *major* city on the entire course of the Colorado including the Green. It may surprise even westerners to learn that, according to the 1980 census, Yuma, Arizona, with 42,000 people, is the largest city on the river and it is only twenty miles from Mexico. Upstream, there is the "instant" city, Lake Havasu, Arizona, with 15,000 (the 1970 census did not even list it), and Grand Junction, Colorado, with 28,000. And that is it; the remaining communities on the fourteen hundred miles of the Colorado are, literally, villages. The banks of no other river in the temperate latitudes of the world are so lightly populated.

American interest in the environmental values of the Colorado River watershed lagged behind nature appreciation in other parts of the nation. In fact, the canyons and deserts of the Southwest were the last landscape Americans learned to love. Throughout the eighteenth and nineteenth centuries, landscape aesthetics focused on wooded, well-watered environments, preferably adorned with spectacular snow-clad peaks: postcard scenery. The nineteenth century also favored pastoral landscapes with lush vegetation, meandering brooks, and contented flocks. Of course, the higher parts of the Colorado Basin fit this pattern quite well. It was the lower elevations, the treeless slickrock expanses burning in the sun and the deep slot canyons, that shocked aesthetic sensibilities. The desert seemed to be an arid wasteland as devoid of vegetation as it was of truth, beauty, and divinity. The old biblical dread of the desert as a cursed land proved hard to shake. The Colorado Plateau seemed strange and hostile, or at best indifferent, to people and their values. Lieutenant Joseph Christmas Ives summarized the general feeling at the end of his 1857 trip into the western part of the Grand Canyon. His report spoke of the "dismal abysses" and "arid table-lands" as "altogether valueless," and he predicted that "ours has been the first, and will doubtless be the last, party of whites, to visit this profitless locality." For Ives, "after entering [the canyonlands] there is nothing to do but leave."[8] F. W. von Egøffstein, the painter who accompanied Ives, created nightmarish and surrealistic landscapes in which evil seems to brood in black canyon depths. Ives spoke of the canyons as "portals of the infernal regions," and Egøffstein illustrated the feeling. Hardly a Walden Pond, the wilderness along the Colorado did not initially support the transcendental assumption of the divinity inherent in nature. Understandably, tourists bypassed the canyon lands for stereotyped monumental scenery such as that of Yosemite or Yellowstone national parks.

John Wesley Powell's account of his 1869 and 1871 trips launched a new viewpoint. To be sure, Powell occasionally feared what he sometimes thought of as a "granite prison," but glimmers of appreciation appear in his journals. "Barren desolation is stretched before me," he wrote of western Wyoming, "and yet there is a beauty in the scene." Farther down the Green and Colorado rivers, Powell exalted in the way the canyon "opened up like a beautiful portal to a region of glory," but, ambivalently, he could add that as night fell the same place became "a black portal to a region of gloom." Clearly, ideas were in transition. But the overall impact of Powell's very popular writings was to invest the canyon lands with unprecedented aesthetic and spiritual value. It was Powell, after all, who popularized the name "Grand" for a canyon that others had just called "horrid."[9]

In putting his finger on the problem of loving the arid West, Powell recognized that for the person accustomed to "verdure-clad hills" the carved and colored world of rock along the course of the Colorado was hard to appreciate. But a few of Powell's contemporaries were starting to make the aesthetic transition. One was Powell's colleague, the artist Thomas Moran. His 1873 painting of the Grand Canyon is open, sunny, and vibrant with color—a direct contrast to the gloomy slots of Egøffstein fifteen years before. When Congress purchased Moran's canvas for hanging in the capitol in Washington, D.C., appreciation of the canyon lands passed an important milestone.

Photographers added to the aesthetic exploration of the desert. Timothy H. O'Sullivan was one of the first to work in Nevada, Utah, and Arizona. He participated in Clarence King's survey of the fortieth parallel in 1867 and joined George M. Wheeler on a reconnaissance of the lower Grand Canyon in 1871. While others defined the desert in negative terms, O'Sullivan found positive value in the rocky austerity in which light and shadow, in association with stone and sand, created a new kind of landscape beauty. He led the way for later photographic interpretation of the canyon lands by Eliot Porter, Philip

Hyde, and David Muench, to name only three. Magazines such as *Arizona Highways* brought their work to a large audience.

The strangeness of the desert, previously repulsive, attracted an extraordinary group of intellectuals and artists in the twentieth century. John Marin and Georgia O'Keeffe came to New Mexico to catch the subtle colors and shapes with their brushes. Mary Hunter Austin wrote her classic, *The Land of Little Rain,* in 1903. Here and in her autobiography, *Earth Horizon,* she made it clear that the essence of the desert was "not the warm tingling presence of wooded hills and winding creeks." Instead, it was "something brooding and aloof, charged with a dire indifference." While she did not fear the arid lands, Austin never forgot that their beauty was of a kind "to watch [man] feels himself a stranger." Another woman who loved the desert, Willa Cather, called it, in *Death Comes for the Archbishop* (1926), one of "the bright edges of the world."

In 1938, the noted literary critic Joseph Wood Krutch abandoned a comfortable rural life in Connecticut for Arizona. His graceful essays did for the desert what Rachel Carson's work later did for swamps and estuaries. The "poor relations" of the American environment were finally receiving a share of the limelight previously dominated by snowy peaks. Krutch made no attempt to understate the harshness of the desert. Instead, he built a philosophy of environmental value based on harshness. According to Krutch, the desert's "beauty is no easy one. It suggests patience and struggle and endurance. . . . In the brightest of its sandstone canyons, even in the brightest colors of its brief spring, there is something austere." He knew that "life is everywhere precarious, man everywhere small." The desert, Krutch concluded, "brings man up against his limitations, turns him in upon himself, and . . . inclines to contemplation men who have never contemplated before."[10]

In the 1960s the Colorado Plateau began to receive increasing praise for its environmental value. This was the decade of Canyonlands National Park (1964) and the successful defense of the Grand Canyon from dam-building proposals (1968). In 1960, Wallace Stegner wrote about the "spiritual renewal" available in the canyon lands. "It is a lovely and terrible wilderness," he wrote, "such a wilderness as Christ and the prophets went out into; harsh and beautifully colored, broken and worn until its bones are exposed, its great sky without a smudge or taint from Technocracy, and in hidden corners and pockets under its cliffs the sudden poetry of springs." For Stegner, "recreation" was an inadequate term for expressing the value of such places; he called on his society to recognize the desert as "part of the geography of hope."[11]

Another landmark of the 1960s was the publication of Edward Abbey's *Desert Solitaire* (1968). His interpretation of the desert avoided any attempt to link it to a conventional kind of beauty and morality. Abbey had no patience with fantasies of "apple trees and golden women . . . a garden of bliss and changeless perfection." For him paradise was the "real earth," and the arid West contained that reality in a form least obscured by either vegetation or myths. Again and again, Abbey warned nature lovers and those seeking God to stay away from the desert. It was, for him, "a dangerous and terrible place . . . a fearsome mostly waterless land of rock and heat, sand dunes and quicksand, cactus, thornbush, scorpion, rattlesnake and agoraphobic distances." For those who would, in spite of these things, visit the desert, Abbey offered straightforward advice: "Enter at your own risk. Carry water. Avoid the noonday sun. Try to ignore the vultures. Pray frequently."

So why go to the Colorado Plateau? Why be concerned about the protection of its environmental values at all? Abbey addressed the question in a 1977 essay in *The Journey Home.* He described a climb up a canyon rim somewhere in northern Arizona to a point he believed no one had ever reached. But he was wrong. "Someone had. Near the summit I found an arrow sign, three feet long, formed of stones and pointing off into the north." Looking that way, Abbey could only see "more canyons, more measas and plateaus, more mountains, more cloud-dappled sun-spangled leagues of desert sand and desert rock." A walk in the direction the arrow pointed only led to a five-hundred-foot drop, and Abbey returned to the enigmatic sign, concluding that "there was nothing out there. Nothing at all. Nothing but the desert. Nothing but the silent world." And then it struck him that this was precisely why he went to the desert. In pointing at nothing, the arrow in fact pointed at something of great value.

It took a long time for American culture to reach this conclusion. For centuries, since Coronado's men stood confused and frustrated on the rim of a very un-grand canyon, the desert was an environmental embarrassment. But, in time, the ideas of Powell, Austin, Krutch, Stegner, and Abbey spread through American thought about nature. In the 1960s a surprisingly large clientele appeared for the wilderness values of the Colorado River watershed. Desert and river "rats" from every state and many foreign countries sought out the canyon lands for an experience impossible to find in other environments. Visitation statistics began to climb dramatically, and nowhere more so than on the Colorado River in the Grand Canyon. Table 4 tells the story of how an experience changed from risky hardship to family fun. Four revolutions explain the shift.[12] An *intellectual revolution* transformed wilderness, in general, and the canyon lands, in particular, from an environmental liability to an environmental asset. People began to *want* to go to run the Colorado and explore its canyons, but that alone is insufficient explanation for the unprecedented surge of visitation after 1964. An *equipment revolution* facilitated the transformation of desire into experience. Post-World War II technology made possible lightweight backpacking and, with special importance to the Grand Canyon river trip, inflatable rafts. A *transportation revolution* also occurred. As late as the 1950s the edges of the canyon lands were several days of travel from transportation centers, such as Denver and Salt Lake City, and virtually unreachable from eastern locations in a two-week vacation. Now, by way of contrast, jet aircraft and a network of paved roads made the Colorado Basin a realistic objective even for a long weekend.

Finally, an *information revolution* brought the southwestern wilderness into national focus and even to the point of its being loved to death. Relevant here are books, articles, films, and the proliferation of commercial guiding and outfitting operations. Literally dozens of guides now vie for the tourist dollar in places like Moab, Utah. Over twenty companies offer river trips down the Grand Canyon, and the story is much the same in Canyonlands National Park (Cataract Canyon) and on the Green and Yampa rivers in Dinosaur National Monument. The Sierra Club and other outdoor organizations schedule regular trips into places few Americans knew existed before 1960. Also important was the publicity associated with the Grand Canyon dam controversy of the late 1960s. It was no accident that the rise of visitation (see Table 4) coincided with a flood of information about the values of Grand Canyon and the tragedy of the lost Glen Canyon.

Table 4. **Travel on the Colorado River through the Grand Canyon of Arizona. Compiled by Roderick Nash**

Year	Number of People	Year	Number of People
1867	1?	1960	205
1869–1940	73	1961	255
1941	4	1962	372
1942	8	1963–64	44
1943	0	1965	547
1944	0	1966	1,067
1945	0	1967	2,099
1946	0	1968	3,609
1947	4	1969	6,019
1948	6	1970	9,935
1949	12	1971	10,885
1950	7	1972	16,432
1951	29	1973	15,219
1952	19	1974	14,253
1953	31	1975	14,305
1954	21	1976	13,912
1955	70	1977	11,830
1956	55	1978	14,356
1957	135	1979	14,678
1958	80	1980	15,142
1959	120		

Today, it is undeniable that there is a growing clientele for wilderness values in the Colorado River watershed. In planning for the future of this part of the West, it is imperative that the interests of this group of citizens be considered with the same degree of seriousness as those of ranchers, farmers, metropolitan water districts, energy developers, and hydropower distributors. While seemingly simple, this has not been an easy point to make in the American political arena. People who like wilderness and free-flowing rivers are generally regarded as less legitimate and less serious than those who deal in acre-feet and kilowatt-hours. But it is arguable that wilderness is just as much of a "resource" as water, electricity, and coal. It just might be the most valuable, scarcer and more sought-after than all the others. The income of the river outfitters and tour operators in the canyon country is one way to measure the value of this wilderness. But it is also essential to recognize that for many people the importance of the Colorado transcends the standard economic indicators. We are talking about religion and the right of a minority to worship as it pleases, which, after all, is guaranteed by the Constitution. And we are also talking about the right of nature to exist irrespective of any human interest.

Presently, the values of wilderness and civilization teeter in uneasy balance on the Colorado. The river has been substantially modified. But parts of it still flow, if not freely, at least with enough of the old wildness to give many visitors the impression of natural conditions. A compromise has been hammered out concerning the Colorado that reflects the ambivalence of the American mind. John Wesley Powell's river does not exist. But neither is the Colorado a string of dams and reservoirs in the manner of the Mississippi. The Colorado River Storage Project Act of April 11, 1956, which dropped plans for dams in Dinosaur National Monument, and the legislation authorizing the Central Arizona Project (September 30, 1968), which killed the Grand Canyon dams, are irrefutable evidence that the American public wants to place a limit on development of the Colorado. Perhaps it is time to really heed John Wesley Powell's advice to stop trying to turn the watershed of the Colorado into the Ohio Valley. Perhaps it is time to recognize that what is different and valuable about the Colorado is its wildness. Let the region do what it can do best—"export" wildness to the nation and the world."[13] Why not allow the scarcity of water in the Southwest to limit growth and possibly point the way toward new definitions of progress and happiness?

The present symposium, meeting at the site of the 1922 deliberations regarding allocation of Colorado *water* should take a firm stand on the alloction of the Colorado's *wilderness*. We need a new Colorado River Compact, adjudicating human needs for nature and for civilization. In the light of the fact that only about 3 percent of the lower forty-eight states retains a meaningful degree of wildness, the new compact should proclaim that enough compromises of the original naturalness of the Colorado have been made. Dams and water diversions are not inherently evil, but they can become ironic—failing of their own success to produce the good life that people desire. Development has gone far enough.

In the interest of environmental diversity and minority rights, *all* that remains of the main-stem Colorado River and its tributaries should be placed in a protective category. The National Wild and Scenic River System is an excellent legislative instrument for this purpose. Deliberately flexible, it can accommodate truly wild sections of a river as well as those with substantial modifications. We store acre-feet; let's also store wildness, banking it against a future that may need it more than we do. Let *all* the remaining free-flowing sections of the river system be protected. For once in American environmental history, let preservation, rather than exploitation, be "grandfathered in." Then, the burden of proof for subsequent change can fall on the developers. Only after careful scrutiny of the real needs of the entire world should withdrawals of the protected waterways from the National Wild and Scenic River System take place.

Protecting wilderness, after all, keeps options open. It is development that closes them off. If future generations should find it impossible to exist without utilizing the Colorado's remaining wildness, that option is still available. But why not let the future make those decisions for itself rather than hand it a fully developed Colorado? It just might be the case that the scarcity theory of value will not only give wildness parity with other resources in the Colorado watershed but make it the most valuable resource of all.

Finally, let me enter a plea to transcend utilitarianism and anthropocentrism when it comes to planning the future of this controversial river. Engineers, lawyers, and politicians especially must try to remember that a river is more than a sum of acre-feet in the same way that a forest is more than a sum of board-feet. With a bow to a former president, I say it is time to quit asking what the already burdened Colorado can do for you and start asking what you can do for the Colorado. The point is that we are not just beneficiaries—"users"—of Colorado water; we are sharers of an ecosystem with the Colorado River.

Notes

1. I have explored this point in *Wilderness and the American Mind* (New Haven, 1982), pp. 1–7.

2. Interview with Ken Sleight, Marble Canyon, Arizona, 30 March 1979.

3. An excellent study, in word and comparative photography, of vegetation history in the Grand Canyon is Raymond Turner and Martin Karpiscak, *Recent Vegetation Changes Along the Colorado Between Glen Canyon Dam and Lake Mead, Arizona,* Geological Survey Professional Paper 1132 (Washington, D.C., 1980).

4. Luna B. Leopold, "The Rapids and the Pools—Grand Canyon," in *The Colorado River Region and John Wesley Powell,* Geological Survey Professional Paper 669 (Washington, D.C., 1969), pp. 131–45; Robert Dolan, et al., "Man's Impact on the Colorado River in the Grand Canyon," *American Scientist* 62 (July–August 1974), pp. 392–401.

5. Philip Fradkin, *A River No More: The Colorado River and the West* (New York, 1981).

6. See Nash, *Wilderness and the American Mind,* chap. 15, especially pp. 330ff.

7. Although definitions of "roads" will vary, it is essentially true that in only three places east of the Mississippi can one get more than five miles from a passenger car. Florida's Everglades are larger but accessible to powerboats and airboats. The other major eastern wildernesses are located in northern Maine, New York's Adirondack Mountains and the great Smokies along the North Carolina–Tennessee border.

8. Quoted in Roderick Nash, "An Unprecedented Landscape: The Problem of Living in the Arid West," in Christopher S. Durer, ed., *American Renaissance and the American West,* Proceedings of the Second University of Wyoming American Studies Conference (Laramie, 1982), p. 71.

9. Powell's account of his trips is most conveniently found in J. W. Powell, *The Exploration of the Colorado River and Its Canyons* (New York, 1961).

10. Joseph Wood Krutch's most important books are *Grand Canyon: Today and All Its Yesterdays* (New York, 1958) and *The Voice of the Desert* (New York, 1955). An excellent new biography is John D. Margolis, *Joseph Wood Krutch: A Writer's Life* (Knoxville, 1980).

11. Wallace Stegner's 1960 letter to the Outdoor Recreation Resources Review Commission is conveniently found in his *The Sound of Mountain Water* (Garden City, N.Y., 1969).

12. For details, see Nash, *Wilderness and the American Mind,* pp. 317ff.

13. For a discussion of the exporting and importing of nature see ibid., chap. 16.

10 A New Confluence in the Life of the River

Gilbert F. White

The symposium at Bishop's Lodge provided a review of experience in managing the Colorado River in the sixty-one years since the signing of the compact by representatives of the basin states; more important, however, it marked the beginning of a new period in the life of the river. It was the first gathering to systematically examine Colorado River activities in a broad framework with a view to assessing the need, if any, for improvement.

There has been an almost religious character to the interpretation of the unfolding collection of sacred testaments—compacts, statutes, judicial decisions, and regulations—that together have come to constitute the "Law of the River." For a long time these dicta and declarations were followed with meticulous concern for the niceties of their meaning and their exegesis but with little challenge to their efficacy in coping with the problems of the basin. By 1983, however, the character of the river and its uses and of the social and economic conditions in which it is managed had changed so substantially that they deserved to be viewed from a different perspective. The new approach to the river, going far beyond the concerns of the 1922 compact, identified a new set of public policy issues and thereby laid the groundwork for consideration of possible institutional changes. While the allocation of the river's water remained central, the management of the river in terms of the welfare of the people of the basin and adjacent areas claimed fresh attention. New concerns were joined with old commitments. Thinking about the river is bound to be different downstream from the symposium.

It may be helpful to summarize the main outcomes and meaning of the gathering under five topics: (1) the ways in which people may look on the Colorado as a system and a resource; (2) changes occurring since 1922; (3) methods of identifying the principal issues that appear to mark the management of the river in 1983; (4) the seven major issues emerging in 1983; and (5) possible institutional shifts and innovations.

Ways of Looking at the River

The symposium begins with an examination of the working of the law of the river, a basically legal point of view and one entirely consonant with the traditional operations of local, state, and federal agencies. As the discussion proceeds, two other ways of approaching the river are pursued.

It may be viewed as a natural system, which has been and is being transformed by human action creating new flow regimens, different water quality and aquatic ecosystems, and new land uses.

It may also be seen in the perspective of the welfare of the people who occupy the basin or are affected by its management. From this perspective it is an aggregation of irrigation farmers, livestock operators, Native American tribes, municipal and industrial water users, electric power consumers (most far beyond the basin limits), skiers, river runners, campers, fisherfolk, and all the others whose well-being is linked in some fashion to Colorado River water.

As these views are sampled, the examination ranges from compact provisions and state legislation to the condition and dreams of people making a livelihood on the land and to the aspirations of people in distant places who come to the basin for refreshment or who regard it as a national resource. These different views establish the frameworks within which the prospects for water shortage, water allocation, river management rules, and numerous other threats and opportunities are appraised.

Changes since 1922

My friend Kenneth Boulding likes to remind me, when we talk about resource futures, that all our knowledge is about the past and all our decisions are about the future. The relatively solid basis from which an assessment of the uncertain Colorado Basin future begins is the record of what has happened since the compact group signed the document at Bishop's Lodge and went home to explain it to their constituencies. Stated only in thumbnail format, the chief changes are formidable.

The mean annual flow of the stream in its lower reaches was much lower than expected.

The salinity concentration in the main stream and a number of its tributaries was much larger than expected. Indeed, there had been virtually no discussion of salinity in 1922.

A series of water control and storage works was engineered and constructed, culminating in the Central Arizona Project.

New techniques of water use—including well drilling, deep pumping, water application methods, laser leveling of fields, desalting, and recycling—were introduced.

Economic analysis moved to a higher level of sophistication in estimating sector and aggregate costs and certain tangible benefits.

Agricultural farming systems were widely revolutionized.

Concern for the environment, partly expressed in a sense of open space and the value of wildness, and the practice of river running as a recreation, burgeoned in the national mental landscape.

Sensitivity to the dignity and place of indigenous people asserted itself at levels where it was virtually lacking until 1933.

Population moved massively into and across urban centers of the basin, bringing with it new cultures, perceptions, and habits.

The whole notion of a national energy policy was called into question and reexamined.

Federal fiscal policy changed radically, introducing new views of the meaning of subsidy and the appropriate roles of state and local governments in the financing of activities formerly considered a primary federal responsibility.

New Institutions

Then there was a progression of institutional changes.

A series of federal project authorizations was enacted.

The rights of state and federal entities were further defined in judicial decisions, ranging from *Arizona* v. *California* to *Sporhase*.

New federal agencies were established, principally the Environmental Protection Agency and with it the provisions under NEPA for environmental impact review.

Major metropolitan water management agencies grew into maturity in southern California and the Denver area.

The Salinity Forum was organized, along with a Committee of Fourteen, to address the continuing deterioration of water quality.

Thus, agencies not fully imagined at the time the compact was drawn came into operation. And innovations in dealing with water currently evolve: the Arizona Groundwater Conservation Act is pioneering in the management of aquifers; the Denver Metropolitan Water Roundtable is yielding preliminary results in its effort to reconcile conflict at the subbasin scale.

Perhaps as important as any of these innovations in recent years was action in the opposite direction—the emasculation of federal agencies and the elimination of state and interstate agencies having some responsibility for the cultivation of consensus on aims and appropriate means of regional development. As the complexity and need for formulating revised basin programs became more evident, the formal instruments to assist that process were weakened.

Identifying the Issues

Against this background, how best may the issues of present and prospective importance in basin management be identified? The symposium proceeded along three courses.

First, it looked at four possible shocks to the system. These might be the following possibilities:

1. An energy crisis renewed
2. Momentous court settlements of Native American water rights claims
3. Large-scale sales of water across state boundaries
4. Extreme drought

It is noteworthy that the participants were not interested in speculating on the implications of a drought of the severity of that recorded in tree rings for the period when the Anasazi culture disappeared, or of a climatic change induced by shifts in the biogeochemical cycles of carbon, sulfur, nitrogen, and trace gases. Other possible generations of shock were considered to be major military installations and national defense claims on basin resources.

Second, participants repeatedly asked what might be the course of events if recent trends were extrapolated and there were no hypothesized case of shock. Underlying much of that inquiry was the question of whether or not any major institutional change would be required if the responsible people and groups were to limp along much as they have during the past decade.

Third, the symposium was pressed to ask how close the projected conditions in the basin would come to meeting articulated aspirations for improvements in the life of the population of the basin and surrounding areas. To make such judgments as to goals for further action requires various criteria as to values to be served. As any person accustomed to analyzing water resources activities might expect, these sets of values were recognized:

1.   Economic development for the Colorado Basin and closely related areas
2.   Economic development for the nation
3.   Social equity (a set of values that had played no role in the 1922 negotiations)
4.   Integrity of natural systems and preservation of the open and the wild

Depending upon the stance adopted, the issues can be stated differently, and some might be omitted entirely, but a relatively small number of issues attracted attention.

Seven Major Issues

At least seven major issues emerge.

1. *Water allocation,* not only in the event of a great drought whenever that eventuates (and surely it will), and neglecting possible climate change, but also in terms of questions that are likely to be significant without such perturbations. These are the questions of what

is meant by consumptive use, by surplus, and by proper allocation among the Upper Basin states.

2. *Salinity* hinges on the selection of appropriate techniques to deal with salt—a wide range of structural and nonstructural measures— and on how responsibility is allocated among the states and the federal government for administering and paying for the control and preventative measures.

3. The definition of *federal reserve rights* is urgent. There is considerable doubt as to how significant the failure to quantify federal reserve rights is in inhibiting development and effective management of the basin.

4. *Native American reserve rights* constitute a cluster of problems: their quantity; their determination; their transferability; and the life and organization of Native American groups as affecting capacity to deal with these issues over a reasonable period of time in local situations.

5. *Instream uses* are in need of specification with a view to recognizing the long-term effects of other uses on wildlife, landscape, and recreation.

6. The question of *water rights transfer and appropriate pricing* procedures between uses and between areas to afford flexibility within the allocations of the compact is not fully resolved.

7. A different type of issue underlying much of the symposium discussion has to do with the *efficacy of basin management*. Some observers argue that the present management of water in the basin, in contrast to the allocations, has been too slow, too cumbersome, too uncertain, and too expensive. Alongside this view is the notion that while day-to-day operations are orderly, there is somehow a loss of a sense of direction for the management of the basin. This situation stands in contrast to the clear-cut statement of the issues in conflict and to be resolved with compromise in the drawing and ratification of the 1922 compact. My personal view is that there is a crisis of confidence in the nation's direction in dealing with basin problems.

These issues now ought to be called to the attention of others in a forthright fashion. This is the first time that they have been stated explicitly for the benefit of larger groups. Their accurate identification and recognition is to be sought. Cultivating understanding of the changes and the issues is a step toward vigorous action.

Possible Institutional Changes

In considering the desirability of any institutional change, the precept that "If it ain't broke, don't fix it" should serve well. Just how much fixing is needed at this stage? What would be the consequences of making no drastic changes?

Some of the arguments about appropriate action are reminiscent of the Missouri farmer who bought a big new mule who wouldn't go in the barn because the mule's ears touched the door. He applied a variety of persuasion—reason, bribery, brute strength—but the mule wouldn't go through the door. Finally, he was sawing off the top of the doorway when the county agent came by, asked what was going on, and remarked, "That's a silly way to deal with the problem. What you should do is dig down under so the mule can go through the door at a lower depth." The farmer favored him with that kind of conde-scension people have for experts from government offices and said, "You don't understand, the trouble ain't with the mule's *legs* being too long, the trouble is his *ears* are too long." A good deal of the discussion about changing Bureau of Reclamation organic acts or state regulations inspires doubt as to single solutions.

Two general comments may be made about possible institutional changes. One of them has to do with the role of crisis. An interesting theme running through most of the meeting has to do with whether it is necessary to wait for crisis before a major change can be achieved in organization, regulation, or statute. Is there any point in calling together the governors unless people are beginning to hurt in making a living in the basin? It is true that sometimes, as with the spectre of earthquakes in southern California, the fear of a crisis is enough to inspire action. Very often crisis is indeed necessary for change, but it has been learned from a good many disasters—natural and social—that if people are prepared for an extreme event they are better able to make constructive changes when the time comes. If they wait for the event they often take frenetic and unsuitable measures.

A second general comment is that the compact is not a management instrument. Many possibly desirable activities don't involve any alterations in the compact.

Eleven institutional changes seem to have been judged worthy of further appraisal.

1. *Modify the compact.* Although a few observers suggested that the compact should be recognized as a mutual mistake and therefore modified to conform to hydrologic and salinity realities, this had little support. Many issues might be faced without modifying the compact.

2. *Broaden Bureau of Reclamation responsibilities.* There may be an opportunity, perhaps by drafting a new organic act, to enable the Bureau to carry out its operations and contracting with more consideration of social aims.

3. *Quantify Native American water rights.* This process might be speeded up or strengthened in a variety of ways, always with due regard for the capacity of Native American tribes to deal deliberately with water rights and land use issues.

4. *Specify federal reserve rights.* This, too, might be speeded up, but with possible social costs as well as benefits.

5. *Declare the Colorado a wild and scenic river.* Under the National Wild and Scenic River System authorization, various reaches might be designated against further encroachment.

6. *Strengthen state permit systems.* The provisions of state statutes and administrative regulations might be altered with a view to promoting water conservation, eliminating perpetuity rights, and allocating water on criteria other than priority.

7. *Facilitate market transfers of water.* This might be achieved through adjustments at several levels of government, with the aim of supporting market pricing while protecting interests of other users than those receiving the rights.

8. *Salinity management fees.* As a means of reducing the output of salt into the river, a system of fees might be established to provide incentives for salinity control.

9. *Harmonize water-use objectives at the local level.* Much of the

actual and latent conflict over water transfers and use might be reduced by energetically supporting at the local or subbasin level informal consultations as to aims and methods of water management. The experience with consultations among members of Native American tribes and with the Denver Metropolitan Water Roundtable offers promising experiments in that direction.

10. *Establish a basin forum or commission.* A means might be found to bring together from inside and outside the basin a group representative of the diverse interests in water and related land resources to assess possible actions beyond those specified in the compact.

11. *Carry out an information program.* Through preparation of issue papers, of a water atlas for the basin, or other media activities, the facts and problems marshaled at the symposium might be disseminated more widely among groups and individuals who are affected by or concerned with the basin's physical and social health.

Considering the number of academic and research people who participated, it is remarkable that the symposium generated no proposals for new research. While any one of the eleven initiatives enumerated above would call for some kind of investigation, the symposium focused on issues and action rather than on further study.

The preliminary appraisal of the various actions recognized but did not attempt to reconcile a spectrum of views of the river as a natural resource and the appropriate place to make decisions about it. At one extreme, the basin was seen as an area where local and state agencies should call the turns, with federal financial and operations assistance. At the other extreme, the river was seen as a national asset warranting vigorous national participation in charting its future.

A Confluence of Views

The symposium was not organized to recommend specific changes in the complex web of institutions dealing with the Colorado. It was intended to identify emerging issues and to canvass the available options in managing the river. It will have achieved its immediate purpose if it leads to a coherent presentation of the information and judgments that were assembled. Thereby, it may point to some number of steps that others may take in the direction of wise use of the basin. A British poet has defined wisdom as the "masterful manipulation of the unforeseen." In a sense, the symposium sought to develop that wisdom within the nation as it looks to the future of the basin. Notwithstanding all their imaginative forays and scenarios or their systematic analyses of possible events, no symposium or learned studies will ever be prescient enough to foresee what lies ahead for the Colorado. But this symposium may strengthen society's capacity to manipulate in some hopefully masterful ways the foreseen and the unforeseen.

The findings should be shared, first by stating the problems and issues precisely, and then by outlining possible institutional changes deemed worthy of exploration. More influential than focusing on any one change would be to cultivate understanding.

A great stream like the Colorado can flow a long distance without any significant input from tributaries. Then it can be joined by a new tributary with fresh flow from downstream headwaters. We are at such a point in the flow of thought about the Colorado. After a long reach in time, during which the main channel has changed only a little, it is swelled by a rush of new perspectives on resources, needs, values, and technologies originating in diverse social and economic landscapes. The basin is physically different than it was in 1922; its national setting has changed; its population is different; and perceptions of it have altered. These inputs are mingling with the views long implicit in the "Law of the River."

The symposium can be a confluence point in the stream of thinking about the Colorado and practicable ways of managing it in the interest of the region and of the nation.

Epilog:
High Water, Carbon Dioxide, and Pig Feathers

Gary D. Weatherford
and F. Lee Brown

High Water

Spring was cooler than usual in the headwaters of the Colorado River Basin in 1983. In mid-May, unseasonably late snowstorms blanketed the upper drainage. Days later, from May 23 to 26, sweater-clad participants at the Colorado River Working Symposium meeting in Santa Fe pondered how a protracted drought might test the agility of the water management institutions in the basin. The attendees were told that runoff fluctuations, resulting from climatic variability, posed potential shocks to the river management system.

The symposium ended under an aura of good will and high resolution just in time for participants to make airplane connections ahead of the Memorial Day weekend traffic. Over that weekend the weather turned from unseasonably cool to unseasonably warm (six degrees Fahrenheit above normal) and the snow—new and old alike—began to melt rapidly. In mid-June the rains came. And in late June there was more rain. Forecasts made earlier in the year of the expected inflow in Lake Powell, which had ranged from 96 to 117 percent of normal, were adjusted from 127 to 210 percent of normal over the month of June 1983.[1] The pulses of inflow topped off Lake Mead where water releases of forty thousand cubic feet per second began to be made. On July 3, water flowed over the Hoover Dam spillway gates for the first time since 1941. Flashboards were hurriedly placed on top of the spillway gates at Lake Powell, where the coursing water was cutting through concrete lining and into the surrounding sandstone. Downstream, rural settlements and subdivisions in the floodplain, from Bullhead City to Yuma, took on water and were evacuated. The water table under Yuma, Arizona, rose to within fifteen inches of the ground surface, damaging wells and septic systems. Millions of dollars of damage occurred to private and public property along the river.[2]

As the water rose and fell in the summer of 1983, public attention focused on the U.S. Bureau of Reclamation and its operation of the dams (see Figure 3). Injured residents of the floodplain charged that the Bureau had failed since January to draw the reservoirs low enough to receive and contain the spring flood flows. Secretary of the Interior James Watt replied that occupants of the floodplain had knowingly assumed the risk of floods. (The Bureau had warned area residents in the late 1970s of the prospect of high flows.) On July 12, Watt called for federal and state officials to meet to review reservoir operations under the law of the river.

The reservoir operations of the Bureau of Reclamation became the focus of oversight hearings held by the House Committee on Interior and Insular Affairs, chaired by Rep. Morris K. Udall, at Yuma and Needles on September 7 and 8, 1983, respectively. The consensus of opinion expressed by state and federal representatives who testified was that the Bureau acted reasonably and within the governing operating criteria, given the weather forecasts it had available to it.[3] River running interests testified that, contrary to legal mandates, the Bureau had been keeping reservoirs too full in order to maximize peak power production, and neglecting flood control in the process.[4] Occupants and entrepreneurs of the floodplain testified, variously, that the Bureau did not reserve enough reservoir capacity for the spring inflows and failed to give clear notice; that the Bureau of Land Management encouraged development in the floodplain, and that the Federal Emergency Management Agency was not responsive.[5] According to one university researcher, the estimated 17 million acre-feet of natural runoff for the spring of 1983 had to be compared to 30.2 million acre-feet in 1884. According to the researcher, the unusual thing about 1983 was the fact that only 5.137 million acre-feet of total flood control storage space was available in Lake Powell and Lake Mead combined at the beginning of the spring runoff season.[6] That amount of flood control space was consonant, however, with

Figure 3.   Political cartoon by Trever from the editorial page of the *Albuquerque Journal*

the 1982 field working agreement between the Bureau and the Army
Corps of Engineers, which calls for 5.35 million acre-feet of storage
space (including upstream reservoirs in addition to Lake Powell and
Lake Mead) to be available on January 1 of each year.[7] There was 6.6
million acre-feet of storage available in the system (from Hoover Dam
upstream) on January 1, 1983.[8] The 1982 agreement resulted from
five years of study, including consultation with the states and the
consideration of numerous alternatives and scenarios.

The congressional hearings helped to set in bold relief some of
the tradeoffs that are unavoidably involved in reservoir operation.
Management of the Colorado River reservoirs unavoidably affects
carryover storage for drought mitigation, storage for regulated irrigation releases, storage for power production and revenues, releases for
river running, storage for lake fishery and releases for riverine fishery,
water quality control, evaporative and seepage losses, temperature,
sedimentation, public access to beaches and shores, flood control, and
relations with Mexico.

In December 1983, a study report issued by the National Center
for Atmospheric Research concluded:

> The highly abnormal meteorological events which contributed
> to the flooding, irrespective of whether or not they could have
> been predicted or prepared for, are not wholly responsible for
> the 1983 flooding. . . . Other factors which contributed to the
> flooding are the maintenance of a system of full reservoirs
> (reflective of societal concern for drought) and physical
> encroachment into the flood plain (made possible by the dams
> along the river). These factors can be managed, but there are
> strong reasons why these choices may not be made in the
> future. Ultimately, the management of the Colorado River is
> the product of political and economic constraints imposed by
> the river's many beneficiaries.[9]

The drought of 1977 in the basin apparently conditioned interest
groups and decision makers to continue their support of a policy fa-
voring full reservoirs. Ironically, one year's drought may have helped
produce another year's flood. Perhaps floods and droughts have become
as linked in policy-making as they are in the flux of nature.

Interestingly, at this writing it appears that the spring runoff of
1984 may exceed that of 1983, but the Bureau cautiously had 7.5

million acre-feet of flood control available in January, and that, plus somewhat more accurate forecasts, led to releases that have avoided damage in the floodplain.

Carbon Dioxide

Concern over variability in the flow of the Colorado was heightened further by a late 1983 report of the Carbon Dioxide Assessment Committee of the National Academy of Science. A chapter of the report focuses on the water-supply effects of a carbon dioxide–induced climatic change in the western United States. If a greenhouse effect (warmer air temperatures and reduced precipitation from the buildup of CO_2 and other gases in the atmosphere) does occur, as many scientists predict, water supply could be reduced 56.5 percent on the lower Colorado and 39.6 percent on the upper Colorado, according to the Academy report.[10]

In short, human activity around the globe, ranging from fossil fuel burning in the industrialized nations to deforestation in the equatorial tropics, may cause protracted droughts for our timeless river within the next century. Severe scarcity, not high flows, could become the dominant reality to which Colorado River management will have to adapt.

Pig Feathers

If a pig has to fly before the Colorado River Compact is changed, we must finally ask whether any signs of wing feathers have appeared on that symbolic sow since the 1983 symposium at Bishop's Lodge was conducted. Arguably, a few feathers have appeared, stimulated by the 1983 flooding.

As the flows peaked in late June and early July of 1983, some key political leaders made notable pronouncements. Governor Richard Lamm of Colorado called upon the basin states to consider new formulas for sharing future shortages, as well as evaporation losses, on the river.[11] Governor Bruce Babbitt of Arizona called for the creation of the Colorado River Basin Commission, composed of representatives of the seven states and the federal government, noting that the full reservoirs on the river marked "a different era" with respect to the

balancing of storage and flood control.[12] In mid-July, Secretary of the
Interior Watt, as already mentioned, initiated a federal-state evaluation of the operating principles and systems that have evolved from
the law of the river.[13] In midsummer 1984, Governor Lamm reportedly
was planning to propose the creation of a Colorado River Forum,
composed of state representatives.

Probably the most provocative event of 1984 was the purchase
by the San Diego County Water Authority in August of an option to
lease upwards of 300,000 acre-feet of water annually from a private
entity, the Galloway Group, which wants to construct a reservoir on
the Yampa River in Colorado. The basin states and many Colorado
River users vigorously opposed the proposal, arguing that such a transfer would violate the "Law of the River." Undaunted, the Galloway
Group in mid-January 1985 extended the San Diego option for two
years. Whatever the final outcome, the proposal has given life and
added relevance to Professor Gardner's discussion of water marketing
in chapter 7 of this volume.

Clearly, events during the remaining years of this century could
lead to changes in the "Law of the River," a body of rules that evolves
in response to the changing complexions of political power, economic
demand, social need, and climate. Until then the river, while noto-
riously controlled,[14] remains part of a larger natural system that is
unconscious of human desires or designs, but is quite capable of shaking
the ground beneath would-be pundits and prophets. The Colorado
has flowed down many gradients in geologic time. Our relationship
with this river is in its infancy. Many lessons in water stewardship
await, compliments of its channels and currents.

Notes

1. Statement of Robert N. Broadbent, Commissioner, Bureau of Reclamation, in Oversight Hearings on Colorado River Management before the
House Committee on Interior and Insular Affairs, 98th Cong., 1st sess. (7–
8 September 1983), pp. 233–41.

2. Ibid., pp. 17, 111.

3. See statement of engineers representing state interests, in ibid., pp.
318, 325, 332, and 477.

4. Ibid., pp. 690, 725.

5. ibid., pp. 77–103, 160–75.

6. Testimony of Dr. Larry J. Paulson, Director, Lake Mead Limnological Research Center, University of Nevada at Las Vegas, in ibid., pp. 542–59.

7. Copy set out in ibid., pp. 285–93.

8. Broadbent, in ibid., p. 224.

9. Steven L. Rhodes, et al., "Climate and the Colorado River: The Limits of Management" (mimeographed, 6 December 1983), pp. 24–25.

10. National Academy of Science, Carbon Dioxide Assessment Committee, *Changing Climate* (Washington, D.C., 1983), p. 423 (table 7.4).

11. J. J Casserly, "Colorado Governor Seeks Western Water Shortage-Sharing," editorial in *Arizona Republic*, 2 July 1983.

12. William E. Schmidt, "Floods Along Colorado River Set Off a Debate Over Blame," *New York Times*, 17 July 1983.

13. Department of the Interior press release, "Interior Calls for Meetings with States and Congress on Colorado River Operations," 14 July 1983.

14. See Phillip Fradkin, *A River No More* (New York, 1981).

Figure 4.   Participants in the symposium. (Photography by Taylor O. Miller)

Appendix 1

Biographical Sketches of Participants and Observers at the Colorado River Working Symposium†

Mr. Ralph Abascal is with the California Rural Legal Assistance in Berkeley, California.

The Honorable Toney Anaya* is governor of the state of New Mexico and previously served as its attorney general. Formerly a senior partner in a law firm in Santa Fe, he received his J.D. from Washington College of Law, American University in Washington, D.C.

Ms. Barbara T. Andrews is an attorney in the Natural Resources department of Davis, Graham and Stubbs, Denver. She is a member of the California and Colorado bar associations, and received her law degree from Stanford. She has written extensively on water matters in California, including a book to be published this spring, entitled *Who Runs the Rivers? Dams and Decisions in the New West*.

The Honorable Bruce Babbitt* is governor of the state of Arizona and previously served as its attorney general. Formerly chairman of the Western Governors' policy office, he is currently chairman of the water management subcommittee of the National Governors Association. He is the author of *Grand Canyon: An Anthology*.

---

†The biographical sketches were current as of the date of the symposium. No attempt has been made to update them.
*Indicates an observer.

Mr. Harvey O. Banks, former director of water resources, state of California, is an internationally recognized water resources planning specialist, professor, lecturer, author, and consultant. He has been in private practice for twenty-two years, serving a wide array of clients nationally and internationally. He has chaired state and federal panels throughout the U.S. and has served on international commissions and committees on behalf of organizations such as the World Bank and USAID.

Mr. Clifford I. Barrett* was appointed regional director of the upper Colorado region, Bureau of Reclamation, in 1981. Prior to this assignment, he had been assistant commissioner—resource planning, of the Bureau, where he was responsible for policy development planning and operation of water resources in the seventeen western United States.

Mr. D. Craig Bell* joined the Western States Water Council in 1974 as assistant director. Acting as an attorney for the council, he has been involved in many activities concerning federal-state relations in water law. In 1980 he was appointed as executive director of the council, a position he now holds.

Mr. Paul Bloom, a Washington, D.C., water law attorney, specializes in water law of the Southwest. Mr. Bloom is the former general counsel of the New Mexico Interstate Stream Commission, was a member of the Committee of Fourteen representing Colorado River Basin states, and has published on the Colorado River Compact.

Mr. Gilbert Bonem is a research associate with the Center for Natural Resource Studies in Albuquerque. His work on the economics of water resources includes an economic base study of the Colorado River Basin, coauthor (with Nathaniel Wollman) of *The Outlook for Water,* and contract work for the Bureau of Indian Affairs on water rights.

Mr. Carl Boronkay* is currently general counsel of the Metropolitan Water District of southern California. Prior to his association with Metropolitan, he was a senior assistant attorney general for the state of California in charge of the public resources section. This included

---

*Indicates an observer.

responsibility for water rights litigation, water pollution, air resources, Colorado River Board matters, the Department of Fish and Game, Department of Food and Agriculture, and Department of Parks and Recreation.

Professor F. Lee Brown is codirector of the Center for Natural Resource Studies water program as well as being professor of economics at the University of New Mexico. He is a former director of the Bureau of Business and Economic Research at that university, the author of many water articles and studies, and coauthor of *The Southwest Under Stress.*

Mr. Russell R. Brown has been on the staff of the Senate Committee on Energy and Natural Resources since 1970 and has served as professional staff for the Subcommittee on Water and Power since 1973. From 1968 to 1970 he was employed on the personal staff of Senator Henry M. Jackson of Washington State. Prior to his Senate employment, he was a career employee with the Department of the Interior in the field of water resources.

Mr. James M. Bush is a private attorney in Phoenix, Arizona. As a member of Arizona's Groundwater Management Study Commission, he was active in drafting Arizona's new Groundwater Management Act. He is vice-chairman of the Western Regional Council's Committee on Indian Reserved Water Rights and a vice-president of the Central Arizona Project Association.

Dr. Edwin H. Clark is an economist and engineer who is currently a senior associate at the Conservation Foundation, a nonpartisan, nonprofit environment policy research organization in Washington, D.C. He is directing the foundation's program on water resources and nonpoint source pollution, as well as the preparation of reports on the *State of the Environment.*

Ms. Jo Clark* is program manager for the water programs of the Western Governors' Policy Office. WESTPO has programs in the area of water project financing, Indian water rights, and interstate ground-

---

*Indicates an observer.

water compacts. She is also responsible for WESTPO's energy transportation study.

Mr. Edward W. Clyde, a Salt Lake City attorney specializing in natural resource law, represented the state of Utah in negotiation of the Upper Colorado River Basin Compact and was a special assistant attorney general representing the Utah state engineers and other water agencies. He has published numerous articles on the river.

Mr. Steven E. Clyde is engaged in the private practice of law in Salt Lake City. He specializes in the area of natural resource law, with a primary emphasis in the area of water law. His clients include municipalities, water conservancy districts, water improvement districts, and many energy and real estate development companies in connection with the acquisition and development of water resources.

Ms. Carole R. Cristiano is currently a private consultant in California. Prior to this, she was a professional staff member of the U.S. Senate Committee on Environment and Public Works, specializing in water resources development. She has also worked as special assistant to the city manager of Santa Fe, focusing on resource development.

Professor Timothy J. De Young, assistant professor of Public Administration at the University of New Mexico, teaches courses in research methods, natural resources management, and program evaluation. His interest in water resources management began as a Peace Corps volunteer in Nepal, where he designed and supervised the construction of rural water-supply systems.

Mr. Roger Eldridge is a senior policy analyst, Office of the Governor, State of Colorado, and has been director of State-Sponsored Organized Research and of the science and technology program for the Colorado Commission on Higher Education. He has been senior researcher for Thorne Ecological Institute, and currently serves as water consultant to the Colorado ski industry.

Dr. Sally K. Fairfax has served on the Board of Agricultural and Renewable Resources of the National Academy of Sciences and on several NAS committees concerned with public range management. Her research interests are focused on legal aspects of resource and environmental policy and the development of public lands and administrative policies in the United States.

Mr. John A. Folk-Williams is president of Western Network, a nonprofit organization examining natural resource conflict and decision making in the western states. He is author of the recent Western Network publication, *What Indian Water Means to the West*, and the forthcoming *Water for the Energy Market*, as well as several articles about natural resources and American Indian issues.

Mr. Jeffrey Fornaciari* has been an attorney with the state engineer's office, New Mexico, since 1980. He was involved with the adjudication of the San Juan River in New Mexico. Formerly, he was director of the Attorney General's Energy Unit for two years.

Mr. Joseph F. Friedkin* was appointed by President John F. Kennedy in 1962 to serve as United States Commissioner, International Boundary and Water Commission, United States and Mexico. He was accorded the personal rank of ambassador by President Lyndon B. Johnson in 1968. He has served continuously in the post under six United States presidents. He and the corresponding commissioner for Mexico are charged with joint implementation of treaties involving the Rio Grande and Colorado River waters.

Professor B. Delworth Gardner teaches agricultural economics at the University of California, Davis. His water publications include the chapter, "Water Management Crunch: An Economic Perspective," in *Economics, Ethics, Ecology: Roots of Productive Conservation,* and the article, "Agriculture and Salinity Control in the Colorado River Basin."

Professor David Getches teaches courses in water law, American Indian law, environmental law, and public land law at the University of Colorado School of Law, Boulder. Before this, he was in private practice in San Diego and Boulder and was the founding director of the Native American Rights Fund. Professor Getches has authored numerous water articles.

Mr. Tom Graff is with the Environmental Defense Fund in Berkeley, California.

---

*Indicates an observer.

Professor Norris Hundley, jr., a historian of the river, is professor of history at U.C.L.A. Two of his major works on the river are *Dividing the Waters: A Century of Controversy Between the United States and Mexico,* and *Water and the West: The Colorado River Compact and the Politics of Water in the American West.*

Professor Helen Ingram has had a continuing interest in water politics ever since publishing a monograph on New Mexico's role in the Colorado River Basin Bill. She is coauthor of *A Policy Approach to Political Representation: Lessons from the Four Corners States,* and is a professor of political science at the University of Arizona.

Mr. Walraven F. Ketellapper is manager of planning and research with the city of Thornton, Colorado, Department of Utilities. He was formerly a staff member on the *California Water Atlas* project.

Mr. Will Knedlik restricts his legal practice primarily to land use, natural resource, and water issues, and to excise, natural resource, and property taxation. Currently, he is director of intergovernmental programs and a member of the faculty of the Lincoln Institute of Land Policy in Cambridge, Massachusetts, as well as a member of the adjunct faculty of the University of Washington School of Law in Seattle.

Dr. Allen V. Kneese is a senior fellow and economist at Resources for the Future, Inc., in Washington, D.C. A long-established authority on the economics of water, he has advised the State of Israel, the World Bank, the National Oceanic and Atmospheric Administration, among others, and has published numerous books and articles on water.

Ms. Penny H. Lewis is a water rights–owning rancher on a Colorado River tributary. She was active in the development of the Copper Mountain ski area. Until 1983 she was a Summit County commissioner, representative to the river district, director of Summit County Water User's Conference, and developer of Headwater Counties Coalition and Front Range Project III Water. Currently, she is on the Colorado Commission of Commerce and Development, and is a regional advisory board member of Silverado Banking.

Mr. Dick Linford is a recognized spokesman for the river-outfitting industry. He has been a guide and outfitter for thirteen years. He is president of the Western River Guide Association, a director of the National Forest Recreation Association, and a member of the National Outfitter Advisory Council.

Mr. Max Linn is founder and president of the John Muir Institute, Inc., headquartered in Napa, California. He previously served as director of information of Sandia National Laboratories in Albuquerque, New Mexico, and on the faculty of the University of Iowa.

Mr. Robert P. Lippman is Southwest representative of Friends of the River, a political, research, and educational organization dedicated to the preservation of free-flowing rivers and conservation of water and energy supplies. He is also on the board of directors of the Western River Guides Association. He received his J.D. from the University of San Francisco and maintains an environmental law practice in Flagstaff. He has been a Colorado River guide since 1972.

Ms. Janet Maughan is a program officer with the William H. Donner Foundation, Inc., in New York City.

Mr. Charles Meyers, now a private attorney in Denver, taught law for thirty-two years and also served as dean of the Stanford University School of Law. Mr. Meyers was law clerk to the Special Master in *Arizona v. California* and served as associate general counsel of the National Water Commission. He is coauthor of the book, *Water Resource Management.*

Mr. Taylor Miller is the director of the John Muir Institute, Inc. He is responsible for overall program direction of the institute. Mr. Miller was formerly assistant secretary for resources of the California Resources Agency, focusing particularly on forest resource management. An attorney, he also previously worked with the Environmental Protection Agency, concentrating on water pollution and pesticide regulation.

Mr. Robert W. Musser is a member of the board of the General Service Foundation. He has been an American Indian art dealer and businessman in Boulder, Colorado, for eleven years. He has been an interested observer in the water problems of the Colorado River.

Professor Roderick W. Nash teaches history and environmental studies at the University of California, Santa Barbara. The best known of his ten books is *Wilderness and the American Mind.* For fifteen years Dr. Nash has been both a commercial and private whitewater boatman on many parts of the Colorado River.

Mr. Michael C. Nelson is special assistant to the chairman, Department of Justice of the Navajo Nation, in Window Rock, Arizona.

Mr. Nelson W. "Bill" Plummer* has been director of the Bureau of Reclamation's lower Colorado region, headquartered in Boulder City, Nevada, since 1981. In this role, he manages the last 688 miles of the Colorado River, overseeing construction of the Central Arizona Project, the Colorado River Basin Salinity Control Project, and the Southern Nevada Water Project.

Ms. Clair Reiniger is president of Designwrights Collaborative, Inc., a nonprofit corporation based in Santa Fe, New Mexico. Designwrights specializes in research, planning, and management of renewable resources (land, water, and energy).

Ms. Joan Reiss is executive producer for California Journal Television, which produces award-winning political documentaries for public television. Presently, the Journal is seeking funding for a Colorado River documentary based on Philip Fradkin's book, *A River No More.*

Mr. Stephen E. Reynolds,* state engineer of New Mexico, is also secretary of the New Mexico Interstate Stream Commission, and New Mexico commissioner on the La Plata, Rio Grande, Canadian, upper Colorado River commissions and the Costilla Creek Compact Commission. He is New Mexico administrator of the Water-Resources planning program, and New Mexico coordinator of the U.S. Army Corps of Engineers floodplain information studies program.

Mr. Donald S. Rickerd is currently president of the William H. Donner Foundation, Inc., of New York City, and has been associated with the foundation since 1968. He is a graduate of Osgoode Hall Law School, Toronto, Ontario. He was appointed Queen's Counsel in 1977.

---

*Indicates an observer.

Dr. Fred Roach is a staff member in the economics group of the Los Alamos National Laboratories. He spent from four to five years examining water resource use in the West, with particular emphasis on water and energy. He has examined conflicts over water use and alternative institutional structures for managing water resources.

Mr. Jerry Sampson, vice-president of Del E. Webb Recreational Properties, has had an active part in owning and operating facilities on Lakes Powell, Mead, and Mojave for the past twenty years. Prior to selling ownership of Halls Crossing to Del E. Webb, he was owner and manager of Halls Crossing Marina and area manager for Nevada Properties on Lakes Mead and Mojave.

Mr. John M. Sayre, a Denver attorney, specializes in water and municipal law. He is general counsel for the Northern Colorado Water Conservancy District and its municipal subdistrict and has been active in representation of many water and municipal clients.

Professor Lawrence A. Scaff teaches political science at the University of Arizona. His major field is political theory and he has written particularly in the area of political participation. He received a Fulbright award for research in social theory in Germany.

Ms. Rita Schmidt-Sudman is executive director of Western Water Education Foundation, a nonprofit, nonpartisan water information organization. A former radio and television reporter and producer, she writes and edits the foundation's bimonthly magazine, *Western Water.*

Dr. Jerry Shapiro has spent most of his professional career to date in the power industry. Trained as a mechanical and nuclear engineer, he has been involved in reactor physics, teaching, and research at Cal Tech, and in implementation of nuclear and environmental aspects of power projects with Bechtel's Los Angeles power division. Currently, he is investigating water and power issues for Bechtel's Research and Engineering Group.

Mr. James Spensley is director of external affairs, University Corporation for Atmospheric Research. He previously was program director of Consortium of Energy Impacts, and acquired broad experience working in environmental areas beginning in the 1960s on the staff of the then newly created President's Council on Environmental Quality. He was in private law practice and serves as counsel on two committees of the House of Representatives in environmental areas.

Dr. James M. Stuckey, founding president (1975–83) of the new Prescott College, is currently a faculty member of Prescott College and director of Prescott seminars emphasizing integrated approaches to environment and economic concerns. His experience with the Colorado River has been kayaking and rafting.

Professor A. Dan Tarlock has taught at the University of Kentucky and Indiana University, and is currently on the faculty of the Illinois Institute of Technology. He has been a visiting professor at the universities of Chicago, Michigan, Pennsylvania, Texas, and Utah. Water law has been one of his principal areas of scholarly interest. He is coauthor of *Water Resource Management,* and has written about water and western energy development, instream flow rights, and the Colorado River.

Mr. John E. Thorson* is director of the Conference of Western Attorneys General, with offices in San Francisco. As a member of the staff of the western office of the Council of State Governments, he also provides staff assistance to the Western Governors' Conference, and the Western Conference of State Legislators. He is a member of the California and New Mexico bar associations.

Mr. Frank J. Trelease III is currently manager of Wright Water Engineers in the Cheyenne, Wyoming, office. He has worked for the states of Wyoming and Colorado in the fields of water-supply engineering, hydrology, and planning. Colorado River Basin work has involved quantification of depletions and water supplies, water-supply acquisition, project planning, and operations analysis. He is a registered professional engineer in Wyoming, Colorado, and Montana.

Mr. Richard Trudell is the executive director and one of the founders of the American Indian Lawyer Training Program. Under an appointment by President Jimmy Carter, he served on the board of directors for the Legal Services Corporation. He currently serves on the board of trustees and executive committee for the Robert F. Kennedy Mem-

---

*Indicates an observer.

orial. He is member of the Nebraska State and American Bar associations, and a member of the Santee Sioux tribe in the state of Nebraska.

Professor Albert E. Utton is editor-in-chief of the *Natural Resources Journal* and codirector of the Natural Resources Center of the University of New Mexico. A Rhodes Scholar from New Mexico, he received his law degree from Oxford University, England. His graduate studies were in international law at the University of London.

Mr. Richard Walden is vice-president of the Farmers Investment Company, Arizona.

Mr. Gary Weatherford is codirector of the Center for Natural Resource Studies water program in Berkeley, California, and former Deputy Secretary for Resources, State of California. An attorney specializing in water law, he has taught at the University of Oregon, U.C.L.A., and Santa Clara law schools as well as having authored numerous water publications.

Professor Gilbert White, geographer at the University of Colorado, Boulder, is the author of *Strategies of American Water Management.* He chaired the National Research Council committees preparing *Integrated River Basin Development* and *Water and Choice in the Colorado Basin,* and he is joint editor of *The World Environment.*

Dr. Scott Whiteford has published extensively on development and underdevelopment issues, with a focus on Latin America. A research fellow at the School of American Research, he is completing a book on agricultural policy, irrigation, and the peasantry in Central Mexico. He is directing an ongoing research project examining the social and political impacts of the salinization of the Colorado River on the Valle de Mexicali.

Mr. Robert E. Wiedemann has been employed with the Denver Board of Water Commissioners for twenty-nine years and presently holds the position of director of finance. He previously served the board as director of water resources, including responsibility for planning long-range water supply, development, acquisition and protection of water rights, and river operation. Prior to coming to the Denver board, he was employed by the U.S. Bureau of Reclamation and by consulting engineering firms.

Mr. Lawrence J. Wolfe is an assistant attorney general with the Wyoming attorney general's office in Cheyenne, Wyoming. He has worked extensively in the areas of water rights and water development law. He receive his J.D. from the University of Wyoming College of Law, where he was managing editor of the *Land and Water Law Review.*

Index

Abbey, Edward, 209
agriculture, 18, 217; allocation measures for, 33; benefits to, 54; competitiveness of, 53, 59, 63, 69, 73, 94, 157, 161; cost reciprocity and, 161, 186; depletion measures and, 123, 130; farmers' control in, 180; historic consumption and, 88, 127, 166; irrigation, 68, 159, 160, 164, 168; irrigation returns, xv, 66, 73, 166, 167; practicably irrigable acreage, xii, 34, 63, 97; upper basin, 165
Albuquerque Journal, 191
All-American Canal, 11, 15, 22, 23
allocation, 163, 212; acrefeet and percentages for, 16–18, 26–28, 31, 36, 39, 58, 122–24, 127; alternate models for, xi; definitions for, 219, 222; institutions for, 156–63;

measures for, 33; misallocation, 157; politics of, 156–58, 162, 168, 172; quality and, 145; reallocation, 166; states charged for Indian use, 130; tensions in, 183
Anaya, Toney, 4
apportionment, 123. *See also* allocation
aqueducts, 11, 30, 37
Aristotle, 179
Arizona: acquiring river rights, 23–25, 30–32, 35–37, and conflicts, 17–25, 28, 30, 35; allocations to, 89, 122, 127, 129, 157; Central Arizona Project, 30, 35, 37, 57, 91, 92, 128, 141, 212; groundwater in, 60, 73, 218; Lake Havasu, 206; Mexico and, 27; Page, 37; Tree Ring Laboratory, 89, 102; Yuma, 18, 39, 121, 206, 226
Arizona Groundwater Conservation Act, 218